World of BCCI

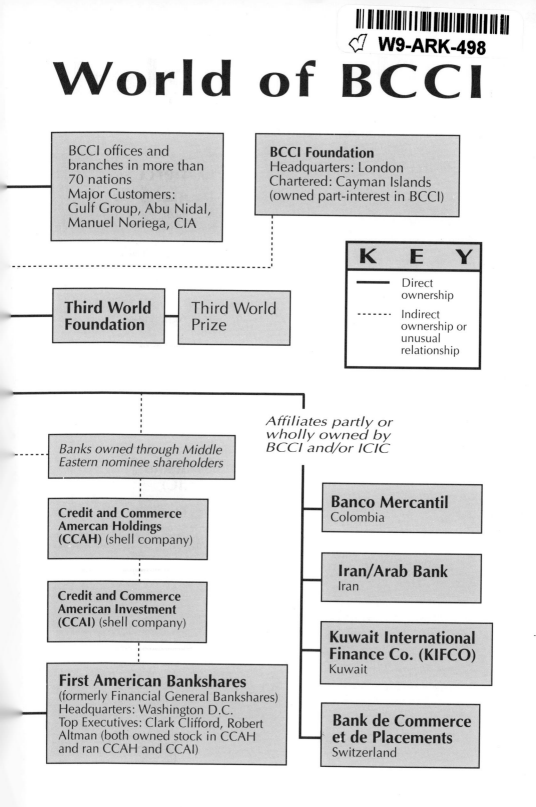

BCCI offices and branches in more than 70 nations
Major Customers: Gulf Group, Abu Nidal, Manuel Noriega, CIA

BCCI Foundation
Headquarters: London
Chartered: Cayman Islands
(owned part-interest in BCCI)

K E Y

—— Direct ownership

------ Indirect ownership or unusual relationship

Third World Foundation

Third World Prize

Affiliates partly or wholly owned by BCCI and/or ICIC

Banks owned through Middle Eastern nominee shareholders

Credit and Commerce Amercan Holdings (CCAH) (shell company)

Credit and Commerce American Investment (CCAI) (shell company)

First American Bankshares
(formerly Financial General Bankshares)
Headquarters: Washington D.C.
Top Executives: Clark Clifford, Robert Altman (both owned stock in CCAH and ran CCAH and CCAI)

Banco Mercantil
Colombia

Iran/Arab Bank
Iran

Kuwait International Finance Co. (KIFCO)
Kuwait

Bank de Commerce et de Placements
Switzerland

DIRTY MONEY

DIRTY MONEY

BCCI:
THE INSIDE STORY OF THE
WORLD'S SLEAZIEST BANK

Mark Potts, Nicholas Kochan
and Robert Whittington

National
Press
Books

Washington, D.C.

First Edition

Library of Congress Cataloging-in-Publication Data

Potts, Mark.
Dirty Money: BCCI, the inside story
of the world's sleaziest bank
Mark Potts, Nicholas Kochan and Robert Whittington
283 pp., 15.25 cm x 22.85 cm
Includes index
ISBN 0-915765-99-3 (cloth): $21.95
1. Bank of Credit and Commerce International—
Corrupt practices.
2. International finance—Corrupt practices.
3. Bank failures.
I. Kochan, Nicholas.
II. Whittington, Robert.
III. Title.
HG 1978.P68   1992
364.1'68--dc20   92-1153
CIP

PRINTED IN THE UNITED STATES OF AMERICA

Acknowledgments

The backbone of this book is Nick Kochan and Bob Whittington's reporting and writing in *Bankrupt*, the British book on which *Dirty Money* is based. Their knowledge of BCCI's history, Third World connections and British operations, as well as the British fallout from BCCI's shutdown, was invaluable.

This book also would not have been possible without the help of the talented team of journalists at with whom I have been privileged to cover the BCCI scandal. Jim McGee's pioneering reporting on the BCCI-First American connection was a superb and, frankly, prescient piece of investigative journalism. Steve Luxenberg has overseen and edited The Post's coverage of BCCI with skill, great patience and an unmatched encyclopedic knowledge of this complicated story. I also am indebted to several other Post colleagues—Joël Glenn Brenner, Steve Coll, Guy Gugliotta, Nell Henderson, Michael Isikoff, Jerry Knight, Steven Mufson, Eric Pianin, Susan Schmidt, Lucy Shackelford, Charles Shepherd, Anne Swardson, Robert Thomason and Sharon Walsh—whose excellent work is reflected throughout these pages, sometimes quite blatantly. Coll's account of Agha Hasan Abedi's background in Pakistan and Knight's reporting on Capcom Financial Services were particularly helpful. Vicki Shannon, the head of the Post's Financial copy desk, did an excellent job of copy-editing the manuscript of this book and making valuable suggestions.

The Post continues to set a standard in allowing and encouraging its reporters to take time to pursue book projects, thanks to Executive Editor Leonard Downie and Managing Editor Robert Kaiser. My immediate bosses, Assistant Managing Editor Peter Behr and his deputy, David A. Vise, generously allowed me the leeway to fit the work on this book around my assignments for the paper. Alan Sultan and Joel Joseph of National Press Books brought this project to me, for which I am grateful and honored, and Jay Acton, my agent, took good care of the contractual details.

An uncounted number of sources have aided my reporting of the BCCI story, providing documents, insight, commentary and guidance, time and time again. For the most part, it would violate confidences to name them, but I thank them, anonymously, for their invaluable help. Finally, my wife, Jane Stiles-Potts, supported the sloppy, frantic author in her midst with love, encouragement and iced tea. She's the best.

—Mark Potts, Washington, January 1992

Many people have contributed to this account of the BCCI story. First, there are the many actors in the saga who were kind enough to spare us their time, without expecting any recognition. Then there are those who have assisted the authors with their time and skills. Among these is Benedict Milne, who contributed extensively to Chapter 9; Loli Cardenoso, who translated *The Kings of the Money Launderers* by Daniel Gonzalez from the Spanish; Laura Lehman, who developed a chronology; Anna Kochan, who translated from the French; and the late great Max Kantor, who gathered research in the United States. Many Asian depositors also have given generously of their time. The antics of the Muslim bank have done nothing but harm for the wider and honorable Asian business community

—Nick Kochan and Bob Whittington
London, November 1991

Table of Contents

Cast of Characters

BCCI Executives

Agha Hasan Abedi—Founder and president of BCCI. A visionary known for his spellbinding oratory, he was more a marketing man than a banker. He commanded fanatical loyalty from his employees and used a formidable list of political contacts to fulfill his dream of creating the biggest Muslim bank in the world. Incapacitated by two heart attacks and a heart transplant in 1988, he resigned from BCCI in October 1990. Now in seclusion in Pakistan.

Syed Ziauddin Ali Akbar—Former head of BCCI's treasury operation and a principal in Capcom Financial Services, the commodities trading company that was spun off from the bank. He was convicted and jailed on money-laundering charges in Britain in 1989, and arrested again on similar charges in 1991.

Amjad Awan—Head of Latin American operations for BCCI and personal banker to Panamanian Gen. Manuel Noriega. Sentenced in 1990 to 12 years in prison for his involvement in BCCI money-laundering schemes. Blurted out details of BCCI's secret ownership of First American Bank to an undercover investigator in 1988.

Swaleh Naqvi—Chief executive and financial brains at BCCI. Credited with some of the bank's more bizarre financial escapades. He kept a separate set of books on the bank's finances, the 1990 discovery of which helped break open the BCCI scandal. Naqvi took over management of the bank after Abedi fell ill, then was forced to resign along with his mentor.

Ghassan Qassem—BCCI executive in London who became a key witness against the bank for British intelligence in 1987.

Masihur Rahman—BCCI's chief financial officer, later a key witness against the bank. Headed an internal task force to examine wrongdoing at the bank in 1990.

Abdur Sakhia—Head of BCCI's American operations, later a key witness against the bank.

Abdus Sami—Abedi's right-hand man before Naqvi. Oversaw the initial attempts to purchase Financial General Bankshares (First American Bank).

BCCI Shareholders

Sheik Zayed bin Sultan al-Nahyan—Ruler of Abu Dhabi. An early friend of Abedi and investor in BCCI, by 1990 he owned 77 percent of the bank along with other family members and Abu Dhabi governmental entities.

Sheik Khalifa bin Zayed al-Nahyan—Son of Sheik Zayed and a shareholder in BCCI and Financial General.

Sheik Mohammed bin Zayed al-Nahyan—Son of Sheik Zayed who as a teenager was an early investor in Financial General.

Khalid bin Salim bin-Mahfouz—Head of a Saudi banking family that bailed out BCCI in 1986 and owned 20 percent of the bank before selling out to Sheik Zayed in 1989.

First American Bank Officials

Clark M. Clifford—Highly respected Washington attorney, adviser to presidents and a former cabinet member. Introduced to Abedi by Bert Lance, he represented BCCI and then the Middle Eastern investment group assembled by the bank in the takeover of Financial General (First American Bank) in the late 1970s and early 1980s, then went on to serve as chairman of First American until August 1991.

Robert A. Altman—Clifford's protege and law partner. Served as president of First American and legal adviser to BCCI. Married to actress Lynda Carter.

Khusro Elley—Former BCCI official who was a top executive of First American's New York subsidiary and an active participant in BCCI's Americas Coordinating Committee.

Nicholas deB. Katzenbach—Former U.S. attorney general appointed as First American chairman to succeed Clifford.

BCCI customers

Abbas, Mustafa and Murtaza Gokal—Three Pakistani brothers who operated the Gulf Group, the umbrella for hundreds of shipping companies that became BCCI's biggest—and most risky—customers.

Manuel Antonio Noriega—Panamanian dictator, indicted by the United States in 1988 on drug charges and captured in 1989. Allegedly used BCCI to launder drug money and in return received the royal treatment from BCCI.

Abu Nidal—Palestinian terrorist who allegedly kept secret accounts at BCCI.

Samir Najmeddin—Financial adviser to Nidal who also allegedly traded arms through BCCI.

Kamal Adham—Former head of Saudi intelligence who was a key shareholder in the takeover of Financial General as a front man for BCCI. Also a shareholder in Capcom Financial Services and BCCI.

Ghaith Pharaon—Saudi Arabian businessman used by the bank as front man in the purchase of National Bank of Georgia, Independence Bank in California and CenTrust Savings in Florida.

Faisal Saud al-Fulaij—Former chairman of Kuwaiti Airways who allegedly acted as a front man for BCCI in the purchase of Financial General. Also chairman of Kuwait International Finance Co., BCCI's Kuwaiti affiliate.

Sayed El Jawhary—Aide to Adham who was a BCCI nominee in the purchase of Financial General. Also a shareholder in Capcom Financial Services.

Abdul Raouf Khalil—Saudi businessman who acted as a front for BCCI in the Financial General takeover. Out of contact with BCCI since 1985. Also a shareholder in Capcom Financial Services.

Mohammed Hammoud—Lebanese businessman who owned stock in BCCI and purchased shares in First American's parent company from Clark Clifford and Robert Altman in 1988, allegedly with financing from BCCI. Died under mysterious circumstances in 1990.

Munther Bilbeisi—Jordanian arms dealer and alleged coffee smuggler.

Regulators

Robin Leigh-Pemberton—Governor of the Bank of England who ordered the shutdown of BCCI in July 1991.

William A. Ryback—Federal Reserve official who questioned Altman about possible BCCI involvement in First American in 1989.

Sidney Bailey—Virginia state superintendent of banks whose early concerns about BCCI's involvement in Financial General were all but ignored.

Pierre Jaans—Director-general of Luxembourg Monetary Institute.

Law Enforcement Officials

Robert M. Morgenthau—New York district attorney who launched investigation of BCCI in 1989.

Lord Justice Thomas Bingham—Leader of British inquiry into BCCI.

Robert Mazur—U.S. Customs Service agent who directed Tampa investigation into BCCI money-laundering and raised early concerns about the bank's operations. Resigned from Customs in 1991 because of frustrations with lack of follow-up investigation.

Accounting Firms

Price Waterhouse—Auditors of BCCI's Cayman Islands operation for most of bank's history and of the entire bank since 1987. Criticized for not discovering bank's problems earlier. Hired by British authorities in 1991 to conduct a separate investigative audit of the bank's operations, which brought details of malfeasance to the authorities and led to BCCI's shutdown.

Ernst & Whinney (now Ernst & Young)——Auditor of BCCI's Luxembourg operation until 1987, when it resigned in protest of sloppy bank accounting practices and trading losses.

Touche Ross & Co.—Appointed by British authorities in 1991 to oversee the liquidation of BCCI.

Congressional Investigators

Sen. John Kerry—Massachusetts Democrat who began investigating BCCI's activities in 1988 and held many key hearings after the scandal broke in 1991.

Rep. Charles Schumer—New York Democrat who strongly criticized federal law enforcement agencies' handling of BCCI investigation.

Jack Blum—Formerly Sen. Kerry's chief investigator. Conspiracy buff who uncovered much of BCCI's wrongdoing but was unable to convince federal prosecutors to act. Went instead to Morgenthau, sparking the New York investigation.

Friends of BCCI

Jimmy Carter—Former U.S. president who accepted millions in charitable donations from Abedi and BCCI, regularly traveled on the BCCI corporate jet and appeared with Abedi at BCCI branch openings and other affairs in the 1980s.

Javier Perez de Cuellar—Secretary-general of the United Nations who accepted rides on the BCCI corporate jet.

Bert Lance—Carter loyalist and former director of the Office of Management and Budget. He resigned amid controversy in 1977 and shortly thereafter was hired as a consultant by Abedi, arranging the purchases of National Bank of Georgia and Financial General. Introduced Abedi and BCCI to Carter, Clifford and Altman.

Andrew Young—Former U.S. ambassador to the United Nations and mayor of Atlanta who accepted loans from BCCI's National Bank of Georgia that were later forgiven and described as consulting fees.

Sergio Correa da Costa—Former Brazilian ambassador to the United States who went on the BCCI payroll as a consultant shortly after leaving the diplomatic service and was instrumental in setting up BCCI's affiliate in Brazil.

Ed Rogers—Former top aide to White House Chief of Staff John Sununu. He became Kamal Adham's lawyer after leaving the White House in 1991 for a retainer of $600,000 over two years, despite having almost no experience practicing law. He was forced to resign the position a few days after being hired following controversy over his role.

Chronology of Events

1922—Agha Hasan Abedi is born a Shi'ite Muslim in Lucknow, India, the son of the administrator for the Rajah of Mahmudabad.

1959—Abedi founds United Bank Ltd. in Pakistan with 10 million rupees from the Saigol family.

1972—September: Fearing the impending nationalization of United and other Pakistani banks, Abedi and a group of investors including Bank of America and Sheik Zayed of Abu Dhabi found BCCI with $2.5 million in capital. The new bank's intention is to provide commercial banking services in the Third World.

1975—Acting through the Pakistani Gokal family, BCCI tries unsuccessfully to purchase New York's Chelsea National Bank.

1976—BCCI sets up International Credit and Investment Co., the Cayman Islands subsidiary that owned stock in its own parent company and was to become known as "the bank within the bank."

1977—BCCI's assets reach $2.2 billion. October: Abedi is introduced to former Carter administration official Bert Lance and hires Lance as a consultant to help BCCI buy U.S. banks.

1978—British regulators, concerned about BCCI's rapid growth, refuse to issue the bank a full banking license.

> **January:** Ghaith Pharaon buys National Bank of Georgia on behalf of BCCI from Lance and other investors. January: BCCI hires Clark Clifford and Robert Altman to be its American lawyers. Acting

through a group of clients, BCCI begins purchasing Financial General Bankshares (FGB) stock on the advice of Lance.

February: Financial General management files suit against BCCI, charging that its clients are investing in FGB as an organized group. The Securities and Exchange Commission soon files a similar suit, and the investors settle it by agreeing to disclose their relationships with each other and make a public tender offer.

July: Credit and Commerce American Holdings (CCAH) and Credit and Commerce American Investment (CCAI) are formed to purchase stock in FGB.

October: CCAH and CCAI, representing BCCI's clients, make a $70 million bid for FGB.

1979—BCCI's largest customer, the Gokal brothers' Gulf Group, is allowed to increase its borrowings from the bank in spite of the group's financial troubles.

February: The Federal Reserve Board rejects the CCAH/CCAI bid for Financial General, citing objections by Maryland regulators about the hostile nature of the takeover.

1980—Bank of America, concerned about BCCI's loan and management practices, sells its stock in the bank. BCCI establishes the Third World Prize, seen by Abedi as the equivalent of the Nobel Peace Prize.

April: CCAH and CCAI bring their attempt to buy Financial General to a vote of the company's shareholders, but it is narrowly defeated.

July: FGB management finally agrees to a takeover by CCAH and CCAI for $180 million, including an injection of new capital.

1981—Terrorist Abu Nidal opens an account at BCCI in London. Former President Jimmy Carter is introduced to Abedi by Lance. Abedi becomes a major benefactor of Carter's favorite charities.

April: The Federal Reserve Board holds an unusual hearing into the FGB takeover attempt. Clifford and Altman pledge that BCCI itself will have nothing to do with the financing or control of the bank.

August: The Fed approves Financial General takeover. September: Abedi creates the BCCI Foundation.

1982—BCCI begins opening offices in Miami, San Francisco and other U.S. cities.

January: Manuel Noriega becomes a BCCI client.

April: After approval by New York authorities, CCAH/CCAI takes over Financial General Bankshares. The bank's name is changed to First American Bankshares and Clifford and Altman are installed as its top executives.

1983—BCCI buys Banco Mercantil, a Colombian bank with branches in Medellin and Cali, centers of the cocaine trade. First American buys two Bankers Trust branches in New York in a deal allegedly negotiated by BCCI.

1984—BCCI's assets reach $16 billion. Capcom Financial Services is founded to handle commodities trading for BCCI and other clients. Shareholders include several investors with close ties to BCCI.

1985—Concerned about BCCI's rapid growth, the Luxembourg Monetary Institute asks auditor Price Waterhouse to launch an inquiry into the bank, but ultimately concludes that any problems are the result of poor management practices. In reality, BCCI is in the process of losing $1 billion from ill-advised and fraudulent treasury trading.

> **April:** BCCI sets up an Americas Coordinating Committee to direct the marketing efforts of BCCI, First American and National Bank of Georgia.

> **October:** BCCI, acting through Ghaith Pharaon, purchases control of Independence Bank of Encino, Calif. A BCCI employee is named chairman of Independence.

1986—

> **May:** BCCI contemplates buying a small bank in Miami through a front man, but the deal is later dropped.

> **June:** Price Waterhouse reports $430 million in losses in BCCI's treasury operation. To cover the losses, Abedi siphons $150 million from the BCCI pension account in the Cayman Islands.

> **June:** The CIA circulates a report on BCCI to law enforcement agencies suggesting that the intelligence agency knows that BCCI illicitly owns First American. The CIA itself is using BCCI to help finance Iran-contra deals and for intelligence operations in Afghanistan.

> **July:** Clifford and Altman buy stock in First American's parent company, CCAH, using $15 million borrowed from BCCI.

July: BCCI brings in the bin-Mahfouz family as investors to help bail out losses at the bank.

December: Concerned that Pharaon's financial troubles may result in seizure of National Bank of Georgia, BCCI arranges for First American to get an option to buy NBG from Pharaon.

December: U.S. Customs Service agents begin the Operation C-Chase money-laundering investigation in Tampa.

1987—British intelligence learns of BCCI's connections with Abu Nidal.

April: Upset with the bank's internal accounting and management practices, Ernst & Whinney resigns as one of BCCI's two auditors. Price Waterhouse becomes the company's sole auditor.

April: Abedi boasts to executives of BCCI's Far East region: "You are now with the First American Group of banks."

August: After the Georgia legislature approves interstate banking law—thanks in part to $1.25 million spent by BCCI on lobbying—First American acquires NBG from BCCI for more than $220 million.

December: International "college" of regulators is created to examine BCCI.

1988—Pharaon, using money borrowed from BCCI, begins purchasing 25 percent of CenTrust Savings, giving BCCI control of the shares.

February: Abedi has a heart attack and later undergoes heart transplant surgery.

March: Clifford and Altman sell a portion of their CCAH shares for a net profit of $9.8 million in a deal arranged by BCCI.

September: BCCI executive Amjad Awan tells an undercover federal officer that BCCI owns First American.

October: BCCI officials are arrested in Tampa at fake bachelor party; the bank and others are charged with money-laundering.

1989—Senate investigator Jack Blum, unable to interest federal prosecutors in information that BCCI owns First American, goes to New York District Attorney Robert Morgenthau, who begins an investigation of BCCI.

October: Bin-Mahfouz family sells its 20 percent stake in BCCI to Abu Dhabi royal family, giving Abu Dhabi a 55 percent stake.

November: Price Waterhouse, in a preliminary report about fiscal 1989, gives BCCI a fairly clean bill of health and says the bank had a profit of $9 million in the first nine months of 1989. BCCI's assets reach a peak of more than $23 billion.

December: Federal Reserve writes Altman asking about rumors that BCCI has made loans to First American shareholders despite assurances to the contrary. Altman tells Fed he knows of no such loans, but doesn't mention loans he and Clifford received from BCCI to buy their stock in the company.

1990—

January: BCCI pleads guilty to money-laundering charges in Tampa and is fined a record $14.8 million.

February: Price Waterhouse tells BCCI it has discovered unusual transactions that may have been fraudulent and declines to approve the bank's annual audit.

March: BCCI sets up an internal task force to investigate the irregularities found by Price Waterhouse.

April: Price Waterhouse reports to BCCI management that the bank lost $498 million in 1989. The accounting firm begins to tell authorities in Britain and Luxembourg about BCCI's problems.

April: Abu Dhabi, apparently oblivious to the full extent of BCCI's problems, takes control of the bank with 77 percent of the stock and announces plans to move headquarters to Abu Dhabi from London. After a personal appeal by the ailing Abedi, Abu Dhabi Sheik Zayed agrees to pump new funds into the bank. BCCI lays off 4,000 workers, about 25 percent of the total work force.

May: Washington business magazine *Regardies* publishes a detailed story raising questions about the overlaps between BCCI and First American shareholders.

July: BCCI chief executive Swaleh Naqvi flies to Abu Dhabi with his secret files on the bank, which are turned over to Price Waterhouse.

October: Sheik Zayed, grasping the problems at the bank, forces Abedi and Naqvi to resign.

November: The Federal Reserve begins a formal investigation into the ownership of First American.

1991—

February: The Washington Post reports that BCCI appears to secretly own First American. The Federal Reserve orders First American to stop doing business with BCCI.

March: The Federal Reserve orders BCCI to sell its secret holding in First American.

March: The Bank of England appoints Price Waterhouse to thoroughly investigate BCCI's finances.

June 28: Price Waterhouse delivers a report to the Bank of England describing massive fraud at BCCI.

July 3: Luxembourg puts the Gokal family's Gulf International Holdings S.A. into receivership.

July 5: The Bank of England and other regulators around the world shut down BCCI.

July 29: The Federal Reserve formally charges BCCI, its top executives, Pharaon and several First American shareholders with the illegal takeover of the U.S. banks and proposes fining them a total of $200 million. Simultaneously, New York District Attorney Morgenthau indicts BCCI, Abedi and Naqvi for fraud, larceny and money-laundering.

August: Clifford and Altman resign from First American. Nicholas Katzenbach, former U.S. attorney general, takes over as chairman.

September: Several BCCI executives, including Naqvi, are arrested in Abu Dhabi. Extradition to the U.S., however, is uncertain.

September: Clifford and Altman appear before a congressional committee investigating BCCI and its relationship with First American. "Our consciences are clear," Clifford says.

November: Tentative plans set for liquidation of BCCI. The bank's total losses are said to exceed $9.4 billion.

December: Federal and state authorities settle charges against BCCI, which pleads guilty to racketeering charges involving money-laundering and the illegal takeover of First American and other U.S. banks. The bank agrees to forfeit more than $550 million in U.S. assets, some of which will be used to bail out financially troubled First American and Independence banks. The plea agreement does not cover any individuals, and state and federal investigations continue.

1992—

January 14: British court approves liquidation plan, under which BCCI creditors and depositors will get 30 to 40 cents on the dollar.

Introduction

The dignified, gentlemanly world of British banking had never seen anything like it. As employees of the Bank of Credit and Commerce International returned from lunch on the warm Friday afternoon of July 5, 1991, they were met at the door of BCCI's London branches by stern-faced bank managers. The employees were told to collect their belongings from their offices, remove no papers and leave the premises in an orderly fashion.

At the bank's British headquarters at 101 Leadenhall Street in the heart of London's financial district, the notice to leave came as the bank's predominantly Muslim staff was returning from a special room set aside in the bank for prayers. At first, the employees were bemused, but then reality set in and panic ensued. Some employees rushed around the BCCI offices, looting cash from tellers' drawers, wondering if it might be their last chance to get anything from the bank to whom many had given their careers.

For BCCI, the jig was up. After nearly 20 years of increasingly corrupt business, the Arab-owned bank was being shut down by regulators who had belatedly discovered that it was rife with fraud, double-dealing, money-laundering, bribery and other wrongdoing—a scandal of nearly unimaginable proportions that was proving to be an acute embarrassment to government officials around the world.

There seemed to be nothing that BCCI had not done, or been accused of doing. Some described it as a full-service bank for criminals. Such shady customers as terrorist Abu Nidal, the Medellin cocaine cartel and Panamanian strongman Manuel Noriega used BCCI to launder money and finance illegal activities, knowing that the bank would keep quiet about their business. Internally, the bank was just as rotten, manipulating accounts, forging documents and even stealing its customers' money—a sort of bank robbery in reverse. Contrary to its deep roots in the Islamic community, BCCI regularly pilfered millions from the Muslim customers to whom it offered special "Islamic banking" services designed to meet religious law. From humble origins in Pakistan, BCCI had grown into one of the world's largest banks, with $23 billion in assets.

Under the leadership of its Pakistani founder, Agha Hasan Abedi, BCCI had been founded in 1972 with a noble cause: to become the first major bank to emerge from and serve the Third World. The strategy was brilliant, and BCCI grew with unprecedented speed, fueled by the oil money that was flowing into its primary customer base in the Persian Gulf. Abedi, a visionary who idolized the rajahs of his native India, practiced an unusual form of management that drew heavily on a mystical offshoot of Islam and was devoted to spending buckets of money on philanthropy and customer service. It sounded crazy, but it seemed to work.

Still, the rapid growth had its drawbacks. Sloppy management and business setbacks led to huge losses at the bank. Desperate for new deposits, BCCI opened its doors to anybody with a buck, including terrorists, drug dealers and arms merchants. BCCI took advantage of both its unprecedented connections in the Third World and the virtual lack of regulation it enjoyed from its bases in Luxembourg and the Cayman Islands, where bank secrecy rules reigned and nobody in power asked too many questions. As BCCI spread its tentacles around the world, it found less, not more, regulation. International banking law is notoriously uncoordinated, and farflung operations can go virtually unchecked—especially if a bank is willing, as was BCCI, to routinely lie to government overseers and even its internal auditors about what it is up to. Abusing the trust that most people place in banks, BCCI was rotten to the core.

But BCCI couldn't hold onto all of its secrets forever. American officials had caught it red-handed in a drug-money-laundering "sting" operation in Tampa, Fla., in 1988, and other regulators had begun sniffing around BCCI. The bank's problems and shady dealings had been whispered about in the world banking community for years, although no one in power seemed too eager to take any drastic steps to stop them. Now, in the summer of 1991, regulators had little choice. Over the past few months, the bank's auditors had uncovered increasingly serious signs of wrongdoing that indicated that BCCI secretly had lost billions of dollars over the years and in the process had run afoul of almost every banking regulation and practice. On June 28, banking officials in London had received the most damning piece of information yet. A detailed audit done for the British government by the accounting firm Price Waterhouse laid out minute details of BCCI's fraud. The auditors provided regulators with a financial document that read more like a crime novel. Sprinkled with quaint code names for the bank and its customers, the report was a compelling account of fraud run amok.

In addition to uncovering many of BCCI's illegal activities, the audit demonstrated to authorities that the bank was in the terminal stages of financial collapse. Officials feared that if they did not take some action to stanch the bleeding at the bank, worried depositors would begin a frantic "run" on BCCI—attempting to withdraw money that the bank, frankly, didn't have and possibly endangering other banks in the process. For a week after the Price Waterhouse report arrived at the Bank of England, phone lines buzzed between regulators in London, Washington, Luxembourg and elsewhere, as authorities attempted to coordinate their actions against the bank. Finally, the decision was made to shut BCCI down on July 5.

Officials at the accounting and consulting firm Touche Ross had been told by regulators that morning to drop whatever they were doing and be ready to handle a "major business failure," forcing the firm to call off a management strategy conference that it had spent weeks preparing. On orders from a court in Luxembourg, where BCCI had its corporate headquarters, and from regulators in London and the Cayman Islands, where BCCI had its main bases of operations, Touche Ross set out to close the bank in London and elsewhere that Friday afternoon and over the next few days. Regulators around the world seized BCCI's assets—

which turned out to be far less than what the bank had claimed.

The shutdown of BCCI caused consternation among the bank's employees and depositors. Bewildered BCCI employees in London—some of them facing the loss of both their paychecks and their deposits—gathered on the doorsteps of the banks' offices in the days following the closing, angrily demanding to know what was going on. British depositors, many of them Muslim immigrants who had put their money in BCCI out of allegiance to the bank's Pakistani founders and its strong ties to the Third World, discovered that their deposits were insured only up to £15,000, or about $25,000. That limit all but wiped out many small businesses that were customers of the bank and had a devastating impact on a number of small local governments around Britain that had deposited millions of pounds in taxpayers' money in BCCI.

As the extent of its crimes became known, the timing of the BCCI shutdown by the British government and the Bank of England became a subject of great debate in Britain. Critics charged that authorities had known about BCCI's wrongdoing for years and done next to nothing about it.

With the lid finally blown, newspapers and magazines in Britain and elsewhere in the world carried lurid reports on what was emerging as perhaps the largest financial scandal in history. The headlines accused BCCI of everything from running its own terrorist squads to bribing some of the world's mightiest politicians. Some of the most outlandish allegations proved unfounded, but there was no doubt that BCCI had earned the title bestowed on it by *Time* magazine: "The World's Sleaziest Bank."

Three weeks after the shutdown in Europe, the burgeoning scandal jumped the Atlantic to the United States. Over the weekend of July 27 and 28, the Federal Reserve staff circulated among its governors and senior officials at other federal agencies an extraordinary 108-page document—the draft of formal charges alleging that for several years BCCI had secretly and illegally owned or controlled First American

Bankshares, the largest bank in the nation's capital, as well as two other U.S. banks and a now-defunct savings and loan. (The latter charge, on top of everything else, put BCCI in the middle of the gigantic U.S. savings and loan debacle.) The Fed had been building its case for months, and on Monday, July 29, it went public. The formal complaint called for a record $200 million fine against BCCI and a lifetime ban of nine key BCCI executives and associates from the U.S. banking business.

The Fed's complaint contained shocking details of how BCCI had controlled the four American financial institutions right under regulators' noses, providing money to a group of sham investors from the Middle East who were listed as the institutions' owners. BCCI also was alleged to have manipulated First American's closely held stock on several occasions, siphoning hundreds of millions of dollars out of the Washington bank to keep financially ailing BCCI afloat. As the Fed's accusations splashed across front pages around the U.S., distressed and disgusted depositors removed more than $1 billion from their accounts at First American and the other BCCI-owned U.S. banks, greatly weakening them.

Simultaneous to the Fed's release in Washington of its thick civil complaint against BCCI, criminal charges were announced against the bank by New York District Attorney Robert M. Morgenthau, who had been conducting his own aggressive investigation into BCCI's operations for two years, sometimes to the chagrin of slower-moving federal officials. Morgenthau charged the bank and its two top executives with a laundry list of offenses that included fraud, money-laundering, grand larceny and even the alleged bribery of government officials in Peru. And the feisty veteran D.A. promised in a press conference that there was much more to come—the current indictment included "maybe 20 to 25 percent of what will ultimately result from this investigation," he said. As had happened in Britain, there were accusations that American authorities had failed to see BCCI's obvious problems. They apparently had missed BCCI's ownership of First American and the other banks for nearly a decade, and several government agencies had failed to heed increasingly specific warnings from the Central Intelligence Agency during the 1980s that BCCI was a corrupt operation. Even a record $15 million fine against the bank in the earlier money-laundering case in Florida had not tipped off regulators to the broader scope of BCCI's alleged wrongdoing.

"This indictment spells out the largest bank fraud in world financial history," Morgenthau said. "BCCI was operated as a corrupt criminal organization throughout its entire 19-year history. It systematically falsified its records. It knowingly allowed itself to be used to launder the illegal income of drug sellers and other criminals. And it paid bribes and kickbacks to public officials."

Morgenthau was not alone in his dramatic description of BCCI's wrongdoing. "The culture of the bank," declared Bank of England Governor Robin Leigh-Pemberton, "is criminal." Those who had scented trouble at BCCI along the way now could only nod knowingly: The CIA's half-serious internal description of BCCI as the "Bank of Crooks and Criminals International" never seemed more fitting.

The publicity of the indictment also cast a spotlight on the many important and politically well-connected friends that BCCI had cultivated over the years. Part of the bank's modus operandi had been to develop strong relationships with powerful people who might help it gain business or escape regulation. Some of these contacts were paid well by BCCI for their friendship, but others were sucked in unwittingly, including such world leaders as former President Jimmy Carter and U.N. Secretary-General Javier Perez de Cuellar. BCCI appeared to have bought, sold and wielded political influence on a scale scarcely seen before. It kept political leaders and ambassadors on its payroll and made loans at favorable terms or forgave loans to others, including Andrew Young, the former U.S. ambassador to the United Nations and mayor of Atlanta.

Abedi and other BCCI officials seemed to have a special knack for understanding how to use their powerful friends, knowing that an innocent photograph of Abedi and former President Carter standing together carried important symbolic clout in the Third World, giving BCCI instant political cachet. Similarly, when Carter or Perez de Cuellar alighted from one of BCCI's corporate jets in some developing nation's capital, the message was clear: this bank was OK to do business with. Men like Carter and Perez de Cuellar may have been inadvertent accomplices to such schemes, but they often were indirectly compensated in the form of huge BCCI donations to their favorite causes.

BCCI's political dexterity, in fact, led to its foothold in United States. When Bert Lance was forced out of the Carter administration in 1977, he was contacted almost immediately by Abedi, who employed him as a consultant to look for U.S. investments. Lance soon introduced the BCCI head to one of the grand old men of the Democratic Party, lawyer and political fixer Clark M. Clifford, and Clifford's protege, rising superlawyer Robert A. Altman. BCCI hired Clifford and Altman to handle its legal work in the United States, and after federal regulators made it clear that they didn't want BCCI to own an American bank, the two men shepherded through the Federal Reserve the takeover of First American by a group of Middle Eastern investors assembled by Abedi— and allegedly acting as front men for BCCI.

For Clifford, a former secretary of defense and adviser to every Democratic president since Truman, the relationship with BCCI was to be the sad end to an otherwise distinguished career. As the BCCI scandal unfolded, Clifford and Altman claimed repeatedly that they had been unaware of their client's illegal activities, particularly the alleged secret ownership of First American. But many observers wondered how two lawyers so smart could have been so dumb. "My heart wants to believe you, but my head says no," Rep. Charles Schumer (D-N.Y.) told Clifford and Altman during a congressional hearing in September 1991. Many observers expected Clifford and Altman to be indicted for their roles in BCCI's secret ownership of First American Bank.

Ultimately, of course, the cost of the BCCI scandal will be much more than reputations, like those of Clifford and Altman. Estimates of the amount lost by BCCI depositors around the world have risen steadily from $5 billion to $10 billion to $20 billion, and accountants at Touche Ross estimated in December 1991 that at least $9.4 billion is unaccounted for. Thousands of bank employees and depositors in Britain and elsewhere lost almost everything they had. Also victims, apparently, were BCCI's principal owners, Abu Dhabi leader Sheik Zayed bin Sultan al-Nahyan and members of his family and government, who had taken control of the bank in late 1989, just as its malfeasance was being discovered. Sheik Zayed was an old friend of Abedi, but when he learned what was going on at the bank, he fired BCCI's founder and other top executives. By the end of 1991, the sheik's representatives were working with court-appointed liquidators in Britain to come up with a plan to partly repay some of BCCI's depositors and creditors. It appeared that the best that these victims could hope for was about 40 cents on the dollar.

How, it is now asked, could a bank have gone so disastrously wrong? Where were the regulators and auditors who were supposed to keep watch over the bank's books? Why, most importantly, was a financial institution known by some to be corrupt allowed to go on taking deposits and conducting business?

The regulators and accountants who supervise banks have a lot to answer for. For 10 years, there was solid evidence building up against BCCI—for those who wanted to see it. The Bank of England saw the danger signs of reckless growth early on and refused BCCI a full banking license, but BCCI still convinced the central bank to let it stay in business. Luxembourg officials made inquiries when the bank lost hundreds of millions in an ill-fated commodities trading scheme in the mid-1980s, but they were assured by Abedi and his henchmen that everything was fine at the bank. Similarly, in the United States, some federal and state banking regulators asked the right questions in 1981 about the takeover of First American, only to be promised by Clifford and Altman that BCCI was in no way directly involved. In the wake of the BCCI scandal, some critics have suggested darkly —and so far without proof—that the bank's powerful political connections kept it from being more closely scrutinized and delayed actions against it. British officials are scrutinizing the Bank of England's actions, while congressional committees are looking into the roles of the CIA, Justice Department and other U.S. authorities in uncovering the bank's wrongdoing—or failing to. Even as the BCCI affair was unfolding, Congress was considering legislation that would address many of the loopholes in federal banking law that BCCI took advantage of to operate in the U.S. and elsewhere, and it later passed laws giving the Federal Reserve more control over foreign banks operating in U.S. territory. No less than Clark Clifford, ironically, endorsed the proposed tightening of the rules. Investigators hint that there are many more stories of wrongdoing still to come about BCCI's activities, some of which are expected to be shocking. As these revelations ripple around the world, it is likely to become painfully clear that any change in banking laws will have come too late to stop BCCI from ripping off billions of dollars.

Chapter 1

═══════════════════════════════════

The Man from Mahmudabad

For anybody else, the situation might have represented a social and diplomatic gaffe of major proportions. To Agha Hasan Abedi, it was an opportunity to make the best of a bad situation—and to cement an important friendship. The occasion was a 1967 state visit to Pakistan by the new leader of Abu Dhabi, Sheik Zayed bin Sultan al-Nahyan. Abedi, a leading Pakistani banker, was in charge of the arrangements for the trip, and he had suggested to Pakistani leader Ayub Khan that it might be a fine gesture to present the sheik, an avid outdoorsman, with a horse. But the gift embarrassed Zayed, who had brought along nothing with which to reciprocate.

Abedi didn't miss a trick. He quickly extended his wrist, slipped off his diamond-encrusted Rolex watch and indicated that Zayed should present it to Ayub Khan. Honor was restored, and Abedi, who was angling to open branches of his United Bank in Abu Dhabi, had crept up another rung in Sheik Zayed's estimation—especially since the sheik himself had given Abedi the watch at a previous meeting.

In the grey-flannel world of banking, Agha Hasan Abedi had a flair for the dramatic—especially if it would help him win a rich and powerful customer. Even as a young banker, Abedi was known for the zeal with which he cultivated contacts with potential customers—or with those who could bring him customers. In the world of banking, the development of such relationships can be the secret of success, and Abedi's ability to make—and use—important friends was uncanny. From the start, Abedi had felt a natural affinity with the privileged people whose business he courted. Despite his own humble beginnings, or perhaps because of them, to him, their fellowship was almost a birthright.

Born in India, Abedi entered the banking business in 1946, as a 24-year-old trainee at the Habib Bank in Bombay. Well-educated, with a degree in English literature, philosophy and law from his hometown Islamic university, Abedi came from a long line of civil servants to the grand rajahs of Mahmudabad. To many who knew him, Abedi's Mahmudabad background was a key to understanding him.

Once one of the most dynamic kingdoms on the Indian subcontinent, Mahmudabad was a center of great wealth, where feudal Muslim rajahs had ruled for centuries from a gold and silver throne in an ornate palace, financing idealistic politicians such as Mohandas Gandhi, plotting against the British empire and giving gifts to their subjects. After Mahmudabad and other kingdoms fell in the mid-20th century, their citizens became a close-knit clan, bound together by history, family, religion and ethnicity. In many ways, friends said, Abedi later attempted to recreate the glamor of the Mahmudabad empire at his Bank of Credit and Commerce International, bringing together many of his old friends, lavishing money upon employees, public officials and charity, wielding political influence and, above all, ruling his financial empire like one of the rajahs of old.

To some in Pakistan, where Abedi and many other Indian Shi'ite Muslims emigrated in 1947 and 1948 following the bloody religious riots that accompanied the partition of India and the formation of Pakistan, Abedi did nothing less than attempt to replace his humble family background with the trappings of a king. "It was Abedi compensating himself for his social origins," Abeda Hussain, a Pakistani politician, told *The Washington Post's* Steve Coll many years later. "He was not interested in the development of Pakistan. But he was interested in being known as a subcontinent mogul." A Pakistani businessman close to Abedi told Coll that to BCCI's executives, "He was their rajah. . . . Privately, we used the word raj-wallah"—man of the kingdom—"many times."

The Mahmudabad connection helped land Abedi the job at Habib Bank: He was recommended for the post by the then-rajah. Early on, he was identified as executive material by the bank, starting work not as an ordinary bank trainee but in a special officer-training program. Abedi quickly made his mark, building a reputation among colleagues as a good marketing man and a persuasive talker, correct and polite. A keen developer of new business, he was willing to do all the early spadework to bring in new clients and was quickly promoted to become head of the bank's development department. Not much given to a social life, the young banker made most of his social contacts at meetings with clients and banking conferences, where he worked the room to build new business.

Aside from a love of Indian classical music, Abedi's only passion outside work seemed to be his religion. He was a devout Shi'ite Muslim, abstaining from alcohol and leading a modest personal life with his wife, the product of an arranged marriage. As his success in business grew, however, Abedi moved away from the traditional Islamic religion to the offshoot philosophy of Sufism, a more mystical variant whose devotees believe they have received special inner knowledge directly from Allah. He used the Sufist charm and charisma outlawed by traditional Islam to mystify his followers both inside and outside the bank with suggestions of infallibility and self-sacrifice. To reinforce his reputation, he would tell colleagues that his great-grandfather had come from the Persian religious town of Om and that his great-grandmother was born in Nishalbur, the home of the Omar Khayyam. One loyal friend later was quoted as saying, "He is the epitome of the high Muslim culture of India . . . there is no personal scandal about him, and he would never speak ill of anyone." Abedi, in turn, received the deference from his employees that he demanded: He was commonly addressed by underlings as "Agha Sahib," a term of great respect and affection.

Abedi's banking career progressed rapidly. He was made manager of Habib Bank's Rawalpindhi branch, then won a prestigious posting to Lahore, the important Pakistani provincial capital, after Habib Bank moved its base of operations to Pakistan. His puritan religious ethic for hard work infected others, and the people Abedi worked with were driven to spend long hours at the bank. But few got very close to the hard-working banker. "He kept a certain distance from the people who worked in the bank. On the other hand, he was much more open than most presidents, because he didn't lead a social life at all," said Nadir Rahim, Abedi's head of human resources at BCCI. "He was dedicated to the bank to the point that when you left at 9:30 or 10 at night he was still there, doing other things, making plans. He would say, 'All right, I think I have given all of you enough time; now I must get on with what I am doing.'"

After just a few years in the banking business, Abedi had developed a formidable list of business contacts, and he knew how to use them. One contact that he had cultivated as early as the mid-1950s was the Saigols, Pakistan's wealthiest textile family and a major political force in the nation. The Saigols were looking to broaden their investments and decided to raise money by selling stock in their company to the public. For guidance, the family turned to their helpful bank manager, Abedi. The Saigols asked Habib Bank if it would allow him to work exclusively for them, and the bank, anxious to please a valued customer, agreed. The temporary assignment eventually became permanent. (A less flattering version of Abedi's parting from the bank suggests that he had extended loans to the Saigols well beyond the bank's limits and thus was told to leave.)

Abedi gained considerable respect for his successful handling of the Saigol stock sale, and within 18 months he had persuaded the Saigols that they should help him start a new bank. The family committed 10 million rupees (about

$500,000) to the venture, and United Bank was launched in 1959 with the Saigols as virtually sole owners.

Many of the practices that Abedi was to apply years later at BCCI were apparent from the beginning at United. The launch of the bank, for instance, was characterized by Abedi's special knack for big names and influence. He appointed the former prime minister of Pakistan, I. I. Chundrigar, as chairman of the United board in the expectation that this would help him to get close to the nation's new leader, Mohammed Ayub Khan, who had come to power in a bloodless coup in 1958.

Abedi also moved quickly to expand his bank outside the boundaries of Pakistan and to tap into riches beyond those of his home country. As an Islamic state, Pakistan had natural religious and political ties to the Arab world, and Abedi sought to exploit it fully. But this was several years before the Arab nations around the Persian Gulf were to win full control of their oil resources from Western companies and begin to pile up petrodollars for themselves. At the time that Abedi made his first visit to scout out the possibility of setting up an Arab joint venture, in the mid-1960s, the nations of the Gulf were pretty much a group of tiny emirates ruled by unsophisticated local chieftains who still took financial advice from the West. When Abedi approached Sheik Shakbut, the emir of the largest nation in the group, Abu Dhabi, about starting a bank there, the sheik rejected his overtures—relying on the advice of the British Bank of the Middle East, which had told him the region did not need another financial institution.

But other forces in the area were aware that the emirates needed to be more open to the outside world, and not just to the powers that had colonized them and their oil resources. In August 1966, Sheik Shakbut's younger brother Zayed, concerned about the economic damage his brother was inflicting on the nascent country, overthrew Shakbut in a peaceful coup backed by a group of British military men. Though unsophisticated and semiliterate, the new sheik was altogether more open to foreign influence and politically savvy about the power his nation wielded. He later asserted command over the seven emirates of the region, and in 1971 joined with Dubai, Sharjah, Ajman, Fujairah, Ras al-Khaimah and Um al-Quawin to form the United Arab Emirates—a small (32,000 square miles), sparsely populated (200,000) but unbelievably rich federation.

Abedi's United Bank and his old employer, Habib Bank, began courting Sheik Zayed soon after his ascension. For the Pakistani banks, the opening of a branch in Abu Dhabi would be an invaluable way to tap into the nation's potentially huge supply of oil money. It also was a potential launching pad for expansion into other oil-rich Arab nations. But attracting the attention of Sheik Zayed required some unusual tactics. The sheik's closest contact with Pakistan was not via conventional diplomatic channels, but through hunting with falcons and bustards, the largest game birds in Pakistan. The sheik apparently was quite a hunter. The travel writer Wilfred Thesiger met Sheik Zayed as a young man when he spent most of his time in the al-Ain oasis and wrote of him and his Bedouin followers: "He had a great reputation among the Bedu. . . . They said admiringly, 'Zayed is a Bedu. He knows about camels, can ride like one of us, can shoot and knows how to fight.'"

Sheik Zayed put together a hunting expedition to Pakistan soon after seizing power. He sent a cable to the Habib Bank— which already had been in touch with him about the possibility of setting up a joint-venture bank in Abu Dhabi—to say that he was interested in coming over to Baluchistan to hunt with his birds of prey. But the Habib Bank fumbled its opportunity, responding that it could promise nothing better than shooting and deer hunting. That gave the canny Abedi an opening. He immediately fired off a cable to the new Abu Dhabi leader: "Excellent falconry here. Don't worry, I can fix everything up." The visit to Pakistan led to some absurd— but critical—rivalry for the sheik's attention and business. When Sheik Zayed and his party were due to arrive at the Karachi airport, both Abedi and the managing director of the Habib Bank showed up to greet him. The Pakistani government's chief of protocol was horrified. Whose guest was the sheik supposed to be? Both bankers claimed the honor. When Zayed landed, the chief of protocol said he would let the sheik decide. But the sheik was tired after his journey and accepted an invitation from the protocol official to rest at a government guest house until he had made up his mind. The bankers shifted their vigil to the house. But after hours of waiting for the sheik to emerge, the managing director of the Habib Bank departed, leaving a disgruntled message that the sheik could contact him when he was ready to see him. When Sheik Zayed awoke and summoned the bankers, only Abedi was still waiting to welcome him to Pakistan. United and Abedi had scored important points with the new leader of Abu Dhabi.

Nothing was too much trouble for Abedi, who personally supervised every last detail of the visit, impressing the sheik and winning his praise. Supposedly, on another visit by the sheik, each of the two banks arranged for a bouquet of flowers for Zayed to receive when he arrived at the airport. The United Bank's representative, upset that his bouquet was smaller than Habib's, switched the name tags on the floral pieces when the opposition wasn't looking.

Abedi worked hard and patiently at cultivating this important new contact, and his efforts paid off: Sheik Zayed ultimately allowed United to open branches in Abu Dhabi several years ahead of Habib Bank. Abedi's bank now had a foothold in a country that was to undergo a most extraordinary transformation. By the late 1960s, oil money was flooding into Abu Dhabi, and Sheik Zayed had become one of the world's richest men. The cultural and emotional shock of his sudden conversion from a man used to the simplicity of a picnic of dried fish wrapped in newspaper to an Arab Croesus must have been enormous. Despite his openness, Sheik Zayed had little exposure to the outside world, and now he was being pursued for his wealth by some very sophisticated operators, whom he had no means to repel.

The newly enriched sheik began to travel, and Abedi established a protocol department at United Bank to look after his every whim. The department reportedly spent as much as 100,000 Pakistani rupees ($5,000) a day to maintain Sheik Zayed's palaces in Pakistan and to serve the sheik's visiting relatives. Several dozen bank employees were assigned to tend to the sheik. Abedi also helped Zayed acquire residences all over the world. To accommodate the sheik on his occasional visits to Britain, the banker established a base in a fashionable London neighborhood. Zayed, who is thought to have had at least 14 wives and more than 40 children, housed his harem across the square from his London home in a luxurious white mansion with gilded gates. He cut a strange figure emerging from that genteel corner.

Abu Dhabi was the first building block in Abedi's plan for United Bank's international expansion, and he now looked to move into Saudi Arabia. Both he and Habib Bank had applied to the governor of the Saudi Monetary Agency, Anwar Ali, for permission to open branches in Jeddah, but both were turned down. Once again, however, Abedi's brilliant opportunism and ring of contacts came into play. He heard that the Saudi royal family had written to Gen. Yahya Khan, who had just overthrown Pakistan's Ayub, thanking him for his support of the Arab cause and asking him if there was anything they could do in return. In normal circumstances, Khan would have declined politely. But Abedi knew that Khan had a weakness for liquor, and he played on this. Abedi ensured that a letter asking the royal family of Saudi Arabia to grant United permission to set up a branch was put in front of Khan after a session of heavy drinking, according to one version of the story. The leader unwittingly signed the application, the request was granted immediately and the first United branch was opened in Dhahran. Officials of Habib Bank complained bitterly, but Anwar Ali neatly explained that his earlier refusal had covered branches only in Jeddah, not in Dhahran.

For all his success in using his political leverage to expand his bank overseas, however, Abedi's connections did not always prove rewarding at home. Following Pakistan's defeat by India in the short, bloody war over East Pakistan—

Bangladesh—in 1972, there was a change of regime in Pakistan, and Zulfiqar Ali Bhutto became prime minister. Bhutto, a socialist, was no friend of the Pakistani banking system in general, nor of Abedi's United Bank in particular. His program included nationalization of the banks, and Abedi was forced to give up control of United.

At the same time, Abedi was falling out of favor with his chief financial backers, the Saigol family. Some sources claim that the Saigols were overborrowing from their own bank and that Abedi was resisting. The family wanted him replaced, but faced an almost complete mutiny from Abedi's devoted staff. To forestall the Saigols, Abedi went to Ghulam Ishaq Khan, the president of the Pakistan State Bank, who intervened to keep Abedi in place until the bank was nationalized. (Ishaq Khan subsequently became head of the BCCI Foundation, Abedi's charitable fund, and now is the president of Pakistan.)

Even as he was losing control of United in early 1972, Abedi was laying plans for his next venture—a bank in which he would have the controlling stake. He went to his old and trusted contact, Sheik Zayed, with a request that the sheik repay with hard cash the help that Abedi had given him on the many occasions Zayed had come to Pakistan on hunting expeditions. As was later to be the case with seemingly every major financial transaction involving BCCI, there is a dispute about how this seed money for the bank was handled. One version has it that Sheik Zayed provided Abedi with the $2.5 million he needed, but other sources indicate that Saudi businessman Kamal Adham, another subsequent supporter, and the Bank of America, an early BCCI investor, may have lent Abedi the money. Bhutto said later that he believed Abedi stole the $2.5 million from United Bank, perhaps by creating some phony loans using a system that he subsequently applied on a grand scale at BCCI.

In any event, Abedi obtained BCCI's startup money and began seeking more, preferably from an American backer. Abedi went first to financial services giant American Express Co., which was impressed by his credentials with the Gulf

Arabs and prepared to back him. However, the company wanted some management control, which Abedi was not prepared to give. Abedi then turned to Bank of America, with which he had a longstanding relationship dating from when BofA was seeking to establish itself in Pakistan and needed an affiliated network of branches there.

BofA had first approached Habib Bank, which refused, but United agreed to cooperate, giving BCCI a beachhead in Pakistan. A little later, Abedi also had helped the big American bank in a small but significant way. The first branch of the new BofA bank was to open on the second floor of a building in Karachi, directly above United Bank, but the building's architects warned that the floor beams could not carry the weight of the BofA safe. The ever-gracious Abedi solved BofA's problem by providing a corner for the safe in United's offices.

Conveniently, Bank of America was now looking for a foothold in the Third World, and it repaid Abedi's persistent friendship by agreeing to take a 30 percent stake in his fledgling bank, providing the final piece of the jigsaw puzzle for the international financial institution that Abedi had dreamed of. On Sept. 21, 1972, the Bank of Credit and Commerce International was registered in the banking haven of Luxembourg, founded by Agha Hasan Abedi with more than a little help from his friends.

When Bhutto heard about the creation of the new bank, he had Abedi's passport confiscated. Winning it back took all of Abedi's powers of persuasion. Among other things, he convinced Sheik Zayed to set up a charitable foundation in Pakistan, to build a hospital in Lahore and to start two newspapers in Bhutto's Sindh province. Abedi had also begun making friends in Iran, and the shah of Iran's brother, Prince Mahmood Reza Pahlavi, is thought to have interceded with Bhutto on Abedi's behalf. Abedi talked openly about creating the biggest bank in the world, and not from one of the traditional financial capitals, such as New York, London or Paris, but from a base in the Third World. His achievement in building United Bank into the second-largest bank in

Pakistan was considered little short of a miracle, and when he regaled his colleagues with his expansionary plans for the new bank, they believed him and wanted to be part of them. In flowery, even mystical language, he described himself to them as a visionary and urged them all to project themselves into the future. Abedi's inspirational speeches to his staff often sounded like twisted religious sermons. "Honesty is magic," he once told staff members. "Money is helpful. Participation is power." Nadir Rahim, who had known Abedi since he was a child, recalled "how he started collecting a team that he thought would take it forward, because he already had a very specific plan for it to become an international bank, a Third World bank, a Third World voice."

In Abedi's vision, the new bank would provide a link between the oil-supplying nations of the Persian Gulf, the industrially and technologically developed countries of the West and the developing countries of the Third World through a worldwide network of branches and affiliates. Abedi also proclaimed a set of ethical principles governing the use of the bank's profits. He said they should be split three ways: one-third for charity, one-third for staff benefits and one-third for promotional activities.

Like his idols, the great rajahs of Mahmudabad, Abedi planned to devote part of his empire to philanthropy. "The management group and the shareholders of the new bank eventually agreed to provide for a minority shareholding by means of a trust which was established for the benefit of staff, and a foundation which would provide aid and services for global deserving causes," Rahim later said. The goals were lofty, and it was left unclear just what the deserving causes should be. But by no definition did they include the people who eventually got their hands on the bank's money.

Chapter 2:

The Bank for the Third World

Abedi opened the Bank of Credit and Commerce International in September 1972 with $2.5 million in capital, a handful of lieutenants from United Bank, a banking license from Luxembourg and a gimmick. BCCI was going to provide banking services to the Third World, particularly the increasingly rich oil nations of the Persian Gulf. The bank would take particular advantage of its own internal Muslim culture to cater to the special banking needs of its Islamic customers, many of whom were uncomfortable—or made to feel unwelcome—at more traditional Western banks.

Given Abedi's close ties with the sheik of Abu Dhabi, along with BCCI's Muslim culture, it was natural for him to particularly focus his attention on attracting business from other Arab nations. The Arab connection was made clear in 1978, when Abedi provided Britain's *Euromoney* magazine with a list of the bank's shareholders. These included the ruling families of Abu Dhabi, Saudi Arabia, Iran, Dubai, Bahrain and Sharjah. But, like so much of BCCI's affairs, the Third World ownership was something of a sham. There is no evidence that major members of the royal families had more than token stakes. Indeed, some of the 39 Arab dignitaries on that list doubtless acquired their BCCI stock as a gift from

Abedi, who wanted to build up a distinguished letterhead to impress potential customers and investors.

Of the five members of the al-Nahyan family of Abu Dhabi who were shareholders, Sheik Zayed had a mere 0.47 percent and his son, Sheik Khalifa, was listed with 1.24 percent of the stock. Ali Shorafa, who was Sheik Zayed's director for presidential affairs, owned 0.44 percent. Small stakes also were held by two Saudi princes. The stakes of Saudi businessman Ghaith Pharaon and his brother, Wabel, came to 15 percent. (Details of Abedi's personal investment in BCCI remained perpetually a mystery, although he purportedly held controlling interest in the bank.)

In reality, BCCI's early stockholder list was by no means exclusively Third World. Bank of America, of course, had a 30 percent stake from the start, and the Union Bank of Switzerland was another early investor, through a holding company, Thesaurus Continental Securities Corp. In addition, not only was BCCI's bank license from Luxembourg, but Abedi had decided after all to put down roots in London rather than the Third World. He was not welcome in Pakistan at the time, and given that English was the second language of all of the bank's leading officers, the British financial center was most comfortable for him. It also was regarded as leniently regulated. From then on, there was a steady flow of Pakistanis to London to join the bank's important-sounding Central Support Organization.

Abedi's basic team at BCCI was very similar to that at the old United Bank. Mesmerized by his success and personality, they had eagerly followed Abedi to BCCI. Not only did they enjoy working with each other professionally, they also shared similar backgrounds. Abedi's executives were for the most part Mahojars—the Urdu word for immigrants—and, like Abedi, they had come from India to Pakistan at the time of the partition of India in 1947. The very fact that the native Pakistanis dubbed them immigrants in this way suggests the instability of their position. Insecure in their new home and rather clannish, the Mahojars took the route of so many new immigrant groups and worked extremely hard to build prosperity. It is little wonder that in Pakistan they set up their own political party, which in recent years has become quite powerful: It contributed to the overthrow of Benazir Bhutto.

Many of Abedi's men were old friends from his home in Mahmudabad. He loyally hired many members of the clan, who in turn treated him with loyalty that bordered on sycophancy. Abedi also sought out relatives of the richest and most powerful men of Pakistan and put them to work at the bank, knowing that their connections might inevitably come in handy—regardless of their competence. "He wanted the sons of somebodies," said Pakistani politician Abeda Hussain. "If you were a civil servant, you got your son hired at BCCI. If you were a general, you got your son hired. They were paid more than they were worth, and they swanked all over the world."

Abedi also bought loyalty, by lavishing generosity of all sorts on employees—picking up medical bills, paying for their children's educations and providing them with low-cost or free loans. Yves C. Lamarche, a BCCI director from Bank of America, once received a loan from the bank for 1.67 million francs ($280,000), according to records found in BCCI's Paris office. Under the heading "Expected Date of Settlement," the loan papers simply said, "Never." "The concept was to extend help. That was why the loyalty of the staff was with him," Abdul Basir, one of Abedi's first managers at BCCI, told Steve Coll of *The Washington Post.* "Mr. Abedi is such a tremendous, charismatic personality, it is not something very easily explained. One must experience it."

The bank made a point of not giving its staff titles, and BCCI's offices usually were a sea of similar-looking desks, with few personal offices or other trappings of power. But this does not mean that BCCI was a flat organization. In fact, it appears to have been extremely hierarchical. There was no question about who gave the orders and when they must be obeyed. In a supposedly title-free organization, Agha Hasan Abedi pointedly held the title of president. Even if he liked to operate on a spiritual plane outside the routine operations of the bank, his finger was on every pulse and his hand in every deal.

But Abedi needed a lieutenant who could convert his vision into operational reality. Swaleh Naqvi, who grew up 100 miles away from Abedi, devised BCCI's banking system and kept the books. He seems to have been relatively unimpressed by the Abedi rhetoric—his interest was to get the mechanics of the bank functioning. If Abedi was the resident visionary, mystic and marketing genius, the workaholic Naqvi provided the pure banking know-how. He was "very creative and inventive in devising projects," according to one former client who later had cause to regret it.

Abedi was totally in awe of Naqvi's brainpower, and there is no evidence that Naqvi ever failed to get his way: He knew exactly how to present information to ensure that Abedi signed off on a deal. Years later, when Abedi became incapacitated, Naqvi took over as BCCI's president. When Naqvi's collection of 6,500 neatly handwritten files was found in Abu Dhabi by investigators probing the BCCI mess, it was clear that some of the bank's more extraordinary accounting and banking procedures were of his devising.

However, Naqvi stepped into the No. 2 position at the bank only after Abedi's former favorite, Abdus Sami, left the bank at the end of the 1970s. Sami came with Abedi from United, where he had been Abedi's deputy, and he eventually went to America to lead BCCI's assault there. Having set up the acquisitions of First American Bank and National Bank of Georgia, Sami expected to be put in charge of the entire U.S. operation. But Abedi gave the job of running NBG to Roy Carlson, a former Bank of America executive with longstanding ties to BCCI, and Sami left with a $400,000 payoff.

From that point on, Abedi and Naqvi completely masterminded the progress of the bank. The rest of the staff members were functionaries, operating at the beck and call of Abedi and Naqvi. The example set by the departure of Sami was to resound through the bank, and anyone who displayed individuality or held a different point of view from Abedi knew that his days were numbered. This highly autocratic, personality-based structure opened the way for abuse and secrecy.

Abedi's Third World strategy started haltingly. The Abu Dhabi connection, built up since the 1960s through Abedi's personal ties with Sheik Zayed, turned out to carry little weight with the rest of the wealthy Arab world. It seemed that the Arab countries either could not grasp Abedi's concept of the Muslim bank or were worried about the men who were behind it. In Saudi Arabia, he had powerful friends such as businessmen Kamal Adham and Ghaith Pharaon, but the king resolutely refused BCCI permission even to set up a finance subsidiary in the country. Bahrain and Qatar were equally inhospitable. Kuwait allowed Abedi a 49 percent stake in a finance company, Kuwait International Finance Co., but no bank, and Oman permitted BCCI a 29 percent investment in National Bank of Oman.

The failure to push deeply into the Arab world made success in London all the more vital, and Abedi and Naqvi aimed the bank at Britain's large expatriate Arab community. The bank was starting from absolute rock bottom. One early salesman said there were "no accounts, no activity, no furniture in the bank. It was desperate—we were visiting hotels and jumping on Arabs to get them to open accounts, no matter what they wanted to put in."

All of the bank's employees and resources were devoted to the relentless drive for accounts. BCCI officers scoured the burgeoning Third World community in London for accounts, offering favorable terms to small immigrant-owned businesses and wooing potential customers with sales pitches in their native languages. To say that the early atmosphere was frenetic would be an understatement. As one executive working at BCCI shortly after the launch put it, "They expected you to be running in the street seven days a week until midnight. Every account was being constantly reviewed, and your performance against target constantly monitored." Meeting and beating targets was rewarded by a mention in the bank magazine; top achievers received letters of commendation from Abedi.

The feverish activity began to produce rewards, as the bank's Muslim message found its way to a number of communities that had money, and between 1975 and 1980, BCCI grew into a bank of substance both in the United Kingdom and globally. Now the financial powers in London had to sit up and take notice of the upstart with the Third World ties. For years, they had assumed that Abedi was a man of no importance and that his immigrant bank would go nowhere. So they ignored him and refused his requests for meetings. He felt excluded from the "Club," as he was later to call the City of London, the British equivalent of Wall Street. So another turning point came when BCCI took headquarters space at 101 Leadenhall Street in the heart of the City and Abedi was in their midst.

Any remaining skeptics could not overlook another consideration: The world was awash with Arab petrodollars, and the City was in hot competition for Arab business with the financial centers in Paris, New York and Tokyo. BCCI's shareholders and links with the Arab world put the new bank in the leading position to win that business. But BCCI also had another advantage—because Third World business was considered somewhat unseemly by more conservative financiers, BCCI's affairs may have been less closely supervised by regulators.

The London base was a bonanza for BCCI. Arabs from the newly enriched Gulf states were coming to Britain in droves to enjoy the casinos, buy property, educate their children, race their horses and shop. On their visits, they banked where they were most comfortable: BCCI branches in prosperous locations in London—Marble Arch, Kensington, Mayfair and so on. Between 1973 and 1977, the number of BCCI branches in the United Kingdom grew from four to 45, and in the United Arab Emirates from eight to 29. The worldwide branch network expanded from 19 to 146. In 1973 BCCI was operating in five countries; by 1977 it was represented in 32.

Every financial ratio used reflects this explosive growth. BCCI's assets grew ten-fold, from $200 million to $2.2 billion between 1973 and 1977, its capital from $5 million to $113 million, its deposits from $19 million to $2 billion and its profits from $335,000 to $25 million. The figures left some bankers gasping and others suspicious.

The ranks of those devoted to BCCI's leadership grew along with the bank. To some degree, they split between Abedi's men and Naqvi's loyalists. The president, for example, put bank executive Dildar Rizvi in charge of hospitality, which meant escorting Abedi's many guests around the world, with money no object. Mohammed Hafiz, the company secretary and monitor of the BCCI share register, also was loyal to Abedi.

A number of the bank's financial executives, however, answered first to Naqvi: Mohammed Azmatullah, who helped him manage his secret files and controlled all contact between Naqvi and the outside world; Saleem Sidiqi, who led the bank's inspection department and is said to have kept files on everyone at the bank; Ameer Siddiki, head of the credit committee; Imtiaz Ahmed, head of the credit division; and Masihur Rahman, the chief financial officer.

Many of BCCI's managers were moved around as the bank developed its operations overseas. Probably the most important job was that of head of the British operation. In the early days, this post was held by Velayat Husain Abedi—no relation to the head of the bank—and later by Basheer Chowdry, who ran it until it was closed down in 1991. Nazir Chinoy was in charge of the French operation until his 1988 arrest for participating in money-laundering in Florida. As the bank grew, it developed regional heads such as Nadir Rahim, who took charge of the small Indian operation. Iqbal Rizvi seemed the highest-flier on the international circuit. He started as a minor functionary in Iran, moved to France and steadily acquired more responsibility until he was in charge of Europe, Africa and South America.

With BCCI's growth came acceptance, not just from the more traditional London financial establishment, but from the Arab leadership that had at first shunned it. "Top people, such as members of royal families, came and opened accounts in those days," said Ghassan Qassem, one of BCCI's top branch managers in London. "So did leaders from Nigeria, Syria, Iraq." Qassem's entree to the fabulous funds of the Saudi Arabian royal family came via the manager of the funds of Prince Faisal, a cousin of King Fahd. Qassem was told that the prince was staying in his residence near Hampstead Heath in Britain and that he should visit him the same day. Apparently, Prince Faisal had horses and property in Britain and needed management of the funds for their upkeep. Qassem, a Jordanian, established instant rapport with the prince and eventually brought the accounts of four of his brothers to the bank as well.

But the helter-skelter quest for accounts led the bank to abuse procedures, according to Qassem. "They made the staff open an account for anyone, just for the sake of reaching targets," he said years later. "They never went through proper opening procedures, and that was an invitation for crooks to join the bank."

The bank flourished by handling large numbers of overseas accounts for private individuals, many of whom had rather more dubious reasons to be storing their money in the United Kingdom than the Saudis' need to fund the upkeep of their estates and horses. With its Luxembourg corporate charter and cross-border ownership, management and customer list, BCCI was all but unregulated.

Certainly, no single regulator directly oversaw the bank's operations. This allowed just about anything to fall through the cracks—especially if the bank's executives wanted it to. With its ability to offer such a cloak of secrecy and discretion, BCCI attracted powerful individuals who needed somewhere to squirrel their wealth away from the prying eyes of their home countries' tax or law enforcement authorities. "Flight capital" of this kind came from places like Nigeria,

Panama and Peru and was welcomed by the bank that could afford to ask no questions.

BCCI also set up a special operation to handle the large quantities of cash that moved between the Indian subcontinent and the emigrant community in Britain. This system is widely known as Hundi, or Hawalla, and its primary aim is to break rules on the export of foreign exchange. The global Chinese community has a similar system called Chitty banking. These are age-old practices that traditionally use corner shops and family networks, but BCCI developed it to a fine corporate art. At its simplest, the bank arranged for a deposit in the local currency at one end and a withdrawal in a different currency at the other, without an audit trail or paperwork—a basic form of money-laundering. As the bank grew and its expertise developed, more sophisticated versions of this system would be applied to the needs of the professional money-launderer and the international arms trader.

The bank also sold itself to traders who needed letters of credit to speed up the transfer of funds around the world. This was to become a very substantial business for a number of Asian businessmen who found in the bank kindred spirits prepared to take trade finance a lot further than is conventionally possible.

Abedi also found a profitable way to achieve a nearly perfect synthesis of top-level political connections and banking. The bank's Third World image gave it natural access to the treasuries and political powerhouses of many developing nations that had large sums of money to deposit and were having difficulty winning badly needed lines of credit from more traditional lenders. Abedi laid on the charm and hospitality to curry favor with politicians and fledgling central bankers in these nations.

The bank eventually succeeded in persuading a number of governments in Africa and South America to fill holes in their balance of payments by taking loans from BCCI rather than from the International Monetary Fund or the World Bank. Abedi also persuaded them to place some of their national treasury funds in BCCI. This was one of BCCI's most important strategies, and potentially one of its most corrupt: Investigations already have begun in Peru, Brazil and Nigeria into alleged bribery of officials by BCCI, and there has been testimony by former officials of the bank that payoffs occurred in many other nations in exchange for business. "This bank would bribe God," one former employee told the *Financial Times*. BCCI even bankrolled a magazine, called *South*, which churned out favorable profiles on Third World nations and leaders from whom the bank was seeking business.

Abdur Sakhia, a longtime BCCI executive who for several years oversaw the bank's American operations, told congressional investigators that the bank made payoffs to the family of Indian leader Indira Gandhi, General Zia al-Haq of Pakistan, and leaders of Bangladesh, Zambia, Kenya, Nigeria, Zimbabwe and other African nations. A Pakistani government report on corruption in the nation's March 1977 elections cites Abedi's use of huge amounts of money to secretly influence the balloting; at one point, the report refers to the BCCI chief as having been "loaded . . . with bagfuls of money."

Sakhia testified to a congressional committee that political payoffs were made "either in the form of cash or hiring of the relatives, a contribution to their favorite charities, a payment for their medical bills. It took various shapes. So in some cases their charities were funded, their projects were financed at favorable rates, [by] loans at favorable rates. So it took different shapes and forms." Whatever the method, Sakhia said the intention was the same: "To buy influence."

Sakhia said a BCCI officer had made the rounds at a meeting of the World Bank during the mid-1980s handing out cash to the staff of the Central Bank of Nigeria in an effort to win business. And he testified about one episode in which he gave a BCCI colleague in London a ride to a hotel at which some Zimbabwean politicians were staying prior to the nation's independence. "He went [in] with a briefcase and he came back without a briefcase," Sakhia recounted. "I asked him, 'What happened to your briefcase?' And he smiled at me, and he said, 'This was for those people.' I said, 'What did you carry, gold bars?' He said, 'No, some cash.'"

There are indications that BCCI may even have hedged its bets when it paid bribes to Zimbabwean officials, greasing the palms of both ends of the Zimbabwe political spectrum so that the bank would be guaranteed an entree when the newly founded nation picked an international bank for a relationship with its treasury. Sure enough, BCCI was the first foreign bank to win a banking license in Zimbabwe.

The development of a Third World customer base, legally and otherwise, was one building block for the bank's survival. But Abedi and Naqvi had to ensure that they controlled the ownership of the bank itself.

One way of creating a market in BCCI shares would have been to issue publicly traded shares in the company, but that would have required opening up the ownership of BCCI to regulatory scrutiny, which would certainly have been resisted by some of the bank's more shadowy backers. The individual likely to resist most would have been Abedi himself, who claimed for many years to control the ownership of BCCI. The alternative was to seek other locations in which BCCI's finances and stock ownership could be registered, away from the prying eyes of British or even Luxembourg regulators.

Bank executives therefore developed a network of offshore companies that would hide BCCI's ownership. They set up a second company to operate in parallel to the Luxembourg-registered BCCI Holdings, to guarantee Abedi's and Naqvi's control and to ensure that transactions and shareholders' identities could be kept secret from regulators and the public.

The parallel company, International Credit and Investment Co., was set up in the Cayman Islands, another haven of lax banking regulation, in 1976. ICIC was to be the umbrella for a number of other shell companies, including ICIC Holdings and ICIC Overseas, and some of Abedi's pet charities. Despite mounds of documentary evidence to the contrary, Abedi would later claim that there was no connection between ICIC and BCCI. Even now, a source close to

Abedi maintains that "There was no link between BCCI and ICIC except that ICIC Overseas lent against shares of BCCI. In some cases where the shareholders were not able to repay the advance for a long time, it was even selling [their] shares." However, Masihur Rahman, BCCI's former chief financial officer, told a congressional hearing in 1991 that ICIC was intended to provide a way for BCCI's longstanding employees to own a piece of the bank—although they never actually got the stock in BCCI that was promised to them by Abedi.

The shadowy ICIC had many other uses. BCCI used ICIC to make loans to shareholders in BCCI and related entities to enable them to hold on to their shares or to indemnify them against any losses. BCCI also borrowed against its own shares through ICIC and even purchased its own stock through the affiliate. This happened when Bank of America wanted to dispose of its BCCI holdings in 1980. BCCI arranged for ICIC to buy the BofA shares, making the subsidiary a stockholder in its own parent. Because of this cozy relationship, ICIC has come to be known as "the bank within the bank."

The Federal Reserve Board's written complaint against BCCI in July 1991 made the murky connection between BCCI and ICIC much clearer. "ICIC Overseas operated under the control of and at the direction of senior BCCI management, including Abedi and Naqvi, to further the business interests of BCCI, and acted as the alter ego or agent for BCCI in connection with the acquisition of CCAH [the vehicle used to buy First American Bank] and a number of other transactions," it stated. "The ownership, management and business activities of BCCI and ICIC Overseas were intermingled and interrelated in such a way that the two groups generally operated as a single entity."

Even without the luxury of a detailed examination of balance sheets and company records, which is precluded by Cayman Islands law, the complexity of the arrangements creates suspicion.

The ownership connections between the various entities with "BCCI" and "ICIC" in their names are incredibly tangled and obscure. For example, a subsidiary called BCCI Overseas, based in the Cayman Islands, was 100 percent owned by BCCI Holdings in Luxembourg. The senior Cayman company was a British charity, called ICIC Foundation, which owned an investment company, ICIC Foundation (Cayman), which owned 35 percent of BCCI's Geneva-based bank, Banque de Commerce et Placements (the rest was owned by BCCI Holdings S.A.—the main Luxembourg company—and Union Bank of Switzerland). The ICIC Foundation also was an investor in BCCI; it borrowed $74 million from an affiliated company, ICIC Overseas, to acquire 9 percent of BCCI shares. Other Cayman investors in BCCI Holdings were the ICIC Staff Benefit Trust and the ICIC Staff Benefit Fund—pension funds for BCCI employees that later were milked dry by Abedi and Naqvi to keep the main bank afloat in the 1980s.

By the late 1970s, the curious personality-based management structure, the questionable basis for the bank's growth and the unfathomable nature of the offshore web of companies were beginning to attract attention and concern from regulators and backers alike. The Bank of England appeared to admit that there was a question mark over the bank when it refused to grant it a full operating license in 1978, stalling its expansion in Britain. Yet in May of that same year, *Forbes* magazine described BCCI as "unquestionably the most successful newcomer to Arab banking in London." At about the same time, Abedi told *Euromoney* magazine, "The Bank of England probably hasn't given permission because of the atmosphere surrounding BCCI and the propaganda that has been spread about us. . . . It's not only the Bank of England that is against us, but the Club."

Previous fans at Bank of America, who in the early days had been willing to back Abedi's freewheeling management style, also were getting cold feet about the bank's rapid rate of growth in the late 1970s. BofA had begun as an enthusiastic backer, with a 30 percent stake, but it had allowed its holding to decline over the years by not taking advantage of addition-al sales of BCCI stock to investors.

An internal BofA report on BCCI's loan practices in August 1978 criticized BCCI's management style, and in June 1980 BofA sold its remaining 24 percent stake. In a press release, the San Francisco banking giant said it was ready to establish its own presence in the Middle East. But in fact, sources say, Bank of America had become concerned about the BCCI style and wanted nothing more to do with it. (BofA also apparent-ly was annoyed by BCCI's practice of hanging Bank of America's logo in the windows of at least one of its branch offices, thus misleading potential customers into thinking they were dealing with the American banking giant rather than BCCI.)

Bank of America's ownership position had given BCCI early respectability on which to build growth. Another im-portant early cornerstone was BCCI's relationship with the Gokal brothers, the Pakistanis who operated a huge shipping business.

The Gokals' Gulf Group was among BCCI's first major customers, and the relationship was highly beneficial to both sides. Their oil-shipping traffic was spiraling upward along with world oil prices and demand, and BCCI was pumping money in to help fuel the growth. The Gokals were more than just BCCI's biggest customers; they were also brother Shi'ites and fellow Pakistanis. Both the Gokals' Gulf Group and Abedi's BCCI were led by charismatic, powerful individuals, and both shared a culture of opulence and optimism. They would travel very similar courses over 19 years, booming in tandem and declining together. Indeed, the Gokals' main holding company, Gulf International Holdings S.A., went into "controlled management," or bankruptcy court super-vision, on July 3, 1991, just two days before BCCI was closed.

The story of the Gokals is another tale of growth from unlikely beginnings. The Gokal family had its origins in Gujarat, Pakistan, and, like another great Pakistani business family—and Abedi client—the Saigols, the Gokals are Khojas, or converts to Islam. In the wake of Pakistani independence in 1947, the Gokals moved to Iraq, and the family prospered there. They had a trading business in Basra that became the world's largest exporter of dates, and a religious member of the family arranged transport on Gokal vessels for Muslim pilgrims on their way to Mecca.

But prospects soured for the family in Iraq; the uncle of the brothers who now run the business was hanged in 1969 following an accusation from a business competitor—later proved unfounded—that he was an Israeli agent. The younger generation fled the country for their lives. The eldest brother, Mustafa, went to Pakistan and set up Gulf Shipping and Trading, while his younger brother, Abbas, established a shipping company in London. Within three years, Abbas was exporting great quantities of cement to the Persian Gulf, where a building boom had started in earnest, as well as to Nigeria and India. Over five years, Abbas's companies built up the world's largest private shipping fleet: some 300 vessels, half owned, half chartered. In 1976, Abbas moved his business to Geneva to avoid having to pay British taxes.

Abbas Gokal was undoubtedly the family entrepreneur. A workaholic who put 20 hours a day into the company, he had a charismatic presence as well as a quick brain. Abbas also was very strong-willed, and anybody who came to him with a problem went away believing that they had caused it themselves, and so would have to solve it. Elder brother Mustafa was a quite different personality. Deeply religious, he was thrust into Pakistani politics by Abedi, who convinced the president of Pakistan, General Zia, to appoint him as his shipping adviser. A third brother, Murtaza, also was involved in running the family shipping business.

The 1970s oil boom in the Persian Gulf region provided a growing market for the Gokals' company, but the Gulf Group also carved out a less savory niche for itself in the shipping world, with a willingness to carry anything anywhere for anyone. For example, it set up a subsidiary, called Tradinaft, that is said to have broken sanctions and traded with South Africa. One of the best deals Gulf did in the mid-1970s was the shipment of military tanks from the

United States to Egypt. The arms were listed as "industrial machinery," but they reportedly were loaded by the U.S. Army and unloaded by the Egyptian army under a massive cloak of secrecy. In another escapade in international politics, it is understood that the Gokals employed Eddie Kamil, a former Seychelles minister of internal affairs, as its personnel manager for four years. In fact, his actual task allegedly was to organize the financing of a coup in the Seychelles that ultimately failed. The Gokals continue to own a number of hotels and other real estate in those islands.

During this period, the Gulf Group worked closely and profitably with BCCI, which was desperate for big customers and prepared to go to great lengths to accommodate their needs. Most Gulf ships were mortgaged by BCCI at extremely high and unrealistic values. BCCI also remortgaged many Gokal ships using similarly inflated estimates. In many cases, the Gokals used ships as collateral for loans from BCCI when the ships actually were already mortgaged to someone else for another loan. BCCI dealt with Gokal officials in a friendly, informal manner. "We used to go 'round to BCCI and pick up a bag of money to pay somebody off," one former Gulf employee later said. "I would go to 101 Leadenhall Street [the BCCI headquarters] and see a man [who] would smile at me, and say, 'Sign this piece of paper.' I would write 'Mickey Mouse' on a piece of tissue paper, which was then thrown away. He handed me a bag of money, which I would then take back and distribute."

It appears that early success went to Abbas Gokal's head. Riding high on a business that seemed to promise infinite expansion, he entered areas quite outside his competence, particularly the highly risky arena of futures and commodities trading, and lost heavily. The man Abbas Gokal put in charge of Gulf Group futures trading was a 26-year-old brought in from the commodities pits in Chicago at a salary of $480,000. He was given a completely free hand to wheel and deal. According to a colleague, "When he lost money, he went on holiday, and when he made it, he traded it again until he lost it, and then he went on holiday." Gokal also liked to encourage enterprise within his own family. It is said that he gave his son a Reuters news-ticker machine and an active credit line of $100 million to learn the futures trading business.

There were other signs of uncoordinated diversification as well. Gokal bought into the Christian Dior clothing company, only to sell it at a loss. He also acquired a chain of butcher's shops that subsequently failed, and he took an interest in companies associated with British designers Alistair Blair and Uzbeck. The Gulf Group's core business was hurting, too. Diversification into shipping cargo other than oil and construction material was less than successful, and the sharp drop in oil prices in the early 1980s torpedoed the company's tanker business.

The Gulf Group's troubles were BCCI's as well. Contrary to standard banking practices that advise spreading a bank's loan exposure among many customers, BCCI had most of its eggs in the Gokal basket. Fully half of its outstanding loans in the late 1970s were to the Gulf Group. But BCCI, apparently out of loyalty and fear, continued to pump money into the company in an attempt to bail out the business and help the Gokals make good on their outstanding debt.

Late in 1979, managers of the Gulf Group gathered in Monte Carlo to discuss problems in the business. The meeting lasted for two days, and it seemed to all present that there would soon be widespread layoffs and office closings. At the end of the second day, Abbas Gokal took the podium to deliver his closing speech. Its tone took all of the managers by surprise. Instead of reflecting the downbeat mood of the meeting, he announced a major expansion of the business and the creation of a large number of offices in the Gulf and the Red Sea areas.

According to one manager, Gokal left the meeting that Sunday and went straight to Kuwait. He returned to Geneva on the following Tuesday with a check in his pocket for a reputed $1.4 billion. "This was his first major influx of pure money, not money against mortgages or money against a particular deal," the manager said. "This time he went out and got pure money." It was assumed at the time that the money came from BCCI.

Even by BCCI standards, the $1.4 billion figure seems excessive for this period, but sources close to BCCI confirm that the relationship between Gulf and the bank changed dramatically at this time. They say the bank was concerned about its official loan exposure to the Gokals, which stood at $80 million, and decided not to increase this beyond $100 million. However, they also claim that an officer of the bank was bribed and, acting without authority, issued a guarantee to the Gokals for an extension of the loan to $400 million. When the matter was uncovered, the officer joined the Gokals' company. Yet BCCI was later to take even more radical steps to keep the Gulf Group—and itself, in turn— afloat.

The increased line of credit had a dramatic effect on Abbas Gokal's personal style. "Prior to that, he had been a quiet man," said a source familiar with the situation. "Even though he mixed with princes, he lived in a maisonette in Ealing [a middle-class London suburb] and he had a nice car. But it was obviously only for business. Then it all changed and he became flash. Instead of just one car, it was matching Rolls Royces in Geneva and London. The office in Geneva was suddenly decorated by an expensive interior designer. His whole personality changed." He also grew increasingly aloof from managers who once had found him approachable and open to new ideas.

The degree to which the shippers sank the bank remains a matter for conjecture. What is certain is that from an early stage, the Gokals were not repaying their loans. The bank appeared not to insist on their repayment and was prepared to doctor its books to show that they were still performing. Ultimately, those loans constituted an untenable proportion of BCCI's balance sheet. According to a Price Waterhouse report to regulators in June 1991, over the 15 years the Gokals banked with BCCI, they had 750 accounts whose total turn-over was $15 billion. By the end, delinquent loans to the Gulf

Group and related companies were believed to have approached, or even exceeded, $1 billion.

The Gokals' Gulf Group seems to have undergone the Abedi experience: uncontrolled growth fueling disproportionate expectations, which could be met only by the creation of funny money. That, in time, would sink them both.

Chapter 3

Mohammed and Mammon

BCCI's founders wanted to create an alternative culture to the traditional Western bank. They were not embarrassed about encouraging the practice of Islam during working hours, they consciously adopted a policy of recruiting practicing Muslims, they naturally favored Arab and Muslim clients and they used the rhetoric of Sufism and the charitable giving that it advocated. The bank's Muslim culture had a powerful appeal for members of a religion that was feeling a surge of confidence during the 1970s and 1980s, and for people who had long felt oppressed and excluded from the Western world.

The Islamic bond was a powerful motivator for employees to feel an unusual degree of loyalty to each other and to their inspirational leaders. But the enthusiasm for all things Muslim also brought BCCI into contact with the dangerous terrorists of the Islamic world, who were to become significant customers as the bank grew.

Islam may have been the predominant culture of the bank, but BCCI's founders were not naive or nonmaterialistic. Although Agha Hasan Abedi was a Muslim, there is plenty of evidence to show that he used the religion's rhetoric to his own ends. This confused faithful members of the staff as much as it did the world leaders who thought they had at last found an ethical banker. Loyalty, nepotism and hospitality are important social tenets of Islam, and Abedi took advantage of them all.

Abedi's loyalty to his staff and friends was legendary, and he went out of his way to protect them. If a personnel mistake was made, he would not fire the individual concerned; instead, he would insist that the employee be moved to a job elsewhere in the bank for the sake of his family. When a member of staff demanded unreasonable compensation, he would insist that the employee be paid. As one friend put it, "He believed in accountability, not punishability."

Abedi was, of course, loyal to Sheik Zayed of Abu Dhabi, but Akbar Ahmed, a Muslim scholar and philosopher from Cambridge University, says the bond between them was that of brothers, and not one based on Abedi's self-interest. Zayed's respect for Abedi was to be demonstrated years later, when he came to the banker's aid after Abedi suffered a heart attack. And when Abedi needed help for his financially struggling bank, Sheik Zayed agreed to pump in billions of dollars. "Are we to see this, as some Western people might, as two shady characters who have got together and made a deal? No," Ahmed said. "What deal can a sheik who is one of the richest men in the world do with a sick bank? What can he offer, except an obligation, [a] code of behavior?"

Nepotism and the devotion to family are an extension of the loyalty principle, which is fine in personal life but can be fatal in a business context. BCCI was an extended family, and its members always were able to find a job. Abedi employed Pakistani leader Zia al-Haq's son knowing full well that it would pay handsome dividends in business terms, and chief financial officer Masihur Rahman's daughter got a job at BCCI even though she knew almost nothing about banking. This was all part of the bank-wide philosophy of back-scratching and glad-handing. In Pakistan there is even a word for it, "sifarish."

There also was the importance of hospitality. In the Arab world, this is part and parcel of doing business. Abedi, of course, always played host to Sheik Zayed on visits to Pakistan, and he was willing to sit for hours discussing hunting matters with a sheik or other well-heeled potential customer if in the end it meant assuming responsibility for his financial portfolio. Business would not even be mentioned, but the unspoken agenda was always clear.

Doing business in this way meant that branches of the bank had to look more like a hotel or a home than an office. BCCI's buildings themselves were located in city centers or in places where they would have maximum impact. When visitors to London were driven in from Heathrow Airport, one of the most prominent buildings they saw was a tall BCCI branch office, located there precisely to impress those visitors. BCCI's buildings were deliberately luxurious, and consistent in their design around the world. This was another of Abedi's marketing ploys: He knew that wealthy customers were impressed by opulence and lavishness. There may also have been a sense that this nouveau riche institution had to be one up on the Joneses, or the Barclays.

"Whether it was in the City of London or a place like Yemen, you knew what to expect the BCCI branch to look like," a colleague of Abedi said. "A certain color of plate glass. You knew there would be a certain desk. It was completely standard right through the world. That was what he wanted to present, and he took a great deal of personal interest in that aspect of the bank."

Keeping the customer satisfied had been Abedi's forte from the beginning of his banking career, and at BCCI it reached its zenith. Customers always commented on the comfort of BCCI's branches, the speed and politeness of service and so on, as compared with local banks.

The Abedi philosophy of management was even more unusual. He was not content just with simple, worthy Islamic qualities, but sought to import some of the more esoteric, quasi-Sufist Islamic principles into the bank's culture. He was fond of making slightly inscrutable philosophic statements--for instance: "Western banks concentrate on the visible, whereas we stress the invisible," he told the *Financial Times* in 1978.

Such mysticism was met with some skepticism inside the bank. What, for example, were staff members to make of his philosophy of the "joint personality," a concept alleged to aid delegation of authority? The theory was that Abedi's most senior associates thought so alike that they acted as one. Therefore, there would be no need to refer back to the head office for decisions. The reality was that Abedi never did anything without referring to second-in-command Swaleh Naqvi. But Abedi used the joint-personality theory to persuade the sheiks who liked to deal with him personally that they should not worry if he was not there in person, because the local manager thought the same way he did, and whatever the manager decided was all right with Abedi. This was a perfect way for Abedi to spread himself out, but it also gave BCCI's managers quite extraordinary freedom of action, which they went on to abuse liberally. Inevitably, eyebrows were raised. "It was not understood," former BCCI official Nadir Rahim said. "There was cynicism within the organization about joint personalities, because human beings are what they are."

The Muslim leadership style even had its own management experts to hone it. A consulting firm, Forum Inc., worked closely with BCCI, and Forum managing director Tom Thiss traveled to BCCI management conferences around the world to expound on the Abedi theory of management. His firm did a study comparing what BCCI called its "Real Management" with more traditional practices.

In the BCCI column there was this description: "Major Purpose: Believes that purpose energizes behavior by engaging spirit. Gives meaning to existence (process of life) by lifting it above routine of daily activity. Ennobles effort by freeing a person from becoming the instrument of another's will. Has four-fold stated purpose: a) Submission to God; b) Service to Mankind; c) Success; d) Giving."

On the other side of the ledger in the study, under the heading "Traditional Management," was a description of a more Western approach: "Does not generally have an equivalent to the BCCI Major Purpose. Some organizations have a few general principles which state that they want to excel in a given field. Others have a value system that gives rise to a central thrust for quality, marketing, or product innovation. Many others talk of making a profit, satisfying the stockholders, meeting the needs of their customers, and providing a high quality of work life for their employees."

Perhaps the Abedi management style reached its apogee of egoism and vagueness at BCCI's annual management conferences, gatherings of managers from all over the world to discuss strategy and philosophy in ways unlike just about any other corporation. For instance, the theme discussed by the management staff at the conference in Geneva in February 1982 was "Submission to God, Service to Humanity, Giving and Success." Abedi told the assembled officers and guests that BCCI would be different: It would be charitable, it would be sympathetic to the concerns of the poor and deprived.

So successful was the discussion in Switzerland that it was followed up a month later with another gathering at the Inn on the Park in London. Less than two weeks later Abedi wrote a letter to each staff member of the bank: "As BCCI has always endeavored to care for your spiritual and psychological needs, no less than your material requirements, it has been decided to implement the theme of '82 by initiating the process of giving. You will be paid 2 1/2 per cent of your present salary for the year on April 8 for giving to any individual or cause in fulfillment of your instinct and good judgment."

Abedi continued the theme, writing to "all members of the BCCI family": "It is in the medium of Giving that life flows into life, and God's divinity in all its embracing fullness, shines and rains softly, smoothly and blissfully on His creation."

This Sufist version of the United Way was by no means unusual for BCCI. At times, the bank seemed as much a religious cult as a financial institution. At BCCI's annual conferences, the previous year's balance sheet was given just the briefest of mentions. The more important topic on the agenda was to instill in those attending the importance of "moving to the spirit of God." Though he spoke of humility, Abedi's gentle domination of these get-togethers was total. Recordings show that he did most of the talking, while the delegates listened to "Agha Sahib" in spellbound silence.

When other voices were heard at the meetings, they echoed the tone set by Abedi. The bank's other top executives would address the conferences with religious fervor about such weighty matters as the psyche and spirit of the bank and the moral and philosophical dimensions of management. Speakers were invited forward to talk when the spirit moved them, with Abedi assuring them that it was not a performance, so no one cared whether they spoke well or badly. Each speaker would not only defer to Abedi himself but would heap praise on the eloquence and wisdom of the previous speaker, while apologizing for his own inadequacies.

Some speakers broke down: "Sir, I am totally overwhelmed by the proceedings of the conference," one executive, Khalid Imran, told one of the meetings, his voice choking with emotion. "After seeing these tears in your eyes, I always have these tears of gratitude. In my moments of silence, I cry that I have been associated with BCCI. Agha Sahib, I am totally overwhelmed. I may sound incoherent, but I would like to say only one thing: I can do anything for this group, this family." When the next delegate was invited forward, he too was overcome by the atmosphere of the moment: "Agha Sahib, frankly I don't find myself equal to it today," he said.

The BCCI conferences were always held in the most stunning surroundings. The 1984 Vienna conference was no exception, with hundreds of BCCI executives and employees along with accountants, shareholders and representatives from other banking affiliates crowding into the magnificent Hoffburg Palace. Tape-recordings of the entire event show how easily Abedi's family, as he liked to describe all associated with BCCI, was swept along. Abedi's tone was hypnotic. He would tell the audience that he wanted to reveal the truth to them.

Speaking without notes, Abedi set the tone for the conference with a lengthy speech about humility. He told his audience that BCCI's achievements would not have been so outstanding "without the support of so many." There was special praise for the Abu Dhabi shareholders. "But for their financial support and, more than that, for the support they have provided through their kindness and by lending us all their influence and prestige, we would not have been what we are and we would not have been sitting here as we are," Abedi said. Every sentence and every phrase was interspersed with long contemplative pauses, sometimes lasting nearly a minute.

Even BCCI's auditors at Price Waterhouse drew praise from Abedi—ironically, as it would turn out. The bank president gushingly offered thanks to "our auditors, but for whose honest and sincere appraisal of the affairs of our bank we wouldn't have got the authenticity that we have today." From time to time, Abedi would ask senior and junior employees if they felt ready to speak. When they did, it would always be to repeat Abedi's message, often with long, apologetic interruptions from Abedi himself as he tried to clarify some point.

At the Vienna conference, Abedi summed up his thanks to all with these words: "Today I am sitting before God and before you all like a child so fearful and so fondly hopeful of the purpose for which we have assembled, for the achievement of the purpose for which we have assembled. I feel so humble and so respectful to you. And I am hoping that during these two days we would have moments when all of us will feel humility in its true sense and in its true value in the same moment."

Not all were carried away by the mood. Abedi's lengthy monologues put some of the bank's more elderly directors to sleep. Some of the American visitors tried to echo the mystical theme, but, as one representative from National Bank of Georgia demonstrated, not all had Abedi's gift of speech. The NBG executive tried to keep the mood, but lapsed into more mundane talk about finances: "I feel totally engulfed at times in the feelings I have for my colleagues and for you [BCCI] as well. I was most impressed by your profit numbers and your growth since the beginning."

Much of the philosophy elucidated by Abedi at these meetings was based on the gentle, charitable principles of Islamic-style banking. The bank's practice, however, was quite different. The teaching of the Koran prohibits Muslims from earning interest, or riba, a rule that was fine for small-time money-changers, but began causing significant problems as the oil boom produced unprecedented wealth. If BCCI was to have Muslim customers, it had to find a way to deal with the religious strictures on interest, or provide some substitute, while still operating competitively in the financial markets of the world.

The solution was not an original one. The Saudis already had solved the problem neatly, simply by calling interest "profit." But there was another, even more sophisticated form of "Islamic banking" coming into use: so-called Murabaha transactions. Under this system, an investor lends his money to a bank, which lends the money to a company to buy raw materials or commodities. The company produces finished goods from the raw materials, then sells them back to the bank at a preset premium to pay off the loan, and the bank disposes of the materials on the open market at a profit over their original cost. Inevitably and not coincidentally, the "profit" made from such transactions is equal to the prevailing world interest rate, allowing Muslims with money to make more without violating Islamic law. Perhaps not surprisingly, this form of Islamic banking showed a remarkable growth during the late 1970s and early 1980s, and BCCI set up a special Islamic Banking Unit in London to handle such business. At its peak, toward the end of 1989, Islamic customers had placed $1.4 billion with BCCI through this division.

Traditional bankers frown on Islamic banking practices—funds produced through Islamic banking are not considered to be genuine deposits under the British Banking Act, for instance. As far as the regulators are concerned, the transaction is asset management by another name and should be accounted for separately. Officially, the depositors are taking too great a risk, since they are so dependent on the success of the producer of the finished goods. To cover the risk that the producing company will fail and be unable to pay back the loan, a letter of credit is usually given by another bank, for which the producing company pays a fee, as insurance.

By 1984, however, BCCI had its own twist on this system: It did not go to a second bank for a letter of credit, but simply issued its own, thereby exposing itself to the entire risk if the producing company went bust. But that was no matter to BCCI—as it turned out, the Islamic customers who placed their money and their trust with their Muslim brothers at BCCI were being brazenly defrauded on a massive scale anyway.

Rather than invest the funds entrusted to it for Islamic banking, BCCI was simply looting these accounts. The money was placed elsewhere within the BCCI empire or on money markets, quite contrary to Islamic law. In its detailed report on the bank's malfeasance in June 1991, auditors Price Waterhouse wrote: "The resulting catalogue of errors with regard to the non-repayment of some placements and the misuse of other placements as security reflects at the very least a lack of any proper independent management control in the U.K. region." That appears to have been an understatement. BCCI, in many cases, was simply stealing its customers' money.

Perhaps the most notable example was the case of a customer that the Price Waterhouse report code-named "Tumbleweed," but which was actually the Faisal Islamic Bank of Egypt, headed by Prince Mohammed bin-Faisal al-Saud of the Saudi ruling family. The Faisal Islamic Bank had begun doing business with BCCI in the late 1970s, and by 1982 it had $171 million on deposit, an amount that continued to grow over the next few years. The bank instructed BCCI to invest its money in commodities that could be bought or sold at a profit under Islamic banking, creating income but not interest, technically.

The Faisal Islamic Bank was one of BCCI's largest customers and, because of its Saudi connections, one of its most important. But Price Waterhouse reported in 1991, "We have seen no evidence to suggest that the bank actually entered any commodity contracts." Instead, BCCI put the Faisal Islamic Bank's money to its own use as an unrecorded deposit that would fool auditors into thinking that BCCI had more money than it actually did or that badly delinquent accounts were actually up to date. The funds were used to cover a loan related to the takeover of Washington's First American Bankshares, to "recreate" another customer's missing deposits of $62 million and to make it appear that interest was being paid on several of BCCI's bad loans, Price Waterhouse said.

If the Faisal Islamic Bank demanded access to its money, BCCI replenished the account, the auditors said. But whenever the auditors came around to check, the account would be emptied, making it all but invisible on the bank's books so that the auditors would not attempt to check the amount on hand with the depositor. Price Waterhouse has estimated that BCCI's liability to Faisal Islamic Bank totaled $358 million, making it one of BCCI's biggest creditors and perhaps the largest single source of the unrecorded deposits that BCCI took from customers and used to pad its depleted books. Other customers of the Islamic Banking Unit were unknowingly abused in the same way. For example, $30 million in Islamic Banking deposits were shifted to an account in BCCI's Grand Cayman branch known as Account 500, which was "used for the purpose of fraudulently routing funds," Price Waterhouse said.

Even when BCCI carried out commodity transactions and other Islamic banking business for its customers as instructed, it listed the bulk of the funds on an "off-balance-sheet" basis, Price Waterhouse said, so that they did not show up on the BCCI books—reducing the company's assets and liabilities by more than $800 million each by 1989 and making the bank look healthier than it was. "From the scale and complexity of the deception it is clear that most of the senior management . . . were or should have been aware of certain elements of the fraud," Price Waterhouse concluded in its 1991 report, which triggered the closing of the bank.

But Abedi apparently went further still. Fundamental to the BCCI philosophy as expressed by Abedi was the bank's charitable activity, the Giving. As usual, he imported lawyers to finesse the tax laws, even while he was planning good works. In September 1981, Abedi established the Cayman-based BCCI Foundation, which was to be funded from BCCI Holdings in Luxembourg through BCCI Pakistan. The good causes it supported were well-publicized. For example, there was the work in the Orangi Project in one of Karachi's worst slums, where millions of rupees went into improving medical and municipal facilities. But the BCCI Foundation may have been as much a tax dodge as it was a charity—it has been reported that the foundation gave out more than it took in only twice in its nine years of operation.

It cannot have been accidental that the offshore connection was highly tax-efficient. The foundation enjoyed a special tax-free status in Pakistan, and within two years of its inauguration it had received huge amounts of untaxed profits from BCCI's activities in that nation. But BCCI's special tax status had to be earned. One of the biggest single beneficiaries of the foundation's largess was the Ghulam Ishaq Khan Institute for Engineering, Sciences and Technology. The institute is named after the president of Pakistan—who as finance minister had approved the tax-free position of the BCCI Foundation.

At the top of the BCCI family tree in the Cayman Islands was ICIC Apex Holdings, part of the mysterious "bank within the bank." It was described as a charity, but for all intents and purposes it was non-operational. Further down the tree was another charitable organization, the ICIC Foundation, whose assets were almost entirely in BCCI stock, thus providing Abedi another way to control the bank's ownership.

From BCCI's London headquarters, Abedi ran another charity using BCCI funds: the Third World Foundation, Abedi's device for receiving in political goodwill and influence as much as he gave to charity. BCCI donated $10 million to the Third World Foundation. Much of it was squandered on lavish conferences held in exotic locations such as Manila and China to discuss Third World issues. Friends, families and their servants, as well as world leaders and journalists, were put up at the finest hotels for the conferences, all expenses paid. The gatherings were always well-attended. Edward Heath, the former British prime minister, was a guest at the Manila conference.

Indeed, Abedi used his charitable work to build his relationships with current and former world leaders— relationships that could only improve BCCI's respectability and business ties around the world. One vehicle for this was the Third World Prize, which Abedi hoped could one day match the Nobel Peace Prize in prestige. The prize, like so much of Abedi's charitable work, looked ethical to those on the outside, but was in fact self-serving. There was the loftiness of the ideal—a prize awarded to people who had contributed most to the Third World, with the support of such figures as Javier Perez de Cuellar, the secretary-general of the United Nations, and Indira Gandhi, the prime minister of India. But there also was the respectability that the prize conferred upon Abedi. The Third World Prize doubtless was an important marketing tool in the bank's efforts to win loan and deposit business from developing nations.

The list of recipients of the $100,000 prize reflects BCCI's drive for international recognition—as does the list of those who presented the prize on BCCI's behalf or who attended the prize ceremony. The first Third World Prize, in 1980, went to Paul Prebish, an international development economist from Argentina. Kurt Waldheim, then the secretary-general of the United Nations, was in attendance. By 1981, the system was in full swing: Indira Gandhi presented the prize to Julius Nyerere, the president of Tanzania. Later winners were Willy Brandt, the former German chancellor; anti-apartheid activists Nelson and Winnie Mandela; and rock musician Bob Geldof, the organizer of money-raising efforts for Ethiopia. Presenters of the award included Chinese Premier Zhao Ziyang—in a lavish ceremony in Beijing—and the leaders of Brazil, Malaysia and Zimbabwe, all good friends of BCCI, with some even allegedly on the bank's payroll.

Yet the British Charity Commission found Abedi's motives in giving the prize suspect, and refused to grant charitable status to the Third World Prize. Abedi had to turn to a Cayman Islands company to acquire a tax break on the prize.

BCCI's charitable activities were not completely corrupted by cynical manipulation and self-interest, however. The bank helped to finance the education of some of the brightest children in the Third World who could not otherwise afford to achieve better academic qualifications. BCCI was a major contributor to Cambridge University's Commonwealth Trust, and the bank's contributions enabled BCCI Cambridge scholars from Pakistan, India, Bangladesh, Sri Lanka, Zambia, Zimbabwe and China to attend the university.

But even then there was a taint. Opposition members of the Pakistani Parliament said that more than 50 of the scholars who had been assisted by BCCI were sons and daughters of politicians. The bank's defense to that charge, however, was that it was inevitable that the best-qualified students would come from well-off families.

Chapter 4

The Persian Carpet Ride

Abedi's pursuit of Muslim money in BCCI's early days led him to look jealously on the legendary wealth of the shah of Iran. The schemes he used to win access to that fortune mirror his subsequent assault on Financial General Bankshares—later First American Bank—in the United States. They show that from the very start, Abedi was determined that his insatiable ambition would not be stopped by local laws barring foreign investors and that he was prepared to obtain sham investments with bribes and other favors.

Links between Iran and Pakistan traditionally had been close; both countries were Muslim and both were members of the Regional Cooperation and Development group. Iran also was the land of Abedi's ancestors, which may have had a symbolic significance for him.

Other connections between the high-flying Pakistani and Iran date back to 1970, two years before he founded BCCI. Abedi was looking for a partner for United Bank in Iran, and he had heard on the Pakistani grapevine that the rival Habib Bank had approached a lawyer and wealthy owner of an insurance company in Tehran, Ali Reza Saheb, for a connection to the shah. Saheb, a former assistant to Mohammed Mossadeq, the Iranian populist leader of the 1920s, was well-connected in political, financial and royal circles and would provide an excellent introduction to the shah. But while Saheb had entertained executives of Habib in Tehran, he turned down their request to open an Iranian affiliate. Abedi thought he would try his luck.

Abedi flew Saheb to London, and the two men met in Abedi's palatial suite at the Hilton on Park Lane. It was the start of a process of blandishment that lasted for the best part of a decade. Saheb had dreams of making Tehran a money center for the region that would attract both Persian Gulf money and American banking business, and Abedi seemed to share some of the same aspirations.

The two men met again in Tehran, where Abedi was accompanied by Swaleh Naqvi and two other close colleagues from United Bank, Dildar Rizvi and Velayat Hussein Abedi. This time there was something more concrete on the table. A private Iranian bank, Asnaaf Bank, had collapsed, and the local authorities were looking for a rescue. Saheb saw a joint venture between United Bank and the collapsed bank as the vehicle.

Negotiations between the two groups began. Abedi's hospitality and spending power were formidable. Ali Reza Saheb remembers that during one negotiating session in Zurich, Saheb's wife and Abedi's new second wife, Rabia, went on a Saturday shopping spree. Money was no limit, but the two women ran out of cash, so the ever-resourceful Abedi told Naqvi to find the treasurer of United Bank's branch in Zurich, who opened the office safe for them.

Abedi successfully completed negotiations with Iran, and United Bank won a 40 percent share of the joint venture, the maximum holding that Iranian law permitted to a foreign bank. The Iranian partner kept the rest.

The joint venture appears to have been put into place without the knowledge of the Pakistani prime minister, Zulfiqar Ali Bhutto. When Bhutto heard about it in the course of a visit to Tehran, he publicly berated his ambassador. Bhutto didn't trust Abedi, and he also was concerned that the joint venture would spoil his hopes for building a relationship between Pakistan and Iran. Shortly after, Bhutto nationalized United and the rest of Pakistan's banks and Abedi set up BCCI, registered in Luxembourg rather than Pakistan. Bhutto, convinced that Abedi had obtained the funds to set up BCCI by making improper loans to his friends, withdrew Abedi's passport.

The nationalization of the Pakistani banks ended the Iranian joint venture, but Saheb and Abedi continued to do business together. Saheb had some reservations about working with Abedi, however. At one point, the Pakistani had promised the Iranian a 25 percent stake in BCCI. But Abedi never came up with the stock, instead putting Saheb off by telling him that he could obtain shares in the bank whenever he wanted. That offer never came to fruition.

Still, the dream of a joint Iranian and Pakistani bank persisted, and this time Saheb went to Abedi for help. Saheb planned to allot wealthy Arab sheiks 35 percent of the shares in a new bank and needed introductions. Abedi went one better: He gave Saheb a list of willing shareholders, but said he wanted BCCI to own 17 percent of the shares and the Arab investors 18 percent. Saheb acquiesced.

Abedi's list included Sheik Zayed of Abu Dhabi and his son, Sheik Khalifa, along with the Sultan of Sharjah, Sheik Qabus of Oman and Sheik Rashid of Dubai. The list was cleared by the Iranian security service, and the investments in the new bank seemed assured. But then Abedi introduced a last-minute hitch. He told Saheb, who was to be the new bank's deputy chairman, that unless someone from the Iranian royalty agreed to become a shareholder, the participation of the Arabs was in danger. This surprised the Iranians, since the issue had not arisen before, but Saheb went to the head of the Iranian central bank, who in turn went to the shah. The latter eventually named his brother, Prince Mahmood Reza Pahlavi, to join the board of the newly formed Iran/Arab Bank.

Abedi and Naqvi, who were staying in Tehran at the time to keep a watchful eye on the proceedings, insisted on visiting Prince Mahmood. Within 10 minutes they were in the prince's office. "They talked to him as if they were talking to a god," Saheb remembered. "They made themselves subservient, bowing profusely. Then Abedi said to the prince, 'Your

Highness, we would like to present you with 2,000 shares in Bank of Credit and Commerce.' The prince asked Abedi, 'How much do I have to pay?' but Abedi and Naqvi said, 'This is your bank, don't worry. We'll arrange it.'"

Several years later, in 1976, Saheb asked Sheik Hamdan of Abu Dhabi—Sheik Zayed's uncle—about the unexpected request by the Arab shareholders that a member of the royal family sit on the new bank's board. The sheik said this had never happened, and he put it down to "one of Abedi's tricks. Sheik Zayed and myself don't like the shah," he said. "He's too arrogant for us. We sit on the floor and eat without servants, not in palaces like him."

The shah's brother, Prince Mahmood, had now become part of the BCCI circle of big Arab names. When Abedi furnished *Euromoney* magazine with the list of BCCI shareholders in 1978, the prince's holding was listed broadly as belonging to the "Iranian royal family"—to the dismay of the shah, who knew nothing about the shares.

BCCI gave its new royal Iranian investor the Persian carpet treatment for several years, and then firmly pulled the rug out from under him. Early on, he was allowed to borrow $200,000 to acquire a penthouse in London, furnished at BCCI's expense. Whenever Prince Mahmood was in London, he was attended by Abedi's assistant, Dildar Rizvi, who took him shopping to buy shirts and ties in the fashionable shops of Jermyn Street and also organized all his hotel accommodations and travel.

Then came the Iranian revolution, and BCCI's openhanded generosity turned into a tight fist. The squeeze on Prince Mahmood took two forms. First, Saheb, who had been given power of attorney over Mahmood's financial affairs, recalls that late in 1978, when the crowds were on the streets of Tehran baying for the shah's blood, Velayat Hussein Abedi, Agha Hasan Abedi's assistant, came to him and told him that BCCI would like the prince's account to be closed. Saheb asked what he owed, and was told that the prince owed the bank for the price of the BCCI shares and the cost of antiques the bank had bought for his apartment, a total bill of $350,000. The prince agreed to sell the London penthouse to cover the debt.

The coup de grace came a few months later, when Naqvi and V. H. Abedi went to see Prince Mahmood while he was a fugitive from Iran in Morocco and highly demoralized. They delivered the customary large bouquet of flowers and then told him that it was no longer in his interest or theirs for Mahmood to remain a shareholder in BCCI. They warned him that the new Iranian government might accuse him of using Iranian government money to buy BCCI shares and offered to protect him by holding Mahmood's shares in trust. BCCI would transfer the prince's shares to its books in the trust arrangement, they said, and pay the prince a $6,000 monthly dividend on the stock. Mahmood agreed to the deal, which effectively gave BCCI control over his shares using a method not unlike those it was later to use to control others' investments in American banks.

The prince learned he had been tricked a year later, when the dividend payments stopped, and Mahmood went to Saheb to ask for his help. Saheb approached Naqvi, who observed that the prince hardly was hurting for money. BCCI knew that the prince had $4.5 million in Citibank in New York, Naqvi said, adding that Saheb should mind his own business. Saheb was powerless, and a deeply resentful Prince Mahmood, who now lives in California, is planning to sue BCCI for the value of his misappropriated shares and other funds.

Meanwhile, Abedi was taking advantage of his position in the joint Iran/Arab Bank. Saheb quickly learned that Abedi voted all the Arab sheiks' shares as if they were part of the BCCI block and that all the money used by the sheiks for their initial share purchases had come from BCCI—another trick Abedi later was to use to great effect in the United States.

But the BCCI shareholders were not content to have just their 35 percent stake in the Iran/Arab Bank, and they started to increase their holdings by purchasing additional shares. Iranian law allowed a foreigner to own up to 40 percent of an Iranian bank, but Abedi was pushing 40 percent and still not stopping. He began buying shares in the bank using the names of sympathetic Iranians who would vote the shares for BCCI. The bank had some formal documentation drawn up outlining how the nominees would keep half the shares for themselves, while the other half would go into a secret BCCI account.

One of the primary participants in the share-buying scheme for the Iran / Arab Bank was Rahim Irvani, an Iranian acquaintance of Saheb's, who had a major business manufacturing shoes for export. Saheb invited Irvani to buy 1 percent of the shares, but Irvani, using his Alvand Investment Co., quickly increased his holding to 6 percent by buying shares allotted to the bank's managing director.

Irvani struck up a close social and business relationship with Abedi over the years, entertaining him whenever he came to Tehran. Irvani later served briefly as a director of Credit and Commerce American Holdings (CCAH), the company BCCI used in its attempt to buy Financial General Bankshares. Abedi repaid Irvani for this and other favors by extending to him loans worth tens of millions of dollars to set up shoe-manufacturing plants in Georgia. Many of these loans became delinquent, according to a BCCI officer, collecting no interest or principal payments, indicating that they may have been gifts or sham transactions.

In addition to his attempts to increase his stake in Iran / Arab Bank, Abedi sent BCCI employees to Tehran in an effort to influence day-to-day management of the bank. The first was longtime bank official Iqbal Rizvi, whom BCCI set up in considerable style in Tehran. He joined the Iran / Arab Bank as a consultant to the managing director, but the board refused him an executive role, and he left within six months. Then Abedi sent over Azizullah Choudry, another banker from his close circle. Choudry stayed longer, but never moved out of the credit department.

BCCI made sure that its Persian Gulf shareholders and their families were properly looked after when they passed through Tehran. On one occasion in the mid-1970s, Sheik Hamdan, a BCCI shareholder, was due to visit Tehran, and

Abedi asked Saheb to provide cars and a driver. Saheb also had a dinner appointment with the sheik, but the venue was changed from a restaurant to the sheik's hotel suite. When Saheb arrived, he asked one of the sheik's companions if the arrangements were working out all right. He was told that "the sheik is taken care of." Saheb went to the suite and discovered "four or five of the prettiest girls I have seen in my life serving the guests wine. They were very young and some came from Morocco and only spoke Arabic." Saheb made his apologies and left, but he suspected the involvement of Savak, the shah's secret police, since the foreign women would have needed permission to enter the country. Saheb later heard from a Pakistani minister that Abedi was the source of this entertainment for the valued Abu Dhabi shareholder.

Abedi skillfully left Saheb guessing about his intentions toward him. On one occasion he even suggested that Saheb might be interested in being a nominee shareholder for BCCI in its attempts to buy a bank in the United States. Saheb says he flatly refused.

Saheb was imprisoned in Iran after the revolution that toppled the shah, and upon his release in 1981, he traveled to Pakistan, where he was entertained by Abedi. Saheb was warmly welcomed as Abedi's eternal brother. Saheb discussed his finances with Abedi and explained that his financial holdings in Iran had been frozen after the revolution. If BCCI would lend him money, Saheb said, he would repay it once his Iranian holdings were released. As a token of good faith, Saheb said he would not touch $1.3 million of his personal funds, which he had deposited in BCCI in London, and Abedi reciprocated by saying he would pay him a monthly fee of $6,000.

But like Prince Mahmood before him, Saheb discovered that his money was being kept from him by BCCI. In 1989 Saheb tried to get at the $1.3 million, as a result of legal advice that there was no connection between his business accounts still locked in Iran and his personal finances. However, he was told by the bank that the money had been moved to

BCCI's Grand Cayman branch and was no longer accessible. A letter from BCCI's legal department stated in no uncertain terms:

"We find your allegations and claims to be false, frivolous and wholly unjustified, and it appears that you are trying to make unconscionable gain at the expense of the bank. . . . We have been instructed by the management not to advert to the contents of your letters under reference as they are false, and/or frivolous and/or extraneous, and are motivated to harass. Kindly therefore refrain from communicating with the bank or with us, as no further correspondence shall be entertained on matters raised by you."

This was the reward for a man once described by Abedi as a "brother" and who had given so much of himself to help BCCI in Iran and elsewhere.

Chapter 5

The World's
Sleaziest Bank

Islamic banking and the duping of the shah's brother and businessman Ali Reza Saheb weren't BCCI's only scams as the 1970s became the 1980s. Whatever else it may have been, BCCI was a pretty lousy bank—it did things with its customers' money that the customers never would have imagined. As the Price Waterhouse reports and other internal documents were to spell out in detail later, BCCI regularly defied the most common-sense rules of finance, particularly when the bank ran into severe financial problems in the late 1970s and early 1980s. To even out BCCI's accounts, bank officials began cooking the books and breaking the law in ever more creative ways.

Depositors had no way of knowing that the bank they thought was safe was actually a black hole for their funds. BCCI mocked the trust that customers place in their banks, frequently diverting clients' deposits to cover other shaky bank operations, commingling customers' money with its own and making unauthorized loans to itself in customers' names without their knowledge.

To cover up its actions, BCCI created a "special duties" department in London, whose responsibilities included falsifying documents, creating fictional financial backgrounds for clients and opening bogus accounts. Whenever the auditors or regulators came near, the bank juggled its books, moving money into those accounts that the overseers were inspecting and then quickly draining them and shifting the funds elsewhere as the auditors moved on. In 1986 alone, investigators later determined, the "special duties" department handled $1.6 billion in spurious funds.

It is hard to tell, investigators say, whether BCCI intended to operate illegally when Abedi founded it. But by the late 1970s, the bank's internal audit reports and other documents make clear, sour loans to the Gokal brothers' Gulf Group and other deepening financial problems were accelerating the bank's plunge into extraordinary and illegal solutions. Other, more law-abiding banks might have set aside reserves to cover their potential losses. But the disclosure of such reserves would have exposed BCCI to public scrutiny. Instead, the bank fiddled with its books "to create the image of success," Price Waterhouse said in its final report on the bank before its shutdown. "They apparently believed that the disclosure of the full extent of the losses . . . would have jeopardized the very existence of the bank."

Such problems help to explain BCCI's willingness to seek out deposits wherever it could find them, from Third World central banks to unwitting bank customers in the United States to drug dealers in Central America. With its chronic undercapitalization and flowing red ink, BCCI was constantly in need of fresh funds, regardless of their origin.

Many of BCCI's problems stemmed from the bank's unusual loan practices. While other banks typically spread their loan business around a large number of customers to avoid putting all their eggs into one basket, BCCI concentrated its largess on a small number of loan customers, to its peril. At one point in 1989, it had lent $3.3 billion of its $20 billion in assets to just 22 customers, with the Gokal shipping empire the single biggest recipient, with more than $700 million in loans. That actually was an improvement from a few years earlier, in 1981, when the equivalent of more than half of the bank's $462 million in consolidated capital—$254 million— was tied up in loans to the Gokals' Gulf Group.

Such exposure to a single customer was a recipe for disaster, and when slumping oil prices and shipping rates rocked the Gokal empire in the late 1970s and early 1980s, BCCI ran into trouble too. But it was afraid to let anyone know. "The bank believed that the failure of Gulf Group would have crystallised large losses which would have eroded the bank's capital base and put its very survival in doubt," Price Waterhouse later said. So BCCI began taking steps to cover up the problem.

To hide the troubled loans from auditors and regulators, BCCI began shifting funds in the Gulf Group's accounts so that it appeared that the interest and principal payments on the group's loans were current if anyone checked. "It appears that account manipulation began at this stage," Price Waterhouse said in 1991. "This was a full-time occupation which involved the manufacture of documentation, inflation of account turnover, concealment of fund flows, etc." But even that wasn't enough. "The position of the bank was so compromised," Price Waterhouse said, that "more complicated manipulation was necessary."

BCCI's Cayman Islands subsidiary began in the mid-1980s to take money from other depositors and shovel it into the Gulf Group accounts. To cover the missing funds, bank officials shifted money over from still other customers' accounts. Sometimes, the bank would create new depositors out of whole cloth—with documentation from the "special duties" department—to make it appear that additional funds were available to pour into the delinquent Gulf Group accounts. As BCCI's affairs were unraveled, many of the bank's large customers discovered that they had loans on the bank's books that they knew nothing about—loans that BCCI had created to make itself look stronger and to provide paper money for movement elsewhere in the bank.

The extent of the deception was not apparent until Price Waterhouse raised red flags in 1990 after finding 47 Gulf Group subsidiaries to which BCCI had lent $191 million but "for which we have seen no loan agreements." BCCI's dealings with the Gulf Group had truly been a case of throwing good money after bad. Dozens of Gulf Group subsidiaries, most of them shell companies, had received loans from BCCI. Many of the loans had been "parked" at BCCI subsidiaries to make them harder for auditors to trace. And recovering money from the Gulf Group for the bad loans seemed all but impossible: many of the Gulf Group assets listed as collateral on the loans had previously been "mortgaged to other banks in priority to BCCI," Price Waterhouse said.

The Gulf Group's total loan exposure to BCCI was at least $705.5 million, according to a 1990 report by an internal task force of BCCI executives. These investigators noted "common patterns of initiation, activity, fund flow, weak documentation and vague explanations." The bottom line: "This part of the bank's activity is perhaps the most depressing part of our findings."

BCCI's loan department wasn't the only source of problems. Like other banks, BCCI invested its cash on hand in a variety of financial instruments in an effort to return added profits. Such "treasury" trading usually involves the most conservative investments. But BCCI, pressed for funds, played for much bigger stakes and took much bigger risks. The result, according to former BCCI chief financial officer Masihur Rahman, was a "disaster" that would prove a watershed in BCCI's history.

At one point in 1985, according to Rahman, the treasury department allowed its exposure from the speculative investment of bank funds to run as high as $11 billion—virtually the entire assets of the bank. The money was used to play the markets in commodities, treasury bonds, foreign currency and other instruments—including options trading, in which profits and losses can be limitless. This adventure cost BCCI $430 million in losses in four months, the final spasm in an eight-year trading nightmare in which the bank frittered away a reported $849 million, and perhaps even more. "We were literally stripped of capital," Rahman said later.

BCCI became involved in the trading debacle when the head of its treasury department, Syed Ziauddin Ali Akbar, sold Abedi and Naqvi on the idea of commodities and futures speculation as a quick fix for the mounting losses from the Gulf Group. A separate unit was set up within the bank's treasury department to conduct this trading, according to Price Waterhouse, further masking what was going on. The treasury department apparently went after big game: A June 1986 CIA working paper said that as of a year before, "BCCI was said on good authority to be manipulating to its advantage the Eurodollar certificate of deposit market" —the trading of savings accounts deposited in European banks in American dollars. The CIA report suggested that BCCI was "augment[ing] its trading strength by bribing a key firm making a market in these securities."

In addition to trading on the bank's behalf, the treasury department conducted unauthorized business in customers' names, using their money and names to trade for the bank's own account. This trading was done by a separate group of officers who worked in desks set aside from the usual treasury trading operation. These shadow trades, known within the bank as "Number Two accounts," thus escaped normal audit procedures and exposed BCCI "to significant risks and lost considerable sums of money," according to Price Waterhouse. As the losses mounted, treasury department staffers exacerbated the problems by making bigger and bigger bets in the bottomless pit of the options market. The more they lost, the more they had to speculate in options in an effort to catch up, and the trend seemed to go nowhere but down.

The losses from the treasury account trading nearly erased the bank's capital base. But no one noticed. Akbar and other members of his department simply covered up the massive losses, according to Price Waterhouse, Rahman and others. They would routinely report profits from the treasury operation even though it was losing money, and they wouldn't report the results from the Number Two accounts at all. Sometimes the losses were hidden elsewhere in the bank's ledgers: They were booked "against client accounts, bogus loans or the other unorthodox forms of funding," Price Waterhouse later reported. "It is clear that there was a major misappropriation of funds and falsification of accounting records in the early 1980s," the auditors said. "We had formed the conclusion that the accounting methods adopted were due to incompetence. However, with the benefit of hindsight, it appears more sinister in that it now seems to have been a deliberate way to fictitiously inflate income."

Through the Number Two accounts, Akbar and the treasury department had access to money from customer accounts all over the bank. If the auditors came snooping around, BCCI officials sometimes offered the bilked customers preferred treatment to get them to confirm false fund levels in their accounts when the auditors sought them out each year to double-check the bank's accounting. As Price Waterhouse was later to report to the Bank of England, the overall scheme to hide the treasury losses involved "an enormous and complex web of fictitious transactions in what is probably one of the most complex deceptions in banking history."

One might think that the executive responsible for such huge trading losses and misappropriations of funds would have been fired for irresponsible management and for endangering the bank, once the losses became apparent to BCCI's top management in the mid-1980s. But he was not. Akbar was first transferred elsewhere in the bank, then "gently" allowed to resign, according to Rahman, "with car and benefits." That's not all: According to Price Waterhouse, Akbar also received $32 million from BCCI when he left the bank. Some called it a bonus; Price Waterhouse described it as "blackmail" to buy Akbar's silence about his activities.

Akbar has denied receiving such a payment and told the *Financial Times* of London in August 1991 that he was being made a scapegoat for the trading losses. "I was simply a coordinator among several departments. I never originated any deals," the newspaper quoted him as saying. According to Akbar, he had only followed orders from above, and he described how a committee chaired by either Abedi or Naqvi met every morning to discuss the treasury operation. Naqvi was said to have monitored all the trading, including the bank's Cayman Islands operations, through which the treasury trading was booked. That version of events may explain why Akbar's "punishment" was so limited—and it may go a long way to explaining what happened next.

A few months after leaving BCCI, Akbar resurfaced in a new role with close ties to BCCI, as a key executive in Capcom Financial Services, a London-based commodities trading company that was to have a history almost as clouded as that of BCCI. Not coincidentally, Capcom had handled much of BCCI's treasury trading during the mid-1980s, when the bank was losing so much money on speculation, and it shared several key stockholders with the bank. Once Akbar moved to the firm, he brought along BCCI and Abedi as customers—unusual, perhaps, given Akbar's role in BCCI's problems—and Capcom became little more than the successor to the BCCI treasury department.

All by itself, Capcom is an intriguing footnote to the BCCI saga. The company was founded in 1984 and set up offices in London and Chicago to trade foreign currencies, government bonds, gold and other commodities. Among its dozen shareholders were three of the investors alleged to have purchased First American on behalf of BCCI—Saudi businessman Abdul Raouf Khalil; Kamal Adham, the former head of intelligence for Saudi Arabia; and Sayed El Jawhary, a longtime aide to Adham. A fourth Capcom investor was Hatton Pharaon, the younger brother of Saudi financier Ghaith Pharaon, who later acted as a front man for BCCI in the purchase of National Bank of Georgia and Independence Bank of California.

Also involved in the founding of Capcom was a group of American investors. One was Bob John Magness, founder and chairman of Tele-Communications Inc. (TCI) of Denver, the nation's biggest cable television company; another was Larry Romrell, a TCI vice president. Apparently neither Magness nor Romrell had an active role in the day-to-day running of Capcom, although reports filed by the company with British regulators listed Romrell as chairman in 1987 and 1988 and said Magness was a member of the company's board in the same period. Both also were significant stock-holders before selling their shares and resigning from the company in October 1988 after Capcom was implicated with BCCI in the Florida money-laundering case.

Another American who invested in Capcom was Robert "Mo" Powell, who has a long history of owning companies doing business with the U.S. and foreign governments dating back to the Vietnam War. Powell now runs a small defense contracting firm in California and lives in Oman, where he operates several other businesses. Powell, also apparently a passive investor in Capcom, told *Washington Post* reporter Jerry Knight that he had had business connections with Adham for more than 20 years and also had longstanding business ties to BCCI. He said he had invested in Capcom because "it was in my interest to please BCCI." The offer to invest came not from Adham, Powell told Knight, but from Akbar.

Obviously, even though it was not owned by BCCI, the trading company had strong ties to the bank: several common shareholders and indirect bank relationships with other Capcom investors, not to mention BCCI's role as one of Capcom's chief customers. When Akbar came aboard as manager and part-owner of the company, the link was complete.

Capcom soon had its own problems. By 1988, suspicions surfaced about the company's ownership and trading practices, and in August 1988, British commodities regulators expelled it from trading in the London futures markets. Among other things, the regulators said the company was unable to satisfactorily identify all of Capcom's owners. In addition, there were questions about tens of millions of dollars in payments found on Capcom's books, for which Capcom conceded that it was "unable to provide the company's auditors with relevant supporting documents." Some of this money appeared to be the result of money-laundering for the drug operation run by Panamanian dictator Manuel Noriega. Capcom later was indicted by the U.S.

government for its role in money-laundering on behalf of Noriega and others.

Mystery remains about other entries on Capcom's books—a subsidiary called Brenchase Ltd., listed in corporate records as being a taxi and car-rental operation, received $68 million from BCCI for what examiners described as "an unknown purpose."

Shortly after British regulators moved on Capcom, the company was kicked out of the Chicago futures markets by officials acting on a tip from their British counterparts. Capcom eventually shut down its American operations entirely. British regulators fined the company $700,000 and American officials fined it $500,000. Akbar himself was in trouble: He was convicted by a British court in 1989 of conspiring to launder money through Capcom and served nine months in jail. In August 1991, he was arrested again in Calais, France, after stepping off a ferry from Britain, where he had been ordered to stay for a new investigation. He allegedly was carrying a fake passport and planning to flee prosecution. Shortly after the arrest, Akbar was indicted along with Capcom and several former BCCI officials in a new federal money-laundering case in Tampa.

Meanwhile, back at BCCI, the magnitude of the trading losses in the treasury operation had become too large to hide by the mid-1980s, and officials in the bank's headquarters nation of Luxembourg began privately urging Abedi to clean up the mess. As a stopgap, the bank recapitalized in June 1986 by taking $150 million from a BCCI employee pension fund held at International Credit and Investment Co., the BCCI subsidiary in the Cayman Islands that has been described as being like "the bank within the bank."

But even that was not enough for the long term. As the bank's financial condition continued to deteriorate, BCCI turned to even more elaborate and desperate schemes to keep its books balanced and to hide its problems from auditors and regulators. It accepted deposits, but did not record them on its books, instead applying them directly to other cash-poor bank operations. When the customer demanded the money that had been deposited, the bank would shift it from somewhere else in a sort of internal "Ponzi" scheme. According to Price Waterhouse, BCCI held $569 million in unrecorded deposits by the end of 1990.

These shifts of funds seemed certain to show up in the bank's regular end-of-year audits. But BCCI had a scheme to handle that, too. Just before a particular account was due for an audit, BCCI officials would fill it with money from another account to make it appear whole—and then move the money elsewhere after the auditors had moved on. Or it would drain an account almost to nothing, tricking the auditors into thinking the account was too inconsequential to need an audit. To cover up bad loans, BCCI would move money rapidly from account to account to make it appear that nonperforming loans actually were earning interest. Through these and other schemes, BCCI convinced its auditors that the bank was solvent during the 1980s.

How were the auditors so badly fooled? One of the answers lies in the peculiar role of corporate auditors, who on the one hand are supposed to identify financial irregularities but on the other are financially beholden to their employers: the company's management. An auditing firm that delivers bad news can be out of a job. As a result, many critics have charged, some auditors don't push very hard with their questions about a company's finances. In BCCI's case, it also helped that the bank wasn't telling the auditors from Price Waterhouse anywhere near the whole truth about its finances.

Chapter 6

Coming to America

Being the bank for the Third World was all well and good, but if BCCI was to be taken seriously as a major international banking power, it needed to have a presence in the world's largest and most lucrative banking market, the United States. Even with its $2.2 billion in worldwide assets by 1977, BCCI was strictly minor league in the world of banking without a U.S. subsidiary. Lacking that, BCCI's operations in the United States would be limited to representative offices that could not take deposits from Americans and would be restricted by law in terms of what banking services they could perform. Moreover, the U.S. presented a potentially rich source of new funds for the perpetually cash-strapped bank.

Almost from the start, Abedi was plotting to introduce BCCI into the U.S. But American regulators made it clear early on that BCCI, with its lack of any central regulator to oversee its operations, wasn't welcome in the U.S. banking business. As a result, the history of BCCI's involvement in the U.S. market is one marked by secrecy and skullduggery, right up until the end—when the scandal over BCCI's illegal ownership of several American banks bolted BCCI onto front pages all over the country.

The takeover of what became First American Bank and other U.S. institutions by BCCI reveals a deviousness on the part of BCCI and a laxness in regulation matched only by the zeal displayed by some American investigators in attacking the scandal after the fact. BCCI's American history also demonstrates the bank's uncanny ability to cozy up to the politically powerful and to use them, wittingly and unwittingly, to achieve the bank's nefarious ends.

Abedi made his first pass at an American bank in 1975, when BCCI attempted to buy the small New York-based Chelsea National Bank, which was a subsidiary of a larger institution, Financial General Bankshares Inc. Actually, BCCI didn't bid openly for Chelsea—in a precursor of things to come, it talked the Gokal family into attempting to purchase the bank on behalf of BCCI. That idea didn't wash with New York regulators, who were concerned that the Gokals didn't know enough about the banking business. The regulators also were wary about what role, if any, BCCI would play as the Gokals' chief adviser. As the questions about the deal became more and more penetrating, the acquisition plans were dropped.

But Abedi continued to look enviously at the wealthy U.S. market. In 1977, BCCI became interested in another Financial General subsidiary in New York, the Bank of Commerce, a medium-sized institution that would give BCCI a solid foothold in the huge New York banking market. New York was a plum because of its position as the world's financial center—trillions of dollars pass daily through New York banks, to and from all corners of the globe. Ownership of a bank there would give BCCI access to that financial pipeline, allowing it to offer its customers a whole new level of money-changing services.

At about the same time that Abedi began to focus on Bank of Commerce, a minor American political scandal was playing itself out in Washington that would prove to be instrumental to BCCI. Bert Lance, the folksy Georgia banker who was a close adviser to President Carter and director of the Office of Management and Budget, was embroiled in a flap over alleged improprieties in his pre-government career running National Bank of Georgia. Facing a nasty congressional hearing into his actions, Lance hired two of the best legal minds in Washington to defend him: Clark M. Clifford and Robert A. Altman.

Clifford was a legendary figure, a former secretary of defense and adviser to every Democratic president since Harry S Truman. Still possessed of a razor-sharp mind in his mid-70s, Clifford was acclaimed as one of Washington's master political fixers, a man who knew how to play the political angles and get a client out of a jam. He was Mr. Integrity, the man who would put his considerable reputation on the line for a client, with the implicit signal being that if Clifford thought the client was worthy, perhaps the other side in the dispute should reconsider its position. This talent proved lucrative—his small law firm was one of Washington's richest and most powerful, with a blue-chip list of corporate clients, and Clifford was regularly called upon to put out tricky political fires like the one that was threatening Lance. He made millions, but lived frugally. A workaholic, his only recreation appeared to be golf, a game that he reputedly played with what might kindly be called a liberal view of the rules.

Clifford even looked the part of the elder statesman: tall and silver-haired, his face seemingly chiseled from granite. In moments of contemplation, Clifford was given to bringing his hands together in front of him, fingertip to fingertip, in a prayer-like gesture that became known around Washington as the "Clifford steeple." Age scarcely slowed Clifford down—when he was called before congressional committees and grand juries investigating the BCCI affair in his 85th year, he testified patiently and lucidly for hours, the only concession to his years being a noontime nap.

Clifford's partner and protégé Altman was a sharp lawyer in his early 30s who came from a monied Washington family and was making a name for himself as a political and legal power in his own right. Clifford and Altman often worked as a good cop-bad cop team, with Clifford playing the genteel Midwestern lawyer and Altman acting the part of tough guy. Altman later added a measure of glamor unusual in button-down Washington by marrying Lynda Carter, the star of the "Wonder Woman" television series, and building a gigantic house (it was said to have 16 bathrooms) in the ritzy Washington suburb of Potomac. Clifford, the father of three daughters, often described Altman as the son he never had. Altman named one of his sons after his mentor, and in times of stress, Altman's hands even occasionally mimicked the Clifford steeple. In a couple of instances during their congressional testimony on BCCI, they looked as if they were praying together before the panel of congressmen that faced them.

In 1977, this high-powered legal team sat with Lance as he faced the tough questions from Congress. By most accounts, they eased him through the difficult situation, but Lance, realizing his political effectiveness to Carter had been severely damaged by the publicity from the scandal, decided to leave the administration shortly after the hearings. He was licking his wounds and looking for financial consulting work in late 1977 when Abedi came calling.

In retrospect, Abedi's interest in Lance is not surprising. Here was an opportunity for the BCCI founder to strike up a friendship with a former top U.S. government official who still had strong connections to the Carter administration—just the type of powerful friend that Abedi had cultivated so well elsewhere in the world. Lance and Carter went way back. Lance had backed Carter when he first campaigned for governor of Georgia at the beginning of the 1970s and later when he ran successfully for president (Lance himself ran unsuccessfully for governor of Georgia in 1974). He also had helped run Georgia's finances for Carter. Lance knew the power of money in the political process—he had seen to it that his bank, NBG, became the single largest lender to Carter's peanut farm. What's more, Lance knew the American banking scene, in which Abedi had such a burning interest.

Abedi set up an introduction to Lance through a Georgia politician who was a mutual acquaintance. Lance met with Abedi and Swaleh Naqvi for the first time at the Waldorf-Astoria Hotel in New York in late October 1977, and he liked what he heard. Abedi told Lance of BCCI's commitment to economic development in the Third World and of his plans to expand BCCI around the world—specifically, into the U.S. "My rejoinder to him [was] that obviously you cannot be a global bank, an international bank, without some sort of presence in the United States," Lance said. Abedi had Lance on the hook, and he wanted the former OMB head to work for BCCI as a consultant on U.S. expansion—just the kind of job that Lance was looking for.

But Lance was also leery of jumping from one controversial situation into another. So he called his new lawyer friends, Clifford and Altman, and asked them to check out Abedi and BCCI—to do what Lance later described, using a legal term, as "due diligence." "I said, 'Mr. Clifford, I have made the acquaintance of Mr. Abedi,'" Lance recalled in congressional testimony more than a decade later. "'His bank is BCCI. He has some interest in talking to me about future relationships, whether that is in regard to being merely a consultant or being actively involved in one of his operations somewhere. . . . But before I do that, it is absolutely imperative and incumbent upon me to make sure that we know what kind of people that I am getting involved with.'" With that conversation, Lance had unwittingly begun to bring together the three key players on the U.S. side of the BCCI scandal: Abedi, Clifford and Altman.

Clifford brought back good news, confirming what Lance had been able to determine on his own: Abedi appeared to be the genuine article, a highly respected banker running a hot young bank. Lance later said:

"Every instance of report that I . . . got, or from what Mr. Clifford told me, came back that Mr. Abedi was a man of integrity and character, that BCCI was a new kid on the block, so to speak, in regard to trying to make inroads into the banking community in London and Europe and so on, but that they were people of integrity and character."

Further endorsement came from Bank of America's two representatives on BCCI's board, who also vouched for the bank—even though Bank of America was beginning the process of reducing its involvement in BCCI because of management concern over the bank's sloppy business practices. Indeed, there is question about just how diligent Lance's and Clifford's "due diligence" was—Lance later said, for instance, that he was unaware that BCCI had unsuccessfully tried to acquire Chelsea National Bank in 1975 through the Gokal brothers. "There was never any comment, as I recall, by Mr. Abedi about any previous effort to take a position in any U.S. bank," Lance said.

Nonetheless, Lance went to work for BCCI as a consultant on U.S. banking. He quickly recommended two banks to Abedi as potential American takeover candidates. One, conveniently, was his old bank, National Bank of Georgia, in which Lance still owned a 12 percent stake. "I said to him, 'Look, you have these investors that you have said you represent who want to be involved in U.S. investments and so on,'" Lance recalled. "'Now, what about the National Bank of Georgia? . . . It's in a fine community, it's in a growing area, it's had the opportunity to grow and develop, but there's a lot of potential there in Georgia and the Southeast in the Sunbelt.'"

The other bank Lance recommended to Abedi was Financial General Bankshares, which in addition to owning Chelsea National Bank and the Bank of Commerce, also coincidentally had owned NBG before Lance. There was dissension within the group of investors that owned Financial General, Lance knew, and he convinced Abedi to shift his sights from the Bank of Commerce subsidiary to the entire bank. Besides, Lance pointed out to Abedi, Financial General had a unique position in the highly restricted world of U.S. banking: Because of a quirk in the law, it was one of a handful of banks then able to do business in more than one state. From its base in Washington, Financial General owned banks in Maryland, Virginia, New York and several other states. "So from an economic standpoint, from a practical standpoint, it made more sense to me to talk about the acquisition of

Financial General instead of the acquisition of the Bank of Commerce," Lance recalled telling Abedi.

Abedi listened to his new friend's advice, although he had to be careful, since banking laws precluded BCCI from directly owning a U.S. bank because of Bank of America's large holding in BCCI, which in turn would give BofA a stake in any bank BCCI purchased. Abedi began BCCI's foray into the United States by purchasing National Bank of Georgia for BCCI for $20 million—in the process, giving Lance a handsome profit on his 12 percent stake in the bank. But Abedi did not buy NBG directly; instead, he went through a front man.

Ghaith Pharaon was a Saudi Arabian businessman with growing ties to the United States who seemed bent on single-handedly smoothing Arab-American business relations. At a time when the fallout from the Arab oil embargo of 1973— and the subsequent embargo of 1979—still fanned American anger toward newfound Arab oil wealth, Pharaon just kept plowing Arab money back into the United States. He even lived in the U.S., in a palatial mansion once owned by Henry Ford near Savannah, Ga.

Smooth, articulate and educated, Pharaon had traveled in high circles from an early age. The son of a Saudi doctor, he had come to the U.S. in 1959 to study mining and then earned an MBA from Harvard, later serving as Harvard's only Muslim trustee. Pharaon was the perfect choice to act on BCCI's behalf in the United States, and NBG was only his first investment on BCCI's behalf. He later fronted the purchase of other financial institutions for BCCI, including Independence Bank of Encino, Calif. (where a former BCCI executive was named chairman), and Centrust Savings in Miami. With Pharaon up front, BCCI's secret purchase of NBG sailed right through the regulatory process, providing a tidy windfall for Lance, who sold his shares to Pharaon. The same day the sale went through, BCCI lent Lance $3.5 million to repay a loan that Lance had outstanding at First National Bank of Chicago.

But owning a small bank in Georgia was not enough for BCCI and Abedi. He still wanted a major presence in the U.S., and with Lance at his side, he began stalking Financial General. Lance introduced Abedi to a number of dissatisfied shareholders who wanted to bail out of the bank. They included the late Armand Hammer, the legendary octogenarian chairman of Occidental Petroleum, who owned around 5 percent, and some associates of his, who also owned 5 percent. There was another 10 percent on the market, and Abedi wanted to snap up the lot. But he ran into U.S. banking regulations that required that owners of more than 5 percent of a company's shares be publicly identified.

Abedi didn't want to tip his hand too early in what he knew would be a difficult takeover struggle. So he quickly rounded up four Arab supporters of BCCI whose names could be used to front the purchases. The four were Adham, the former Saudi security chief; Faisal Saud al-Fulaij, the Kuwaiti businessman and onetime head of Kuwaiti Airlines who had longstanding ties to BCCI and ran its Kuwait International Finance Co. affiliate; Abedi's old friend Sheik Zayed of Abu Dhabi; and Sheik Zayed's teenaged son, Mohammed bin Zayed, who at the time was too young to conduct his own business and was represented by Abdullah Dharwaish, the financial adviser to Sheik Zayed. (Sheik Zayed himself later dropped out of the initial group, but came back in as an investor in 1983 and, ironically, wound up owning First American when he took over BCCI in 1990.)

Adham became the de facto leader of the investor group and by far its most controversial figure. He had little experience in banking, but he was a past master of political intrigue. Born in 1929, Adham is the half-brother of a wife of the late King Faisal of Saudi Arabia, and was a close confidant of the king. He was given the job of chief of the Saudi Foreign Liaison Bureau, with the responsibility of looking after Faisal's security, at a time when radical elements in the Middle East were beginning to threaten the area's autocratic barons. In Anthony Sampson's book on oil and the Middle

East, *The Seven Sisters,* Adham was described as Faisal's "chamberlain."

As head of the Saudi equivalent of the CIA, Adham also acquired prestige in the shady world of the intelligence community, where ruthlessness is more highly prized than democratic instincts. When he made a visit to Iran in 1975, Adham was feted by Savak, the much-feared secret police. He also had close contacts with the CIA and sought to influence the policy of Anwar Sadat in Egypt by pushing large sums of money his way to encourage Sadat to expel Soviet advisers. He also is understood to have been behind Saudi Arabia's policy of backing the Palestine Liberation Organization in the mid-1970s.

Adham's business career seemed to be a logical extension of his intelligence career. As early as the mid-1960s, Adham was representing some of the world's largest arms companies, and at the end of the decade he was the intermediary for Saudi Arabia in arranging the purchase of French weapons by Egypt. Later, he represented Boeing Co.; in the mid-1970s, U.S. government agencies investigated "questionable payments" made to Adham by Boeing following a massive aircraft sale to Egypt, apparently kickbacks to help secure business in Egypt and elsewhere in the Middle East. Somehow, most of Adham's past seemed to escape the attention of regulators as they considered BCCI's application to buy Financial General, even though the Boeing allegations, for instance, had been reported by the Wall Street Journal and others.

Lance relished his new role as dealmaker, which put him back in a position to rub shoulders with the rich and powerful. Abedi took him to Pakistan to go bustard hunting with Sheik Zayed. "Let me try to describe Sheik Zayed for you," Lance later recounted in his Georgia drawl. "He's an interesting man. At that point in time when I met him, not only did he not speak English, I don't think he understood the first word of English. And that's one of the few people that I've ever run into that didn't understand anything that I was saying. I know I talk funny, but it was obvious that he didn't have the slightest idea of what I was saying. He did respond to a smile. And I decided that might be the best way to communicate."

Sheik Zayed, however, wasn't the only one who didn't seem to understand what was going on. Lance apparently was in the dark about the arrangements made between BCCI and its clients. BCCI made the purchases of the stock, but told regulators in various filings that it was doing so on behalf of the four investors.

It appears that BCCI decided to purchase the stock on behalf of the four even before it had determined who the investors would be. In January 1978, Abedi's deputy and chief U.S. representative, Abdus Sami, sent his boss a telex to brief him on the status of the purchase of the Financial General shares. Sami told Abedi that U.S. law required that the individual shareholders' stakes in the company must be kept below 5 percent apiece, and asked for the names of two other investors "immediately" to go along with Adham and Fulaij. Sheik Zayed and his son were then added.

Secrecy was clearly of the essence. "We must be careful that our name [BCCI] does not appear as financier to most of [the investors] for this acquisition," Sami wrote. Indeed, it later came out, BCCI had lent several of the investors the money to acquire the Financial General shares, even though they claimed the money had come from their own pockets. This was to be the crux of the fraud charges brought by the Federal Reserve in 1991.

In the same telex, Sami told Abedi that "our friend"— Lance—had advised BCCI to hire an American lawyer to handle any litigation arising out of the takeover effort and to supervise any filings with the Federal Reserve seeking approval of the acquisition of Financial General. The lawyer's name: Clark Clifford. "I met with Mr. Clark Clifford and explained to him our strategy and our goal," Sami wrote Abedi. "He was happy to know the details and has blessed the acquisition." Clifford has denied advising BCCI to do anything to skirt U.S. regulations.

Clifford and Altman were now to play increasingly important roles in the Financial General takeover and the eventual running of the bank. Why would Clifford and Altman become involved? This question was asked by many in the wake of the scandal. Perhaps both saw BCCI's stalled attempt to purchase Financial General as a chance to apply their considerable skills as legal and political fixers. For Clifford, this was a particularly interesting case—the BCCI investors clearly were in need of someone of considerable repute who could guide them through the thicket of the U.S. regulatory and legal system, and Clifford fit the bill perfectly. He later said that he agreed to stay on after the takeover and manage the bank as its chairman because, at age 75, he had decided he needed a new challenge. "There was nothing particularly interesting going on at the [law] firm at this time, and this was a challenge to me," Clifford said. "It was another mountain to climb." For his partner, Altman, there was also the chance to spread his talents into the commercial world from the legal arena. Others later saw a simpler, darker motivation in the two men's involvement: the opportunity to make a financial killing on the bank takeover. Whatever the reason, it appears that Clifford and Altman wound up getting much more than they had bargained for.

Shortly after the two lawyers were retained by BCCI, Financial General's management sued BCCI, Abedi, Lance and the four investors who had bought into the bank, alleging that they were acting as an organized group, not on their own, in acquiring Financial General shares. Such a distinction is important in securities law—as individuals, the investors each held less than 5 percent of Financial General, less than the legal reporting requirements. But if considered as a group, their holding was almost 20 percent, requiring them to disclose their holdings and declare their intentions for the bank.

A month after Financial General filed its suit, the Securities and Exchange Commission filed similar charges against BCCI, Abedi, Lance and the investors. The case was settled the same day by a consent agreement in which the defendants admitted no wrongdoing but agreed to abide by SEC rules in the future—and to make a public offer for Financial General shares, as a group, if they wanted to buy the bank. Altman and Clifford told their clients that they'd been caught in a technicality that was easier to settle than fight. But a federal court, issuing a preliminary injunction against the BCCI investors in April 1978 in the suit brought by Financial General, said there was more to it: The court ruled that BCCI had been deeply involved in the abortive takeover attempt, had sought to buy more shares than it had clients for and held unusual power over some of the shares the investors had purchased.

Checkmated by regulators, and facing stiff opposition from Financial General's management in any event, BCCI tried a new tack. In the summer of 1978, it formed Credit and Commerce American Holdings (CCAH) and a related company, Credit and Commerce American Investments (CCAI), to mount a new effort to take over Financial General. (There is some documentary evidence that CCAH may have existed as early as 1976 as a BCCI acquisition vehicle.)

The two companies were registered not in Washington or London, but in the regulatory and tax havens of the Netherlands Antilles and the Cayman Islands. The Netherlands Antilles, home of CCAH, had considerable appeal at this time because of a favorable taxation treaty between the United States and the Netherlands. In a letter to the Federal Reserve, Altman promised that "neither BCCI nor any other organization related to BCCI contemplates owning any equity interest in CCAH"—even though BCCI's secretive Cayman Islands affiliate, ICIC Overseas, was listed as one of the shareholders, with a 4.5 percent stake in CCAH. This new takeover effort was minus Lance, who apparently had been jettisoned to reduce controversy.

With the new corporate structure in place, the next bid for Financial General came in October 1978, with the filing with the Federal Reserve of an application for prior approval of a takeover of the bank by CCAH and CCAI. In the increasingly complicated corporate shell game being used in the takeover effort, CCAH was listed as the parent company of CCAI, which in turn was to make the formal bid for Financial General. The offering price was $70 million, which was to be obtained from a group of investors in return for stakes in CCAH, thus expanding the original group of four Arab investors to around a dozen. The investors, the application vowed, would use their own money.

The group of investors assembled by Abedi to bid for Financial General was a combination of powerful Saudis and minor dignitaries in the Arab world. Trading on the influence of his patron, the sheik of Abu Dhabi, Abedi had trawled the Gulf and further afield for supporters who would have little idea of his purpose or methods. In this way he added to the group Humaid bin Rashid al-Naomi, the ruler of the small nation of Ajman; Sheik Hamad bin Mohammed al-Sharqi, the ruler of the Emirate of Fujairah; and Ali Mohammed Shorafa, the director of presidential affairs for the United Arab Emirates and a top aide to Sheik Zayed.

Officially, BCCI was no longer part of the group in any way, although it continued to act as investment adviser and communications link to the investors, as Clifford and Altman were to argue repeatedly in their defense. (Former BCCI executive Abdur Sakhia was later to point out to a congressional committee that the bank's purported role as an intermediary between Clifford and Altman and the investors was somewhat odd. "I fail to understand that it was difficult to communicate with the Middle Eastern investors," he said. The investors were "people who did business in the United States, who came to the United States. It was not Bedouins who lived in the desert. ... These were big, prominent people.")

The application to the Federal Reserve for prior approval indicated that CCAH was planning to attempt something almost unheard of in the hidebound world of banking—a hostile takeover attempt. The men who ran Financial General angrily fought back with a legal barrage led by Chairman William Middendorf, a pugnacious former secretary of the Navy. Once again, regulators tripped up the acquisition attempt: This time, Maryland officials ruled that it was a violation of state law for a bank doing business in the state to be acquired without its consent.

The Fed dismissed the application for the takeover in early 1979, ruling that the Maryland objections were enough to scuttle the bid, and not commenting on anything else in the application. BCCI and its investors had struck out again. Still, in an interview with the *Financial Times* at the time, Abedi asserted that he was not giving up. He was "not sure yet who will make the offer, but whoever makes it and if it succeeds, BCCI will probably manage Financial General."

CCAH pitched another takeover try in 1980. This time around, the group led by Adham solicited proxies, or votes, from Financial General shareholders to support their offer. The measure was narrowly defeated at the bank's 1980 shareholders meeting. But shortly after, CCAH came up with a sweetened financial offer and the management group led by Middendorf caved in.

The investors now had permission to buy Financial General from its owners. But they still needed the blessing of regulators, and that proved to be difficult. In the wake of the 1979-80 oil embargo, anti-Arab sentiment was running high, but the bigger problem appears to be that the regulators simply didn't trust BCCI. Since its far-flung holdings left it virtually unregulated by any central body, the mere mention of BCCI made the Federal Reserve and other authorities queasy. They were anxious to be reassured that BCCI, whatever its ties to CCAH, would have nothing to do with Financial General. "I could not for the life of me figure out what the relationship was between BCCI and their investors and [Financial General's Virginia subsidiary]," said Sidney Bailey, Virginia's commissioner of financial institutions and a persistently suspicious critic of BCCI.

New York banking regulators feared that "the Arab investors might have been acting for BCCI," according to Geofredo Rodriguez, who oversaw the deal for the New York bank superintendent's office. But Altman promised in a letter to regulators: "With regard to the stockholders of

CCAH, all holdings constitute personal investments. None is held as an unidentified agent for another individual or organization."

The Federal Reserve, as the primary regulator of U.S. bank holding companies, had final say in the matter. After listening to written arguments, it convened an unusual "informal private hearing" on April 23, 1981, at its stately headquarters in Washington to examine the proposal to acquire Financial General. "We wanted to establish that BCCI was not going to be acquiring a controlling interest" in Financial General, Donald E. Kline, the Federal Reserve's associate director of regulation and supervision, later told *The Washington Post* .

Present at the hearing were 16 regulators, including Bailey, Rodriguez and other officials of states in which Financial General did business. On the other side of the table were Clifford, Altman and their clients: Adham, Fulaij, Saudi businessman Abdul Raouf Khalil and Sayed El Jawhary, an adviser to Adham, all representing themselves and others in the 14-member investor group. Taken as a group, most of the investors had two things in common besides their Middle Eastern roots—they were part owners of BCCI and they had suddenly and, supposedly coincidentally, developed interests in owning Financial General Bankshares.

Clifford began the hearing by again reassuring the regulators that BCCI had no direct part in the takeover. The bank and Abedi were merely acting, he said, as communications links and investment advisers to the investors. Clifford then called upon the investors to speak for themselves, introducing Adham, the largest shareholder, to the regulators as "a prominent businessman in Saudi Arabia." "I have come to have the deepest respect for his character, for his reputation, for his honor and for his integrity," Clifford said—notwithstanding the fact that a Federal Reserve staff report completed the day before but not brought up at the hearing had concluded that Adham had been paid off by Boeing, although his acceptance of the payments did not violate U.S. law. Clifford, who later claimed to have been unaware of any derogatory information about Adham, referred to him at the hearing as "His Excellency," and the regulators followed suit.

The white-haired, distinguished-looking Adham dealt with each of the regulators' concerns in turn, using his most polished manner. While BCCI was the group's investment adviser, he said, "There is, however, no understanding or arrangement regarding any future relationship or proposed transactions between Financial General and BCCI." Adham and the other investors promised that they were passive owners, that they had no intention of getting involved with the management of Financial General, which would be handled by a new board headed by Clifford and Altman. The bank would continue to be "an American company," they promised, and another Washington titan, Clifford's close friend Stuart Symington, a former senator, would be the trustee for 60 percent of the company's shares to ward off any undue influence. Adham even became huffy at the suggestion that the investors were fronting for BCCI:

"I think from the line of questions, it appears there is [a belief that] BCCI is behind all of this deal. I would like to assure you that each [investor] on his own rights will not accept in any way to be a cover for somebody else. . . . We don't need anybody to use us, to be a cover for them. We are doing it for ourselves."

Clifford went even further. When one regulator, Lloyd W. Bostian Jr. of the Federal Reserve's Richmond office, asked, "What precisely is [BCCI's] function, if any, in this proposal at the present time?" Clifford responded: "None. There is no function of any kind on the part of BCCI. . . . I know of no planned future relationship that exists."

Although there also were questions about the similarity between the name of Bank of Credit and Commerce International and that of Credit and Commerce American Holdings, Clifford and Altman assured the regulators that it was simply a coincidence, and for the most part, the applicants were hit with no zingers. The regulators never laid a glove on them.

Clifford, it appeared, had succeeded in working his magic to assuage the regulators' fears. Though Bailey continued to raise questions about the deal—at one point, he wrote a letter to the Fed complaining that, in essence, Clifford and Altman were asking regulators to simply "trust us" that BCCI was not involved in the takeover—the Federal Reserve approved the takeover of Financial General on Aug. 25, 1981. The Office of the Comptroller of the Currency also gave its blessing, saying,

"It has now been represented to us that BCCI will have no involvement with the management and other affairs, nor will BCCI be involved in the financing arrangements."

New York regulators, who had their own qualms about the deal, nonetheless approved it the following spring, after forcing Financial General for technical reasons to sell off the Bank of Commerce, ironically the reason for Abedi's initial interest in the bank. On April 16, 1982, CCAH purchased the remaining shares in Financial General and took over the bank, renaming it First American Bankshares—"The bank for all Americans," as an ad campaign later put it. Clifford became its chairman, and Altman its president. With branches throughout the Washington area (and as far south as Tennessee), First American was well-positioned to take advantage of the economic boom in the region in the 1980s. It grew to be Washington's largest bank holding company, with a peak of $11 billion in assets in 1989.

The regulators later had to admit they had been fooled. "The representations made by the applicants, CCAH shareholders and their counsel before the Board were representations of BCCI because BCCI intended to be, and was in fact, the principal shareholder of CCAH and caused such representations to be made in the application, in related materials, and at the hearing," the Fed said in its July 29, 1991, complaint against BCCI, Abedi, Naqvi and the investors. (Clifford and Altman were not named as defendants in the case; it was believed that investigators were preparing separate charges against them.)

The Fed's complaint painstakingly documented the way that BCCI manipulated the control of the shares in CCAH, using the investors' names to dupe the regulators about the company's independence. The trail of letters and contracts cited by the Fed is extraordinarily complete, which raises the question of why it took almost 10 years for the alleged fraud to be tracked down.

The use of front men, or nominees, to disguise the true ownership and control of First American is really only the start of the scam. Having given the investors' names to regulators as the purported owners, BCCI proceeded to use a series of nominee companies and individuals to fabricate the bank's finances and capital structure and to route money from the investors' accounts into BCCI disguised as capital infusions into First American.

It is not altogether clear whether BCCI owned First American through this scheme from the start. But by no later than 1983, according to federal prosecutors, shortly after the takeover, BCCI had begun to rearrange the ownership in the bank to its favor. It made loans to the CCAH shareholders and accepted CCAH stock as collateral, backed by stock-pledge agreements, blank share transfers, undated powers of attorney and buyback agreements that promised that the investors would not lose money on their shares. Together, these actions gave BCCI direct control of the CCAH shares, and over the next few years, it called the shots in the owner-ship group, even though the stock remained registered in the nominees' names.

The investors never paid any interest on the loans that were made against the stock—a further indication to inves-tigators that the transactions were fakes. What's more, each of the nominees was paid handsomely by BCCI for letting his name be used: Adham received $2 million, Fulaij got $100,000 a year from 1986 to 1989, plus $606,000 in 1990, and Jawhary was paid $150,000 a year for acting as a nominee, according to the Fed charges. (Adham later claimed that the Fed was wrong, that he had paid for the shares himself and had no nominee arrangement with BCCI.)

BCCI owned at least 25 percent of First American by 1983, enough to give it technical control over the bank, by the Fed's definition. It later increased its holding to more than 60 percent through stock manipulation. "The bank for all Americans" turned out to be the American bank for Abedi.

In March 1982, when the takeover of Financial General appeared imminent, one of the investors, Fulaij, sent a congratulatory telex to Abedi. "Kindly accept my heartiest congratulations on the successful conclusion of a hard and long-drawn battle," he wrote. "Special thanks are due to you and Mr. Naqvi and of course our lawyers for the untiring efforts, dedication and unwavering faith which made this success possible. I have no doubt that under your inspiring leadership, any remaining hurdles will also be overcome and the new venture will one day, [praise] Allah, acquire the size and standing we have all been hoping and looking for."

Chapter 7

The Friends of BCCI

Possibly because of tighter regulation, BCCI did not operate quite as recklessly in the United States as it did elsewhere. Nonetheless, the bank carried a good deal of its operating philosophy over to its U.S. operations, particularly in the way it curried favor and built relationships with government officials and other prominent people. Sometimes these friends of BCCI were unwittingly used by the bank; on other occasions, it paid handsomely for their friendship, directly or indirectly. It was a strategy that had worked effectively elsewhere, and it was to have benefits for the bank in the United States as well.

In this respect, Bert Lance proved a valuable contact for BCCI. Not only did he identify Financial General as a target for BCCI takeover and introduce Abedi and the bank to power brokers Clark Clifford and Robert Altman, he also provided an entree for the bank into the Carter administration. The bank's friendship with Jimmy Carter was to last a decade—and left the former president highly chagrined when he eventually learned how badly he had been used, and by whom.

Shortly after leaving office in 1981, Carter was visited at his home in Georgia by Abedi, an introduction set up by Lance. Carter and Abedi apparently hit it off, finding common ground in their concerns for the well-being of the Third World. Abedi contributed $500,000 to the building of Carter's

Presidential Library in Georgia, and he was an even bigger benefactor of Global 2000, Carter's humanitarian charity devoted to promoting self-sufficiency in the Third World by raising health standards and improving the environment. Abedi is said to have contributed $8 million to Global 2000, and he ultimately served as co-chairman of the organization with Carter.

Abedi helped Carter in other ways, making the BCCI corporate jet available when the ex-president needed to travel abroad. Carter, in turn, made appearances at the openings of various BCCI branches around the world. To many Americans who recall Carter's failed presidency, he may not seem a particularly powerful asset for Abedi and BCCI. But overseas, and particularly in the Third World, where Carter still carries a considerable reputation, the former president's association with BCCI and Abedi gave the bank and its founder an enormous amount of prestige.

After the BCCI scandal broke, photographs surfaced of a smiling Carter standing with Abedi at BCCI branches around the world, doubtless helping to bolster BCCI's image. Lance recalled that he had introduced Abedi to Carter when the banker said he wanted a picture of his young daughter with the former president—an innocent enough request, but an important symbol of friendship that could be used by Abedi to build the bank's credibility around the world. "You have to understand the culture of the bank and the global picture of the bank," explained Abdur Sakhia, BCCI's former head of operations in the United States. "Mr. Carter travels with Mr. Abedi to so many parts of the world: He goes to Pakistan, he goes to Kenya, he goes to Zimbabwe, he goes to many other places with Mr. Abedi on Mr. Abedi's plane. What the Kenyans and Pakistanis see is very different—that he is the former most important man in the world; he's a friend of Mr. Abedi. He visits BCCI offices in those countries; the media in those countries see that. So although it does not give [BCCI] any foothold in this country per se, around the world it's a different picture."

Carter wasn't the only world leader used by BCCI this way. United Nations Secretary-General Javier Perez de Cuellar also was given use of BCCI's plane, providing the bank with an important endorsement at a time when it was avidly wooing business from Third World central banks.

When news of BCCI's closing was announced and details of the bank's wrongdoing began to circulate, these relationships proved highly embarrassing to Carter and Perez de Cuellar. The former president said he was "shocked and disturbed," adding that he had been told by the Justice Department at the time that BCCI was a legitimate and respected organization. "We didn't know the facts," Carter said sheepishly. "I don't know how much of the facts was known by anybody in this country." Perez de Cuellar, meanwhile, went to great lengths to deny that his association with BCCI implied any endorsement of the bank. But to customers in the Third World who had been impressed by BCCI's important friends, the connection already had been made.

Even before Abedi hooked up with Carter, BCCI may have played a part in the singular highlight of the Carter presidency: the Camp David Middle East peace accord between Egypt and Israel. According to an extraordinary conspiracy theory whispered in Washington in the wake of the discovery of the BCCI scandal, the purchase of Financial General Bankshares had as much to do with diplomatic motives as it did financial ones.

There is speculation—so far not proven—that the original attempt to purchase Financial General in 1978 was intended as a signal to Egyptian President Anwar Sadat that the Arab world was comfortable with the U.S. attempt to bring Egypt and Israel together. Since the putative investors in Financial General came from all over the Arab world and included the leaders of several nations, the act of making such a significant investment in the U.S. at this critical time is said to have demonstrated to Sadat that the Arab community did not disapprove of his involvement in the U.S.-backed negotiations with Israel that culminated in the landmark Camp David agreement in 1979.

The architect for this plan is said to have been Kamal Adham, the former Saudi intelligence chief who was a leading investor in Financial General. Adham—widely known to have been a close friend of Sadat—is believed to have used his American and Arab intelligence connections to orchestrate the deal, with his banking relationship with BCCI acting as the glue and providing a vehicle for the financial part of the transaction. As a result, according to this theory, which was first postulated by congressional investigator Jonathan Winer, Sadat got his signal, BCCI got its lucrative secret foothold in the United States and Jimmy Carter got his one great diplomatic triumph. Like many of the intricate conspiracy theories that sprung up after the BCCI scandal became public, this one was as tantalizing as it was hard to prove.

BCCI's ties with the Carter administration went beyond Carter and Lance. The bank also had a close relationship with Andrew Young, Carter's ambassador to the United Nations and later mayor of Atlanta. The National Bank of Georgia extended a $175,000 line of credit to Young's consulting firm, Andrew Young Associates, in the early 1980s. The credit line, secured by property owned by Young and a partner, was later taken over by BCCI, which had bought NBG. Young told the *New York Times* that he paid about $32,000 a year in principal and interest on the line of credit between 1984 and 1989, when BCCI agreed to cancel Young's remaining obligation of about $160,000. The canceled loans were described as "consulting fees" that BCCI owed Young for his firm's work in introducing the bank to Third World leaders. There is no indication that there was anything illegal about BCCI's relationship with Young, but given his prominence in the black community, diplomatic circles and Democratic politics, he certainly was a good friend for the bank to have.

As elsewhere, BCCI may not have been above resorting to bribery to accomplish its goals in the United States. An affidavit released by federal investigators in January 1992 to support the arrest of Sani Ahmad, former head of BCCI's Washington office, publicly revealed for the first time that prosecutors were "investigating allegations that former BCCI officers in the United States bribed public officials." The affidavit gave no details, but it added that Ahmad may also have been involved in the coordination of "certain types of industrial espionage on behalf of BCCI, including the giving and receiving of commercial bribes." Given his high-level role in BCCI's Washington operation, Ahmad could be an important figure in the scandal. He had fled the United States for Pakistan, but he returned in late 1991 to negotiate the sale of his suburban Washington home. Shortly after, he was arrested and held without baill under a warrant seeking to force him to testify before a grand jury.

Since the BCCI scandal began, there have been persistent unconfirmed reports that BCCI had Washington politicians on its payroll and that it gave them highly favorable loan deals. Central to these rumors has been the purported existence of a list, supposedly found among BCCI documents, of more than 100 politicians that BCCI paid off. To date, however, no such list has been publicly produced, and even investigators deep into the case say they have not seen it—although they, too, have heard the rumors of its existence and believe them to be true.

Even without that list, there is evidence that BCCI was willing to pay a great deal of money to get its way. In 1986 and 1987, for instance, the bank, through National Bank of Georgia, spent $1.25 million to lobby the Georgia legislature for the passage of a law to permit the purchase of Georgia banks by institutions elsewhere in the United States—a law that was passed just in time for First American to take over NBG in 1987. It's not clear just why BCCI and NBG felt the need to spend so heavily to push for the legislation, since it was not opposed by Georgia's three largest banks or the state banking department.

In any event, the money was used to wine and dine and possibly to bribe state legislators, investigators say. In one instance, a leader of the legislature reportedly received a weekend trip to Fort Lauderdale from NBG just before the vote on the legislation, and he invited other lawmakers to join him on the freebie. The legislator has denied this, and the two men who oversaw the spending of the $1.25 million deny that they bribed anyone or gave legislators trips or other considerations in exchange for their votes.

At the time, it was not against Georgia law for members of the legislature to receive gifts from lobbyists. That law eventually was changed—but too late to stop BCCI from spreading its dollars around. "By the summer of 1987, Georgia law had been amended, due at least in part to the lobbying efforts," the Federal Reserve said in its July 1991 complaint against BCCI. Said one investigator: "There's no one who would look at this and say the legislature in Georgia wasn't bought . . . and in the most blatant kind of way." The Georgia effort is being investigated by the Justice Department as part of the overall probe into BCCI's American operations.

Sometimes, the cultivation of influence didn't cost BCCI a thing. Its secret ownership of the Washington area's largest bank gave it access to all sorts of powerful people who might later be co-opted. Over the years, First American worked to establish itself as the bank of choice for foreign embassies, diplomats, foreign military representatives and others in the Washington area; it also went after banking relationships with United Nations personnel and other foreign officials in New York. First American also carried many Washington accounts for the CIA.

Much of this activity may have been innocent. Given First American's large presence in the Washington market, it was only natural that it would get at least its share of business in competition with other banks. Just because a politician or diplomat borrowed money from the bank to buy a house or car doesn't mean he or she was on the take. Many such loans were made, at normal interest rates and terms, and paid off as scheduled. But First American's big business among such people gave it the opportunity—as in the case of Andrew Young in Georgia—to forgive a loan or provide a lower-than-normal interest rate to special friends. Investigators say privately they expect eventually to find proof that such wrongdoing occurred. It would only have been natural, given BCCI's culture, according to those familiar with the bank.

"There was a pattern to buy relationships and buy influence," Sakhia testified before the Senate subcommittee on terrorism, narcotics and international operations. While he claimed no personal knowledge of BCCI bribery in the United States beyond office gossip about it, Sakhia noted: "BCC's strategy globally had been to be very well-known, to make an impact in the marketplace, to have contacts or relationships—what we used to call relationships—with all the people who matter, whether in the business circle, whether in the academics, in the political circle, in the administration, high net worth individuals, universities, you name it. We would develop relationships with everyone of consequence."

The guest list for the opening of BCCI's office in Miami in 1982 showed how the bank could turn out the big names for what was actually a fairly trivial event. Among the dignitaries on the list were the vice president of Panama, the governors of the central banks of Trinidad, Jamaica and Barbados, and the powerful oil ministers of Venezuela and the United Arab Emirates. That wasn't all: The guest list also promised that Sakhia would invite several ambassadors from Washington and some of BCCI's favorite customers, including Pharaon. The memo containing the list includes a request for a BCCI executive to line up an appearance by Florida Gov. Bob Graham at the opening—and mentions that the opening could be rescheduled for the governor, if needed. A later social event in Miami, a breakfast with a group of Chinese banking officials whom BCCI was then courting, sported a guest list that included Gov. Bob Martinez, several other state officials—including George Bush's son Jeb, then the state secretary of commerce—and executives from most of the major banks and businesses in South Florida. BCCI clearly knew how to hobnob with the rich and powerful.

One particularly curious BCCI relationship was the one the bank had with Sergio Correa da Costa, the former Brazilian ambassador to the United States and a significant figure in Brazilian politics. Shortly after da Costa retired from the diplomatic service in November 1986, he went onto BCCI's payroll, for $150,000 a year, credited directly to da Costa's account at BCCI's New York agency.

"Congratulations from myself and my colleagues on your joining our Brazilian project," a BCCI executive in Miami wired the ambassador at the embassy in Washington in late October 1986. "We welcome you to the fold [and the] BCCI family. I am very certain your experience, qualifications and contacts not only in Brazil but also internationally will go a long way in turning our subsidiary in Brazil into one of the most successful units of BCC."

According to documents recovered from the bank, da Costa became an executive and part-owner of the Brazilian subsidiary—an affiliate for which he apparently helped win approval from Brazilian regulators. A 1986 BCCI memo, marked "Strictly Private & Confidential," outlined a deal with da Costa for the formation of the Brazilian bank—with BCCI's Miami office as controlling partner—using techniques reminiscent of the nominee arrangement BCCI allegedly had pioneered in the takeover of First American.

Da Costa and another man were to be joint owners of a new firm, called "Company X" in the documents, which would hold 17 percent of the stock in the new bank. BCCI would lend da Costa and his partner some of the money needed to buy the bank stock—at less than half the going interest rate—in exchange for the usual share-pledge and buyback agreements that would give BCCI effective control over the shares. The internal memo indicates that BCCI knew that it was skirting the law: "It must be emphasized that the Brazilian economy and bureaucracy are highly sophisticated," according to the document. "As such, any payments made by Brazilians must have the appropriate origination of funds. That is, the Brazilian 'investors' must have the necessary net worth for Brazilian taxation authorities' purposes to

5. *Former Carter administration official Burt Lance (top) and Saudi financier Gaith Pharaon were key figures in BCCI's effort to crack the American market. Lance introduced BCCI and Abedi to Clifford and Altman and helped broker the purchases of Financial General Bankshares and his own National Bank of Georgia. Pharaon was a front man for BCCI in its illegal takeovers of several American banks.*

3. *Sheik Zayed bin Sultan al-Nahyan, the ruler of Abu Dhabi, bankrolled BCCI. The Sheik, members of his family and the government of Abu Dhabi wound up owning 77% of the corrupt bank.*

4. *Below is Masihur Rahman, BCCI's former chief financial officer, who fled for his life after quitting the bank. His Congressional testimony in 1991 provided an early inside glimpse at BCCI.*

2. Swaleh Naqvi, the right-hand man of BCCI founder Agha Hasan Abedi. He is considered to have been the financial brains of the operation, and took over in 1988 after Abedi was incapacitated, only to be ousted along with his mentor in 1990. Naqvi's detailed private files of the bank's chicanery were essential to cracking the BCCI case.

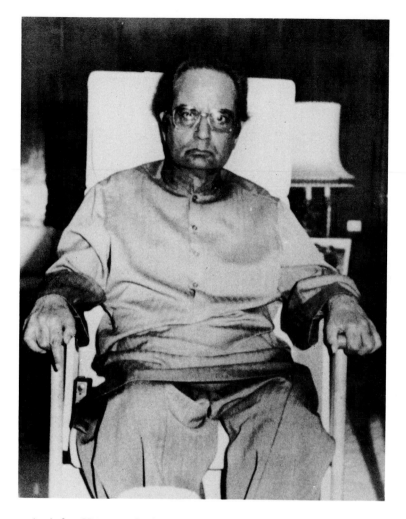

1. *Agha Hasan Abedi, the "Man from Mahmudabad," who founded BCCI and ran it with an iron fist in its heyday. Fond of uttering cryptic bits of philosophy and running business meetings that were more like religious revivals, Abedi oversaw the bank's rapid expansion and most of its wrongdoing before succumbing to ill health and being forced out of the bank in October, 1990. Wanted by authorities from around the world, by 1992 Abedi was living in seclusion in Pakistan, denying everything—and reportedly laying plans to start another bank.*

6. Clifford and Altman (right) with Lynda Carter observing.

7. *U.N. Secretary-General Javier Perez de Cuellar found him-self at the center of controversy after the BCCI scandal broke when it was learned that he had accepted rides on the bank's jet.*

8. *Andrew Young (below), former U.S. ambassador to the UN and Atlanta mayor, was employed by BCCI as a consultant.*

9. *Robert Morgenthau, the feisty, 72-year-old New York district attorney, announcing the indictment of BCCI and its former top executives in July 1991. "This indictment spells out the largest bank fraud in world financial history," said Morganthau, considered to be the most aggressive prosecutor of the bank's wrongdoing.*

10. *Sen. John Kerry (D. Mass.) conducting one of a series of Congressional hearings investigating BCCI's activities.*

11. *Personal attention to customer relations was a BCCI hallmark. Here Abedi (below, right) and other BCCI executives visit important customer Sheik Humaid bin Rashid al Naomi, at a remote desert location.*

support any investments made." Da Costa and his partner were to receive $450,000 from BCCI to help them meet the net worth requirement.

This memo was written two months before da Costa retired as ambassador, indicating that he was already dealing with BCCI while still in office. Another, even earlier, memo, written by Sakhia to BCCI London, said, "Ambassador da Costa has promised Dr. Pharaon to assist the bank in any way he can" and added that da Costa had promised to urge a powerful Brazilian businessman to lobby the president of Brazil on BCCI's behalf.

Da Costa's name appeared on yet another curious BCCI document found by investigators, a list of international loans outstanding at BCCI Panama as of April 1988. Da Costa is listed as having a loan from BCCI of nearly $1.6 million "parked by BCCI Miami," according to the document. In late 1991, shortly after a Brazilian newspaper revealed the contents of these documents, the Brazilian government belatedly moved to shut down the BCCI affiliate that da Costa had co-founded.

BCCI appears to have been skillful at playing other kinds of power games as well. By hiring superlawyers Clifford and Altman to handle its difficulties with the Securities and Exchange Commission in 1978, it demonstrated its innate ability to go for the best hired guns that money could buy, and it continued that pattern in Washington over the next decade. Even as they were running First American, Clifford and Altman handled a significant amount of legal work for BCCI, including coordination of the massive defense of the bank's 1988 money-laundering charges. At one time or another over the years, BCCI seems to have employed most of the high-powered law firms, lobbyists and public relations experts that line Washington's K Street power corridor, and for the money-laundering case, it seemed to be employing all of them at once. Such professionals were another way that BCCI used influence. By bringing such heavy artillery to bear on regulators and prosecutors, the bank often was able to overwhelm its foes, or to find a back-room way of coming to some settlement.

One interesting relationship between BCCI and a notable political power-broker-for-hire was the bank's dalliance with Henry Kissinger's consulting firm. In October 1988, days before the bank was charged with money-laundering in Tampa, BCCI executive Abol Fazl Helmy met with members of Kissinger Associates to discuss the possible hiring of the political and economic consulting firm, apparently to help build contacts and map strategy around the world. Kissinger Associates offered some heavyweight talent—in addition to the former secretary of state, its members included longtime State Department official Lawrence Eagleburger and Gen. Brent Scowcroft, later President Bush's national security adviser. In a description of the firm given to Helmy, Kissinger Associates boasted of its work in discreetly helping large corporations navigate political straits and set strategies around the world. "I am reluctant to be more specific, at least on paper, about the kinds of consulting projects we undertake for our clients," one of Kissinger's partners wrote Helmy. "The key point, of course, is that our consulting and transaction work are rooted in the firm's understanding of geopolitics and economics: A client should not ask us how to build a polyethylene plant, but should ask about what is likely to happen in the various countries where that plant might be sited."

A few days after the meeting, Helmy filed a report on it to Naqvi in London. By then, BCCI had been indicted in Tampa, and the bank was facing serious legal problems. "Judging by the high level of adverse publicity that is being generated by the media, it is imperative that a firm response be made," Helmy wrote. He added that he already had been told by his contact at Kissinger Associates that "Dr. Kissinger recommends that a public relations offensive be made by us," and that Kissinger's firm had offered to make a few phone calls to help BCCI hire a PR firm. "While I am certain we have our fair share of advisers and consultants," Helmy added, "I thought it prudent to pass on the information, considering the importance of its source." It is not clear whether BCCI followed that particular piece of advice, or whether it even actually retained Kissinger's firm, but the company stayed in touch with Kissinger Associates for the next few months. The paper trail on the relationship is sketchy, since Kissinger's firm preferred to deal with clients personally rather than risk any embarrassing written communication.

In December 1988, Helmy wrote Naqvi again to report that negotiations with Kissinger Associates were progressing. Noting that Scowcroft had just been nominated to be Bush's national security adviser and others in the firm seemed destined to play roles in the new administration, Helmy wrote:

"You may agree that this association with Kissinger Associates Inc. needs time to be cultivated. I am working in that direction."

By the next memo, Jan. 11, 1989, things had gotten even more mysterious. Helmy referred to a luncheon meeting he had had with "the gentleman" a few days earlier to discuss the bank's problems. Kissinger Associates is not named in the memo, but investigators believe that the memo refers to the ongoing attempts by BCCI to enter into a relationship with the firm. "It was established that it is in our best interests for both parties to continue with the conversations," Helmy wrote Naqvi:

"They were far more knowledgeable of the details of our situation during this meeting and made several 'unofficial' general recommendations which I shall convey to you at our next meeting. I am meeting my contact's senior partner by the end of January with a view of discussing our overall worldwide activities."

Tantalizing stuff but, unfortunately, investigators say, they have been unable to find additional documents that spell out whether BCCI actually went on to employ Kissinger's firm, which has denied being on retainer to the bank. BCCI also showed an impressive knack for hiring people just out of government to do its bidding. There was nothing illegal about this, but it showed that BCCI had mastered Washington's "revolving door," in which former officials who move into private practice in the same field often find themselves representing clients against former colleagues still in government. The advantage to the client is obvious: A lawyer who intimately knows the way around an agency and its bureaucracy, or who can get top officials on the phone instantly, can be of incalculable benefit in smoothing a company's way through the regulatory maze and in performing damage control. The relationship with Bert Lance was one prominent example of this.

Clifford, of course, with his long Washington resume and many connections, was the ultimate insider, and his personal assurances in 1981 that the investors in Financial General had no connection to BCCI appear to have played a major role in winning approval of the takeover. At Clifford's side in that hearing was another former insider—Baldwin B. Tuttle, who only a couple of years before had been deputy general counsel of the Fed and remained friendly with most of the agency officials who investigated the deal. There's no suggestion whatsoever that Clifford and Tuttle abused such connections—but their presence doubtlessly gave their clients much greater credibility in the eyes of the regulators who knew them.

This chummy use of former government officials continued even after the BCCI scandal was brought to light, as the various defendants lined up legal counsel. Kamal Adham hired as his lawyer the former head of the organized crime strike force for the Justice Department in New York—not a bad ally to have when your adversaries are former colleagues in the Justice Department and the crimebusters in New York District Attorney Robert Morgenthau's office. Sakhia's attorney was Mark P. Schnapp, who only a short time before had been chief of the criminal section of the U.S. attorney's office in Miami, a center of investigation into money-laundering charges, including those against BCCI.

Even more notable, however, was Adham's brief employment of Edward Rogers, the former top aide to President Bush's chief of staff, John Sununu. Rogers, a young lawyer with little experience in private practice, received a $600,000, two-year contract to do legal work for Adham shortly after leaving the White House. When details of the agreement became known in the fall of 1991, the BCCI scandal seemed finally to have touched 1600 Pennsylvania Avenue. Just what would a former aide do for all that money, critics wondered; might he try to lobby his friends in the administration to go easy on his client? Bush, furious, denounced Rogers, and the former aide quickly ended his association with Adham. Rogers returned the down payment on his huge fee, some of which he reportedly had already used to buy a new Jaguar. Nonetheless, the incident seemed to prove that BCCI, in death as in life, knew where and how to push the buttons of power.

Chapter 8:

"The First American Group of Banks"

Ralph Perry, an official of New York's Bankers Trust Co., was confused. For weeks, he had been negotiating with an executive at BCCI, Khusro Elley, about the possible purchase of a handful of Bankers Trust's branches in New York. But now, in May 1983, Elley was telling Perry that he was representing not BCCI, but First American Bank's New York subsidiary (FABNY) in the negotiations—even though another BCCI official, Abol Fazl Helmy, was aiding Elley in the discussions with Bankers Trust.

Even more perplexing, Elley told Perry that any changes in the FABNY bid would have to be cleared with BCCI officials in London. "I went up to the BCCI office and we sat down and talked about the whole thing," Perry recalled several years later. "I remember we wrote on a yellow pad some basic principles we agreed upon and initialed it." Yet when the formal $3 million bid for the branches arrived at Bankers Trust, it was on First American stationery, signed by First American President Robert Altman. Just who was Elley working for, anyway?

That's a question that has epitomized the investigation into the relationship between BCCI and First American. In spite of all the promises by Clifford, Altman and others that there was no meaningful connection between BCCI and the Washington bank, there were repeated indications during the 1980s that the connection was more than meaningful. Indeed, as Perry found out, BCCI often appeared to be deeply involved in the running of First American—and didn't seem to care who knew it.

Over the years, BCCI made important strategic decisions for First American, including the financially disastrous decisions to expand the bank into New York and Georgia; coordinated marketing efforts among its own U.S. offices and First American; used First American branches to perform banking services that BCCI was not allowed to take part in itself under U.S. law; had a hand in hiring executives to run parts of First American; and used the bank as a proving ground for bright young BCCI managers—including Elley, who took over as a top executive of FABNY shortly after negotiating the purchase of the Bankers Trust branches.

Within BCCI, First American was treated as a member of the family—along with National Bank of Georgia and later Independence Bank of California, both of which BCCI also purchased secretly during the 1980s. "It is nothing but one institution," Abdur Sakhia, BCCI's onetime head of American operations, later recalled for a congressional committee. "In any management discussions and any discussions on our future in the United States, we would think of three entities—BCCI, National Bank of Georgia, First American, or then, Financial General—in the same breath. Who would be going where, who would work in which entity, what area of business will be handled by which entity, allocation of businesses, markets, geographical territories—all took place as if this was one entity."

Because First American's New York operations were so critical to BCCI's efforts to get a toehold in the United States, particular attention was paid to the formation, staffing and expansion of the New York arm of the bank, which First American was forced to rebuild from scratch after it was forced by regulators to sell the New York-based Bank of Commerce as part of the initial approval of the takeover of the bank. BCCI seems to have helped in any way it could. When First American of New York needed to find offices, BCCI pitched in, helping it lease space for a large branch on the ground floor of 350 Park Avenue in midtown Manhattan a block from BCCI's New York office.

When FABNY needed executive talent, BCCI helped provide it, sending over Elley and others, some of whom later returned to the bigger bank after seasoning at FABNY. In other cases, applicants for top positions at First American found themselves on a plane to London for interviews with Abedi, Naqvi and others after they had passed muster with Clifford and Altman. Potential board members apparently also had to be approved by BCCI. On at least two occasions, according to documents found by investigators, candidates to be directors of First American or one of its subsidiaries were proposed directly to Abedi and Naqvi by First American officials with ties to BCCI, without, apparently, the nicety of mentioning the candidates to the bank's supposed top executives, Clifford and Altman. Investigators also found a letter in the BCCI files from accountants Ernst & Whinney to BCCI confirming the firm's engagement as CCAH's outside auditors—without any indication that Clifford and Altman, as heads of the American company, had been involved in the hiring process.

In turn, First American did some banking business with BCCI, depositing money in a period when the big bank needed it most. In 1986 and 1987, for instance, First American used $74 million of its funds to purchase uninsured certificates of deposits in BCCI's branch in the Cayman Islands. Similar transactions took place on a smaller scale as late as 1990. All of the money was repaid, with interest, but A. Vincent Scoffone, First American's treasurer, testified in 1991 that Altman had personally instructed him to make the deposits even though safer alternatives were available. Altman's lawyer said the transactions were legal and proper.

The close relationship between the two banks also extended to joint marketing efforts. Because BCCI's offices in the United States were prevented by law from taking deposits and performing some other functions, they frequently referred customers to First American for service—occasionally with very specific instructions on how the customer should be dealt with. BCCI and First American officials also met to discuss ways to jointly build credit card and letter-of-credit businesses and other customer services. While banks occasionally cooperate on marketing, there is no indication that First American had such a cozy relationship with any other large bank.

BCCI even went so far as to create an "Americas Coordinating Committee" to oversee marketing operations among its various U.S. affiliates. This group, which met regularly in 1985 and 1986, exchanged ideas, strategies and business contacts among First American, NBG and the BCCI offices in New York, Miami and Washington. Participants in the meetings acted as if they were all working for the same employer; Aijaz Afridi, First American of New York's executive vice president, acted as the chairman of the first meeting of the committee, in April 1985. According to the minutes of that meeting, the committee's objective was to "coordinate the efforts of different locations of BCC and other institutions so that the President's [Abedi's] desire to have a totality in approach is achieved. ... Only by joint efforts and coordination ... could we be able to successfully meet this challenge."

Something else in the minutes of the first meeting stood out to investigators when they uncovered the documents years later. Elley—by then a top official of First American of New York, but still on BCCI's payroll as well, according to the Federal Reserve—concluded the proceedings by pointing out to the others that "in America we are sitting on $7 billion assets and this is just a beginning. There is much to do, and in spite of the diversity of operations as different agencies and banks, we have to find a common denominator." The $7 billion figure was a giveaway: BCCI itself had only $800 million in assets in its handful of agency offices in the United States at that time, but the addition of the assets of First American and NBG brought the total to $7 billion.

The Americas Coordinating Committee was by no means the only place that bank officials openly discussed the relationship among BCCI and First American and the other U.S. banks. It also apparently came up at BCCI's lavish annual management conferences, held in one European capital or another and attended by executives of BCCI affiliates all over the world—including, according to at least two guest lists discovered by investigators, First American President Robert Altman. At another major BCCI meeting, in Hong Kong in April 1987, Abedi pridefully told executives of BCCI's Far East region:

"You are now with the First American Group of Banks, [with] at the moment, over $27 billion in assets, and we will be $30 billion by the end of the year. We are now being recognized in the brotherhood of international banks as an important factor to the banking system of the world."

The only way BCCI had $27 billion in assets at that time, investigators later pointed out, was if First American was added to the total.

There were other links as well. Not only had two of First American of New York's top executives, Elley and Afridi, come from BCCI, they maintained close ties to the bigger bank: Elley stayed on the BCCI payroll, and Afridi is said to have talked daily by telephone with BCCI executives in London during his four years at FABNY. He transferred back to BCCI after leaving FABNY.

With all this going on, it is not unfair to wonder how Clifford and Altman, as First American's top executives, could not have been aware that BCCI was so involved in the running of their bank. That issue becomes even more acute given the two men's involvement in BCCI's other American affairs as key members of the bank's U.S. legal team. Shouldn't it have occurred to Clifford and Altman, as two of Washington's most savvy lawyers, that they were dealing with the same set of people in two very different—and theoretically conflicting—settings? The two men may ultimately face legal action as prosecutors try to prove that they were aware of BCCI's ownership and the deception that went with it.

But Clifford and Altman have steadfastly maintained that they knew nothing of any secret stock ownership, Americas Coordinating Committee, joint marketing efforts, First American Group of Banks, or any of the rest. As far as they were concerned, they ran the bank themselves.

Sure, they say, they occasionally ran an idea or job candidate past Abedi and Naqvi as representatives of the bank's Middle Eastern owners. But otherwise, they claim, they made all the decisions, set the bank's strategy, managed day-to-day operations and hired whomever they pleased. "They were not making the decisions," Altman firmly told a Senate subcommittee hearing. "The decisions remained with the [First] American group, as we had said to the Federal Reserve." Added Clifford: "The agreement was that I would have total responsibility and I would have total authority. [Abedi] never violated that at any time. He can make suggestions, he can make offers of help, but when the time came to make decisions, he didn't make any one of these decisions in any way. The board and I made them all."

Confronted with the growing pile of evidence to the contrary, Clifford and Altman offered another theory: If BCCI was exercising control of their bank's affairs, they suggested, it was doing so behind their backs. "We never knew these meetings were going on among the BCCI people," Clifford said. "We don't know when they began to acquire First American stock. We didn't know that. Nobody else knew it. So they had plans going on, secret plans, perhaps they were conspiring among themselves. But we weren't conscious of that. The authorities weren't conscious of it. This may be part of the typical operation of the way BCCI does its business, handling it secretly." BCCI's only role, as far as Clifford and Altman were concerned, was as investment adviser and communications link to the Middle Eastern investors who the two men believed owned First American.

That argument has been met with a great deal of skepticism, given the two men's brains and connections.

Whatever they said, Clifford and Altman were clearly close to Abedi and, to a lesser extent, Naqvi, flying regularly to London to visit them and report on First American's business and the state of BCCI's U.S. legal affairs and exchanging friendly correspondence with them on a regular basis. Abedi was even a guest at Altman's wedding to Lynda Carter and presented the new bride with a Jaguar automobile as a gift. Altman claimed that was just the gesture of an unusually generous client in an otherwise arms-length attorney-client relationship. "It's true that he gave my wife a very generous gift," Altman said. "That is the kind of thing that is done in the circles in which he operated in the Middle East, but as far as a personal relationship, our dealings were almost entirely business."

However, investigators into the BCCI mess kept coming across internal bank documents that seemed to indicate that Altman, at least, and to a lesser extent Clifford, knew of BCCI's involvement and cooperated with it. One possible "smoking gun" is a July 1984 memo to Naqvi from a BCCI officer reviewing First American's financial results for the previous six months. The numbers weren't very good, and the official wrote Naqvi: "Perhaps Mr. Altman may require some assistance and guidance in enabling him to reach the budgeted income figures." A handwritten postscript adds: "I have since discussed the half-yearly results of [First American] with Mr. Altman to draw his attention to the areas in which the group's income is falling behind budget." In response, Altman and his attorney argued that any oversight of the bank's finances was in keeping with BCCI's role as adviser to First American's shareholders.

Altman also is said to have participated in BCCI's unsuccessful efforts to secretly take over a bank in Florida. Former executive Sakhia testified that BCCI had wanted to buy a small bank in Miami in 1986, but was worried about regulatory problems. So it decided to buy the bank through yet another nominee arrangement. After failing to set up a couple of deals with various front men, BCCI decided to have longtime customer Faisal Saud al-Fulaij, who ran BCCI's

Kuwaiti affiliate and also was involved as an investor in First American, buy the Florida bank on its behalf. Altman attended a meeting with Naqvi in May 1986, Sakhia testified, to discuss the arrangements for the purchase of the bank, and was asked at that time to look at BCCI's still-secret purchase of Independence Bank of California a few months before as a model for the Florida deal. Altman has strongly denied this allegation, which would have implied that he knew about the secret takeover of Independence. But a memo written by Sakhia for BCCI's internal files, with a copy to Naqvi, shows that the men agreed at the meeting that Altman would handle legal aspects of the deal, including drawing up a purchase agreement and filing a takeover application with regulators. Naqvi, according to the memo, would arrange for staff for the newly acquired bank "on an urgent basis." The deal never came to pass, however.

Also troubling to investigators was the discovery of a memo attached to a document signed by both Clifford and Altman that seemed to suggest that any BCCI involvement in First American's 1987 purchase of National Bank of Georgia would focus "unwelcome attention" from regulators on BCCI's relationship with First American. Altman contends that this document, which was drafted by another law firm, has been radically misunderstood; the mention of concern about BCCI's involvement, he said, had to do with the possibility that regulators would think that First American and BCCI were improperly acting as partners in the NBG takeover; this would have been true if any other major bank had been involved, Altman said.

The National Bank of Georgia takeover has, in fact, been identified by the Federal Reserve and other investigators as being quite suspicious—with some suggesting that BCCI used the transaction to siphon more than $200 million out of First American, and out of the United States, since it allegedly already secretly owned NBG and was apparently just transferring the ownership from one of its American affiliates to another.

The NBG saga begins, once again, with Bert Lance. Lance had run the bank before joining the Carter administration and owned a good-sized chunk of it when he left the government. In his new role as adviser to Abedi, he had urged BCCI to purchase NBG; BCCI passed the tip onto one of its clients and biggest shareholders, Saudi businessman Ghaith Pharaon. In late 1977, Pharaon began acquiring NBG shares, borrowing some of the money to buy the stock from BCCI. By the mid-1980s, BCCI had secretly taken control of NBG, in Pharaon's name. At Abedi's suggestion, Pharaon hired Roy Carlson, an affable former executive at Bank of America with longstanding ties to BCCI, to run NBG; three other former BCCI officers later came to work at NBG at the behest of BCCI. Some of these former BCCI employees received housing allowances or salary increases of as much as $1,500, authorized by BCCI to cover their transfers to Atlanta.

Even more so than with First American, BCCI treated NBG as one of its own: It invited NBG executives to its annual conferences, moved the formerly locally oriented institution strongly into international business, allegedly including money-laundering, and urged NBG to adopt many other practices and accoutrements of BCCI ownership—including a corporate logo closely modeled on BCCI's own hexagonal symbol. "While we were NBG under Pharaon, we all felt we were part of BCCI—or at least kissing cousins," Richard Guthman Jr., who was NBG's senior vice president for government banking, later told *The Washington Post's* Eric Pianin. "As it turned out, I guess we were part of BCCI, but we didn't know it at the time."

BCCI even arranged for a $10 million capital infusion to be made into the bank in 1982 under Pharaon's name to satisfy concerns of the Federal Reserve that NBG was somewhat undercapitalized. But the money, it turned out later, came with a catch. BCCI secretly wired the $10 million to Pharaon, who put it into the bank, as required, in late April 1982. A week later, the regulators satisfied, the money was sent back to BCCI—a clear violation of the Fed's request.

But things were not going well for Pharaon, whose reputation as one of the largest and most visible Saudi investors in the United States was belied by some serious financial problems. To raise money to cover losses elsewhere in his rickety empire, in 1986 he sold his remaining NBG stock to a company controlled by BCCI, which thus wound up with 100 percent of NBG—albeit in Pharaon's name.

That arrangement soon became sticky. Pharaon's creditors were baying at his heels, and BCCI officials apparently became concerned that they might take legal action to grab his shares in NBG. As a result, the Federal Reserve has alleged, BCCI arranged to have the stock transferred to First American's trusty parent company, CCAH. It seemed to be a terrific deal for the cash-strapped Pharaon—CCAH was to pay $220 million for a bank that most observers thought was worth a lot less.

Altman, in a letter to Naqvi proposing the deal—ostensibly so Naqvi could win approval from CCAH's Middle Eastern shareholders—said the high price was necessary because there were other suitors for NBG, including NCNB Corp., the large and acquisitive bank-holding company based in Charlotte, N.C. However, Altman added, "We have never seen a written bid from NCNB"—a statement that some investigators later found strange, given that First American and NCNB theoretically were competing to buy NBG at that juncture. Altman should not have been able to see a written bid for NBG unless someone inside the Georgia bank's ownership—Naqvi perhaps?—was willing to show it to him, the investigators said. Altman later said the statement had been taken too literally and denied any BCCI involvement in the purchase.

In any event, there was a fundamental problem with a takeover of National Bank of Georgia by CCAH: It was illegal under Georgia banking regulations. State law prevented the acquisition of Georgia banks by companies outside the "southern region," which didn't include First American's Washington base. One year and $1.25 million in lobbying costs later, that was to become a moot point. But in the meantime, First American struck a deal with Pharaon late in 1986 under which First American would get first right of refusal to buy NBG, pending the change in the law, in exchange for an $80 million option fee. The purchase price would then be reduced to $140 million. According to the Fed, BCCI immediately advanced Pharaon the $140 million in the form of a loan, which the bank said he did not have to repay. When First American finally bought NBG in August 1987, the $140 million was used to wipe out Pharaon's loan.

In all, the Fed alleged, Pharaon received only a bit more than $14 million of the final $227 million purchase price of National Bank of Georgia, even though he was listed as its sole owner. The rest went to BCCI, used to reduce Pharaon's indebtedness and for other purposes. Among other things, the money helped swell BCCI's capital base and took heat off the bank at a time when regulators and auditors were beginning to take closer looks at the bank's relationships with Pharaon and other large and delinquent customers. But it also succeeded in moving more than $200 million from First American onto BCCI's books.

That wasn't the end of BCCI's involvement with Pharaon in the U.S. banking business, however. In 1988 and 1989, Pharaon, using money borrowed from BCCI, purchased roughly 25 percent of CenTrust Savings Bank of Miami— enough for technical control, according to the Federal Reserve's definition. Once again, he then secretly signed control of the stock over to BCCI, according to the Fed.

Even by the standards of the U.S. savings and loan debacle, CenTrust was a notorious case long before BCCI got involved. The S&L was run by the flamboyant, politically well-connected David L. Paul, and wasted money at such a profligate rate that CenTrust's ultimate and perhaps inevitable failure was estimated to cost U.S. taxpayers $2 billion. BCCI and Pharaon did what they could to keep CenTrust afloat: In May 1988, BCCI purchased $25 million worth of CenTrust debentures to make it appear that the market for the sickly bank's securities was more robust than it actually was. A few weeks later, mission apparently accomplished, CenTrust bought back the debentures.

Pharaon and BCCI also collaborated on the takeover of Independence Bank in California, and top officials of Independence later sued Pharaon, alleging mismanagement of the bank, which was teetering on the edge of financial collapse by late 1991 until it was bailed out with money from the forfeiture of BCCI's U.S. assets.

Indeed, it seems that BCCI had no better luck running the banks it secretly controlled in the United States than it did managing its own affairs. First American, NBG and Independence all wound up in financial difficulty, and CenTrust failed outright.

The version of the First American purchase of National Bank of Georgia provided by the Federal Reserve and other sources indicates that the takeover of NBG was BCCI's idea, not Clifford's and Altman's—a charge they emphatically deny. But perhaps they should let BCCI take the blame, since the acquisition of NBG was pretty much a financial disaster for First American.

The new subsidiary—immediately stripped of its BCCI-like logo and renamed First American Bank of Georgia—was a financial turkey, not nearly worth the price that First American had paid for it. It had suffered $18.3 million in loan losses between 1984 and 1986, and it was paying $2 million a year to operate a glitzy, $29 million headquarters complex that Pharaon had ordered built for it on the outskirts of Atlanta. To just about every independent observer, the $227 million sale price seemed high, especially since First American had agreed to pay cash for the bank, rather than swapping stock. One source familiar with the situation later told *The Washington Post* that it made little sense from an accounting and business standpoint for First American "to give [Pharaon] $220 million in cash for this dog."

First American didn't have much luck running NBG either. NBG continued to suffer serious losses, and First American, which was suffering its own financial problems, was forced to pump more than $30 million into the Georgia bank in 1991 just to keep it afloat. First American of Georgia suffered further later in the year when depositors withdrew tens of millions of dollars in the months after the revelations about BCCI and its involvement in the bank. By then, the bank's value had dwindled to about $75 million—one-third the purchase price—and First American officials were trying to get rid of it.

BCCI's alleged involvement in First American's marketing and other operations and its expansions into New York and Georgia have raised significant questions about Clifford's and Altman's roles in the management of the bank. But there also were questions to be raised, as it turned out, about their roles in its ownership. The two men's all-but-secret purchase of a small amount of stock in First American's parent company, CCAH, and then its highly profitable sale, has created a controversy almost as great as any other part of the BCCI scandal—and raised still another set of questions about their relationship to BCCI.

Clifford and Altman were treated extremely favorably throughout the deal, buying the stock with loans from BCCI at terms available to scarcely any other customer, and then selling it after 19 months for three times what they had paid for it—a price that seemed unjustified by any impartial valuation of the company's shares. The two men made a tidy profit on the deal: Clifford earned $6.5 million before taxes, and Altman earned $3.3 million.

In retrospect, the stock deal looks like a canny move by the two men on several levels. When they took over the management of First American in 1982, they did so for virtually no compensation: Clifford received a salary of $50,000 a year, paltry for the chairman of a bank that size; Altman received nothing for serving as president. The two men were compensated by the bank in other ways—their law firm, Clifford & Warnke, acted as the bank's counsel on many matters, bringing the firm more than $1 million a year in legal fees, not to mention the fees the firm was earning from BCCI. But Clifford and Altman said they hoped that if they did a good job in building First American, they would receive compensation from the bank's shareholders in the form of stock. "What I wanted to do was buy stock in my own company," Clifford later said, "the one that I had put so much of myself into to build."

In July 1986, with First American prospering, that wish came true. CCAH made one of its occasional "rights offerings" to its dozen or so shareholders, selling additional stock to raise new capital for the bank. Existing holders of the privately traded stock were permitted to buy new shares proportional to their holdings, with the new stock priced at "book value"—a bargain-basement calculation based on the value of the company's assets. Shareholders did not have to buy all of the shares offered to them: they could waive some of their rights, for purchase by other shareholders or others designated by the owners. In this case, Clifford and Altman were in luck—Mashriq Holding Co., a CCAH shareholder, bought 8,550 shares in the July 25, 1986, offering and waived its rights to 6,742 shares. The offering "was not fully subscribed, so that gave [us] a chance to come in," Clifford later explained. The two men bought the shares at the book-value price of $2,216 each. Clifford bought 4,495 shares, Altman 2,247.

Mashriq's reasons for waiving its rights to buy shares at the book-value price now puzzle investigators. Just the day before the rights offering, Mashriq had purchased a large block of CCAH shares from another investor at a much higher price: $4,044 a share. "For [Mashriq] not to take advantage of the rights offering just does not make sense," a congressional staff report said in 1991. And that wasn't Mashriq's only unusual stock activity that week. On the same day that it bought CCAH stock at $4,044 per share, it sold some shares at $2,216. By buying stock and then turning it over at a loss and by passing up the opportunity to buy shares at the lower rights offering price, Mashriq appeared to suffer paper losses of $18.9 million in a two-day period.

But Mashriq's losses were illusory, the Federal Reserve has alleged, and there is little mystery about what was going on: BCCI apparently was manipulating the stock sales to its own ends. The bank was going through some financial trouble and had cut a deal with Khalid bin Salim bin-Mahfouz, a Saudi Arabian banker, to bail it out. To do so, BCCI had to assemble a large block of shares for sale to bin-Mahfouz for a cash infusion of $135 million. Sure enough, that transaction came later in the week. Mashriq sold 22,000 CCAH shares to bin-Mahfouz for $6,094 a share—nearly triple the price at which it had sold some shares just a few days before.

In addition to raising the money to bail itself out, BCCI allegedly had also freed up some stock for Clifford and Altman to buy. And BCCI gave them the wherewithal to do it. Although both men were wealthy in their own rights, they borrowed money to buy the $14.9 million worth of stock being made available to them. After being turned down by one bank, they borrowed the funds from BCCI at what can only be described as favorable terms. Clifford and Altman were to pay an interest rate on the loan equal to the London interbank offer rate (LIBOR), a European version of the U.S. prime lending rate. At the time, the LIBOR was about 6.2 percent—almost 2 percentage points below the prime, which generally is available only to blue-chip corporate borrowers.

Indeed, it was unusual for any customer to get the LIBOR rate, as Clifford and Altman later admitted in congressional testimony: No customer at their bank, they conceded, had ever gotten a deal that good. Clifford and Altman were later accused by some in Congress of having been given a "sweetheart" deal, and Clifford, frankly, seemed to agree. "The negotiations for the loan were conducted under very friendly circumstances," he said.

But the cheap interest rate was only the half of it. The loans were also "non-recourse," meaning that if the two men failed to pay them off, all they would lose was the stock itself, which was pledged as collateral. Such loans typically are made at higher rates of interest or with large up-front fees—not at an interest rate as low as the LIBOR rate. Clifford's and Altman's friends at BCCI were treating them very well—and doing so on the orders of First American's satisfied owners, the two men's attorney later theorized, "because they wanted it probably to be easy for Clifford and Altman ... to have a financial stake in the enterprise" as a reward for their management skills.

They soon got their payoff. Eighteen months after buying the shares, Clifford and Altman decided it was time to sell. The reason is not altogether clear. Clifford later explained that the two men were facing sizable payments on their loans from BCCI and needed money to pay them off. They also said they wanted to take advantage of what they saw as favorable market conditions. "In 1988, the market in bank stocks was strong—strong in this country, strong worldwide," Clifford recalled.

Clifford wrote a letter to Naqvi to say that he and Altman wanted to sell some shares and to ask some help in finding a buyer. No price was mentioned in the letter, but Clifford said he told Naqvi that he and Altman wanted to get about 2.5 times the stock's current book value of slightly more than $2,500 a share, or about $6,250 a share. A few weeks later, Naqvi reported back with an offer from another CCAH shareholder, Mohammed Hammoud, of $6,800 a share, or more than 2.7 times the book value. "That was perfectly satisfactory," Clifford later testified before a congressional committee—indeed, it was more than three times what the men had paid for the stock. On March 31, 1988, Clifford and Altman sold Hammoud about 60 percent of their CCAH shares.

Hammoud, a small-time businessman from Beirut, appeared to have gotten the money from BCCI to buy the shares, according to investigators. Strangely, investigators later uncovered an undated power-of-attorney form in which Hammoud seemed to have given Altman authority to sell his shares, raising even more questions about the transaction. Altman said he had never seen the form and questioned its authenticity.

How did Clifford come up with the asking price for the shares that he and Altman sold? The two men said they did not seek an independent appraisal of the stock's value, instead basing the price on what they had heard other bank stocks were selling for. But only a handful of banks were worth as much as 2.5 times book value in early 1988, according to bank analysts. Partly as a result of lingering effects of the stock market crash a few month earlier, the average publicly traded big-bank stock was going for about 1.2 times book value at that time.

Price Waterhouse was similarly conservative. In an audit report for BCCI, Price Waterhouse concluded that a bank stock involved in a takeover would be worth 1.5 times book value, and thus estimated that CCAH stock would be worth around $3,700 per share in early 1988. In the less-charged environment of the sale of a minority stake in a bank—such as Clifford's and Altman's combined 3 percent holding—the multiple would be even smaller, Price Waterhouse said: more like 1.2 times the book value, or $3,100 per CCAH share. "Given the related-party relationship of [the Clifford and Altman] transaction," Price Waterhouse said a few months later, "we do not consider the $6,800 price indicative of the market value of the shares."

Clifford and Altman, however, argued that the price they received for the stock was justified by the value that they had added to First American during their management of the bank. They noted that the $500 million investment by the bank's owners in 1982 had grown to be worth more than $1 billion by 1988 as First American's assets grew from $2.6 billion to $11 billion. "As far as I'm concerned, it was a perfectly proper reward for the unusual service that we had rendered in more than doubling the value of the rest of the stock," Clifford said.

Further proof of the bank's value, Clifford said, came when NCNB made a $1 billion takeover bid for First American in early 1990. "I immediately translated that in my own mind into a billion-two, -three or -four, because nobody ever makes his best offer first," Clifford said. "My guess is that it was worth a billion-and-a-half. So that would have been substantially three times the investment that our people had in it. And that's why we have been perfectly comfortable about the profit we made in the transaction."

But Clifford's analysis doesn't quite stand up to scrutiny. Assuming that First American was worth $1.5 billion in a takeover in 1990, Clifford and Altman still got a better deal. Since CCAH had about 300,000 shares outstanding, a $1.5 billion takeover bid would have been worth roughly $5,000 a share—well below the $6,800 that Clifford and Altman received for their stock. What's more, Clifford's appraisal of the bank's value based on the NCNB bid was somewhat disingenuous.

The NCNB bid was not unsolicited, as Clifford liked to imply. Rather, it was the result of a concerted attempt by First American's management over the previous year to find a buyer for the bank, an effort internally code named "Project Constitution." The investment-banking firm Goldman Sachs & Co. had been inviting large banking companies to make bids on First American, and NCNB was the only one to bite. So its $1 billion offer may have been close to its best shot. The takeover talks ultimately went nowhere, and First American was taken off the market. Clifford and Altman, meanwhile, pocketed the hefty profit from their stock deal and continued to own shares in CCAH—although the stock became virtually worthless after the scandal broke.

There was an interesting footnote to the Clifford and Altman stock transaction. For years, First American had been defending itself in a lawsuit brought against the bank by a number of former minority shareholders in the bank's Virginia subsidiary who argued that they had been shortchanged in the early 1980s when First American bought out the remaining shares in the bank that it did not already own. The case had gone to the Supreme Court, where the shareholders lost on a technicality, even though a lower court had ruled that the investors seemed to have been paid too little for their shares. As it turned out, even as Clifford was arguing in court that the 1.3 times book value paid to the minority shareholders was very fair, he was getting more than twice that for his CCAH shares and arguing that it was just as fair. After details of the Clifford and Altman stock deal emerged, a lawyer for the minority investors attempted to have their case reopened, to no avail.

The favorable terms that Clifford and Altman received in the stock deal was one reason it provoked outrage. Another was that they seemed to have attempted to keep the stock transaction secret. The stock purchase and sale apparently were unknown within First American; the bank's internal auditors discovered the transactions only because they were searching the books for unusual wire transfers between First American and BCCI after an article appeared in the Washington magazine *Regardies* in May 1990 raising questions about ties between BCCI and First American. In the search, the auditors discovered the wire transfers from BCCI to Clifford and Altman of the money lent them to buy the CCAH stock. Further investigation turned up checks from Clifford and Altman to BCCI, apparently to cover interest payments. Only when they confronted Altman about the wire transfers and checks were the auditors and other bank officials told about the stock deal, investigative sources said.

Although the two men said they had reported their ownership of CCAH stock on annual federal Y-6 disclosure forms—which generally go unread by regulators—the first public disclosure of the stock deal came in a May 1991 *Washington Post* story by Jim McGee and Sharon Walsh. They revealed that Clifford and Altman had bought the stock with a loan from BCCI and had sold it for a total profit of $9.8 million. *The Post's* story caused a firestorm of outrage directed at Clifford and Altman. Banking and legal experts described the stock deal as "highly unusual." How could Clifford and Altman have promised that BCCI would not finance the purchase of First American, and then borrow money themselves from BCCI to buy stock in the bank? The two men retorted that they believed the prohibition on BCCI financing of CCAH stock purchases applied only to the initial purchase of the bank, and not subsequent transactions.

The public relations firm Hill & Knowlton, representing Clifford and Altman, put out an eight-page statement defending their stock transactions. The statement argued that "these investments were no secretive ownership," since regulators had been notified and the deal approved by the other two directors of CCAH—former senator Stuart Symington, who was by then deceased, and Gen. Elwood Quesada, who had told *The Post* that he did not remember approving the stock purchase. The statement also argued, fairly, that the profit from the stock transaction was not out of line with compensation paid to top officers of other major banks.

The discovery of the stock deal shocked some regulators and investigators into the then-developing BCCI scandal. No one was more shocked than officials of the Federal Reserve, some of whom thought they had approved the takeover of Financial General 10 years earlier on the grounds that BCCI would not be involved in financing stock purchases. Fed officials had been exchanging letters with Altman for more than a year in an effort to track down the growing number of rumors that BCCI had financed the purchase of First American and owned the bank secretly. "In order to clarify the situation it would be helpful if you would provide information on any loans extended to the original or subsequent investors, either directly or indirectly, by BCCI or any of its affiliated organizations," William A. Ryback, deputy assistant director of the Fed's division of banking supervision and regulation, had written Altman in December 1989.

That description would seem to cover the $15 million in loans made by BCCI to Clifford and Altman to buy CCAH stock, as well as some later loans to buy additional shares in rights offerings. But Altman, who showed in congressional testimony a masterful ability to answer questions only part way if at all, convinced the Fed to limit its inquiries about BCCI loans only to borrowings for the initial purchase of CCAH shares in 1982. Altman answered Ryback that there were no such loans from BCCI—furnishing a stilted-sounding letter from the usually cordial Naqvi to back up this contention. "Mr. Naqvi states flatly that BCCI did not finance the acquisition 'in any respect,' " Altman wrote Ryback in

January 1990. No mention was made of the loans to Clifford and Altman.

But then, Clifford and Altman already had proved that they could keep a secret when they wanted to. They had succeeded in keeping the identities of even the listed shareholders of First American secret over the years, blocking the release of the names of the Middle Eastern shareholders in at least one lawsuit and attempting to convince the Federal Reserve not to disclose the names to journalists seeking regulatory documents that ordinarily would have been part of the public record.

Moreover, when members of First American's board of directors testified before Congress in September 1991, they confessed that even they had been left in the dark on some fairly fundamental matters pertaining to the bank they were supposed to be overseeing. Because of First American's and CCAH's complicated ownership structure, in which a series of holding companies separated First American from its Middle Eastern owners, the directors confessed, they were never really sure who owned the bank, legally or otherwise—even though under federal law, directors are supposed to be working for a company's ownership. Clifford and Altman, the directors said, simply had never told them who the owners were.

Chapter 9

====

The Bank for the
Underworld

Perhaps not surprisingly, given its increasingly corrupt corporate culture and its reputation as a haven from regulation, BCCI came to acquire a long list of shady customers. Chronically desperate for capital, BCCI couldn't really afford to be choosy about its clients—anybody with money to deposit or to pay for financial services was welcome, and BCCI was willing to do almost anything to attract them. Money-laundering, secret accounts, hidden identities, financing of illegal activities—all were available to BCCI customers. That made BCCI, as some wags said later, truly a full-service bank. As terrorists, drug dealers, arms traders, smugglers and spies flocked to BCCI's doors, the Bank for the Third World became the Bank for the Underworld.

The Third World connection was, indeed, an advantage in attracting such business: Because it operated in nations that served as bases for terrorists and homes for drug factories, BCCI was, if nothing else, convenient—a sort of neighborhood bank in some of the world's worst neighborhoods. In some Third World nations, it faced little or no competition from other, more ethically operated international banks, thus offering financial access to markets that otherwise were hard to reach.

Over the years, BCCI's customers included international terrorist Abu Nidal, the Iranian-backed Hezbollah terrorist group, the governments of both Iran and Iraq, and many of the drug dealers of Latin America—including Panamanian dictator Manuel Noriega, a particularly good and valued customer of the bank for many years. With its roots so firmly entrenched in the Middle East, BCCI did well in the arms business, serving people who in public professed mutual hatred and yet in private shared bankers and letters of credit. For its Latin American customers, BCCI offered ever-more creative ways to launder the millions of dollars produced by the drug trade with the United States. Even run of the mill smugglers were able to benefit greatly from BCCI's services.

The bank provided financing and letters of credit to customers that other banks would hardly have let in the door. BCCI played a role in the Iran-contra affair and may have been a key participant in the alleged "October Surprise" designed to keep American hostages in Iran in order to ensure the election of Ronald Reagan as president. Arab terrorists bought weapons from the Israeli intelligence service, the Mossad, in deals run by a BCCI bank manager with BCCI financial support. BCCI staffers also assisted Arab terrorists in smuggling arms between the U.S. and the Communist Bloc by providing fraudulent documentation and finance. The bank even dabbled in the financing of illegal trading in nuclear materials.

After the BCCI scandal was exposed, tales swirled of a so-called "black network" operated by the bank from a base in Karachi. This network was said to be a full-service, in-house terrorism operation, with hundreds of operatives available for espionage, smuggling and other clandestine operations—"a Mafia-like enforcement squad," according to *Time* magazine. More responsible investigators strongly rejected such wild stories. Besides, between its own "special duties" department, its corrupt management and the nefarious doings of many of its customers, BCCI hardly needed a special "black network."

Many of the same attributes that attracted criminals to BCCI also appealed to intelligence agencies and security services around the world. The CIA, British MI5, the Mossad and others also were customers in good standing. The far-flung BCCI banking network made it easy to transfer funds to spies and operatives around the world, and the bank's penchant for secrecy made it easy to keep such transactions under cover. That BCCI was itself dirty was not necessarily a plus or minus for such customers—in many cases, it was just more convenient to do business with BCCI in a Third World capital than it was to use, say, Chase Manhattan Bank. Besides, good guys, like bad guys, have to keep their money some place.

But as the intelligence and law enforcement communities came to understand BCCI and its customers better, they also found the bank to be a handy way to keep tabs on those customers. It appears that, to some extent, BCCI was able to keep out of trouble over the years by trading information on some of its dirtiest customers for a sort of protection from nosy government officials, and intelligence services seemed to have allowed the bank to operate unimpeded as long as it continued to serve their purposes.

Certainly, any major bank with hundreds of thousands of customers around the world will have a few bad apples among the bunch. But BCCI seemed to have more than its share, and many of them had connections to people who were even more questionable. Examined closely, some of the deals provide insight into the murky web of ties among arms dealers, terrorists, renegade government officials, drug dealers and other criminals—and the banks like BCCI that finance their deals. Like so much else in the BCCI affair, unraveling one shady relationship leads to disclosures about many others.

One BCCI client, for instance, was Ben Banerjee, an expatriate Indian and former commercial airline pilot who had obtained a license to deal arms in Britain. Banerjee lived in the small British village of Olney and owned a company called BR&W Industries Ltd. He was a frequent visitor to

BCCI in London in the late 1970s, where staff members came to know him as "the old tradesman." He was a reliable source of letters of credit, and always banked through Shafiqur Rahman Khan, a manager at BCCI's Hyde Park branch, one of the bank's key London offices.

"The old tradesman," it appears, was a typically mercenary arms dealer. "Banerjee would sell anything to anyone, anywhere," said Ghassan Qassem, a young Syrian-born BCCI bank manager who worked on Banerjee's account. Banerjee got along well with Qassem, in whom he often confided after a few drinks. He once told Qassem that "the most beautiful thing was being in a Beirut hotel room and looking at the sky and seeing it red from all these bullets. He said he was desperate to continue seeing that sight because it meant more orders for him."

Qassem recalls that Banerjee once sent a single container to Lebanon carrying two separate shipments of arms—one for the Palestine Liberation Organization and one for its enemies, the Hezbollah. Banerjee was paid for each shipment, and the two groups went at each other with the munitions he had supplied.

Banerjee's contacts were far-flung. He was known to the British intelligence services, and he acted as an intermediary among arms manufacturers, other dealers and customers in France, Turkey, the Eastern Bloc, Argentine and Korea, as well as the Middle East. In one deal backed by a letter of credit from BCCI, Banerjee allegedly arranged the $10 million illicit shipment of 1,250 American TOW anti-tank missiles to Iran—the missiles were listed on bills of lading as "lift trucks." Another Banerjee deal using BCCI involved the $1.9 million sale of Polish rockets, anti-aircraft missiles and launchers and automatic rifles to Dubai. He also was said to be one of the brokers involved in the Iran-contra scandal.

In 1981 Banerjee brought a potential new client to BCCI. Samir Najmeddin said he was a representative of the Iraqi government and wanted to set up an account at the bank. Najmeddin was passed on to Qassem, whose upbringing in Jordan, where his family had moved shortly after Qassem was born, was thought to put him on the same wavelength as the new client.

Shortly after Najmeddin's account was opened, $48 million was transferred from his account at one of Midland Bank's London branches, where it had been for the previous three years, to BCCI. This was no small amount. "At the time, this sum was the size of a branch, not an account," Qassem recalled.

BCCI opened a total of 12 accounts on Najmeddin's behalf. The bank also went to a London accounting firm and organized an offshore trading company for Najmeddin, registered in Panama with headquarters in Warsaw. The company was named SAS Trade & Investment, after the initials of the three named directors of the company—Shakir Farhan, Adnan al-Banna and Samir Najmeddin himself—and was supposed to be a firm specializing in the international trading of computers, facsimile machines and other office equipment.

But SAS Trade & Investment was no office-equipment dealer. Instead, it was a front for one of the world's most odious terrorist organizations. In reality, Shakir Farhan was the feared Palestinian terrorist leader Abu Nidal. Najmeddin also had given Qassem a phony story. Rather than being a representative of the Iraqi government, he was the treasurer and financial brains behind Abu Nidal's organization. The name of the third principal of the company, Adnan al-Banna, a relative of Nidal's, also would have set off alarm bells had Qassem been more politically aware. Abu Nidal had been born Sabri al-Banna and only adopted the *nom de guerre* of Abu Nidal—"father of the struggle"—in the 1960s, when he joined the Palestine Liberation Organization. He later became a Maoist-style communist following military training in North Korea and China, and split with the PLO in 1973 when its leader, Yasser Arafat, suggested that a policy of "progressive moderation" might bring about a peaceful agreement with Israel. Arafat, considered a wild-eyed radical by much of the world, simply wasn't radical enough for Nidal.

Nidal then set up his own organization, the Fatah Revolutionary Council, totally dedicated to the destruction of Israel and prepared to use any means to achieve this. He has been called the most dangerous man in the world; his campaigns of terror have killed more than 900 people in at least 20 countries. Abu Nidal's forte does not seem to have been finance, however; he left that to Najmeddin, although he retained power of attorney over all of his accounts at BCCI. Nidal's direct involvement with the accounts was slight—he came to London in 1981 to transfer $500,000 into his newly opened personal account, and he was to return only twice more during his involvement with BCCI.

Between 1981 and 1986, Najmeddin—and by extension Abu Nidal—was to become one of the most valued customers of BCCI's Hyde Park branch. Najmeddin also developed a close friendship with Qassem, who was struck by the man's shyness: "He was very, very humble, very soft-spoken; he is afraid of his own shadow," the banker later said. "He's very timid and not a man of power or personality. But he treated me as a father does a son."

Once the covert Abu Nidal account was opened, Najmeddin provided a letter of credit for $30 million to Ben Banerjee, who supplied him with ammunition from Turkey and rockets from France. The deal went smoothly and BCCI earned a huge commission. For the next five years Najmeddin used BCCI for all of Abu Nidal's letters of credit. Each one valued at more than $500,000 was approved by the Central Credit Committee, a group of four senior BCCI management figures led by Swaleh Naqvi.

Najmeddin's main European base initially was in Switzerland and later in Poland, but when he was in London he was given carte blanche by BCCI to use its offices for his own business. This involved sending coded messages and receiving replies on a daily basis. Qassem recalled that occasionally bank staff members were employed for whole days simply to deal with Najmeddin's numerous telexes. Qassem was too preoccupied with financial considerations to consider the purpose of these messages. "No one mentioned that this was a terrorist account," he said. "This was the biggest account we had. We had to make sure that they were never upset or we would lose them. If we lost them, we were finished."

While Najmeddin began as an agent for Abu Nidal, he gradually became a trader and broker in his own right, selling arms to governments and terrorists. He is known to have supplied artillery shells to the Iraqi army, handguns, shotguns and ammunition to the Iraqi police, and night-vision devices to Argentina during the Falklands war against Britain.

In spite of his dedication to the violent overthrow of the Israeli state, Najmeddin developed working relationships with several Jewish arms dealers. In 1982 he struck a deal to ship military equipment to Abu Nidal's base in Poland, where the Fatah Revolutionary Council was allowed to operate freely, provided it did not carry out attacks on Polish soil. Najmeddin's associates were two New York-based American Jews: Leonard Berg, the president of a police equipment company named HLB Security Electronics Ltd., and Solomon Schwartz, the director of a firm called Global Research & Development. Both men are said to have had links with Israel's Mossad.

The export of arms from Britain to Poland was illegal, but Najmeddin went with Qassem to a British accountant based in Geneva to arrange a number of letters of credit for SAS Trade & Investment. Najmeddin wanted $10 million, saying that he wanted to export spare pipeline parts to the Eastern Bloc. Qassem told the accountant that an offshore company was needed because this kind of shipment to Poland was forbidden by the British authorities.

On the surface, this seemed in order, and the accountant planned to use an offshore company whose name suggested it dealt in pipeline parts. But he got cold feet when he saw documents making it clear that the eventual destination of the shipment was the Polish Ministry of Defense. The accountant says he reported the incident to the British Consulate in Geneva, which told him, "You're mixing with some very dangerous people." This seems to indicate that British intelligence already knew something about Najmeddin's work.

The deal eventually proceeded through BCCI without the Geneva connection, and a letter of credit was arranged, falsely stating the shipment's destination as Mexico. The arms— along with other devices, such as electric cattle prods used for crowd control and torture—were purchased from Britain, Belgium and the United States through Schwartz and Berg. The consignment was loaded onto a chartered jet at New York's Kennedy Airport in February 1984, but just as the plane was about to take off, U.S. Customs agents moved in and arrested Schwartz and Berg.

As far as Customs officials were concerned, this was a conventional bust. Schwartz was a known racketeer with Mafia connections who had been under surveillance for some time before his arrest. But there were signs that something bigger was involved, perhaps—Schwartz hinted in his defense—involving a covert attempt by American officials to swap arms to Poland in exchange for advanced Soviet tanks. The key to the episode is Najmeddin's involvement. The Poles certainly did not need the munitions being smuggled— it was, after all, fairly routine equipment and they had their own manufacturers and sources—but Abu Nidal most certainly did need it. Nidal also had the money to pay for it.

According to one source, the deal was set up between the CIA and Najmeddin to finance the defection of a Polish general. The general had demanded $1 million to come to the West, and if the deal had worked out, the CIA would have provided Najmeddin with arms, which would then have been shipped on to Abu Nidal in Poland. In exchange, Najmeddin would have paid the $1 million to the Polish general, who would then have defected.

In 1989 Schwartz and Berg were sentenced to 10 years apiece and ordered to pay fines of $700,000 each for racketeering, wire fraud, conspiracy to violate the Arms Export Control Act, exporting arms in violation of that act and related offenses. Early in 1991, a federal appeals court reversed three of the counts, but affirmed the rest of the convictions. The assessed fines were reduced by $277,000 to reflect the reversal of the three counts and the sentences were ordered reconsidered by a lower court.

BCCI financed a number of other arms transactions in the Middle East that brought together some unusual bedfellows. For example, in 1985, Najmeddin set out to acquire some Israeli-made Uzi machine guns, telling one of his contacts, a man who owned a weapons shop in London, that he wanted 200 of the weapons. The shop owner said he knew someone who could oblige, and the following day an Israeli came to the bank branch office to meet with Najmeddin. According to Qassem, "He talked about how he was going to get the guns from Israel. He made a big scene, and said, 'I can only get you 20 now, and 20 every month.' Najmeddin said, 'No, I want them all in one go. Otherwise, I'll go somewhere else.'"

The Israeli agreed to the terms and the payment: $48,000 for the guns and $80,000 for silencers. "They came to my office in BCCI and received the checks from me and gave me the bill of payment. They knew who they were selling to," said Qassem, who later cooperated in great detail with British authorities investigating BCCI. The deal was concluded successfully, and the Uzis were shipped out of London's Heathrow Airport aboard a Swissair jetliner. Qassem said he was later told by British intelligence that the company the Israeli owned was a front for Israel's Mossad intelligence service.

The incident poses a number of questions, since it certainly seems odd that the Israelis would deliberately trade with their enemies. Yet it seems extremely unlikely that the Israelis did not know who was behind Najmeddin. So were they free-lance traders who did not care who bought as long as the money was good? If they were Mossad-linked, could the weapons have carried hidden identification or been sabotaged in some way? The hidden-identification theory may be bolstered by another trade that went through the bank. In April 1986, terrorist Nezar Hindawi made his notorious attempt to blow up an El Al flight from Heathrow to Tel Aviv by planting a bomb in his pregnant girlfriend's luggage. It appears that Najmeddin purchased the electronic exploding devices from Israeli sources, and Qassem reckons that Hindawi was foiled because the devices had been secretly identified by authorities before the sale.

Although Iraq was providing Abu Nidal's Fatah Revolutionary Council with a base, Najmeddin was not averse to selling arms to both the Iraqis and their enemies, the Iranians. In 1984 Najmeddin had meetings in London with members of Iran's Logistics Support Center, which had offices next door to the British Department of Trade and Industry. Contracts eventually were signed committing him to supply $25 million worth of arms to Iran. Negotiations for the deal were carried out using BCCI telex machines. This was contrary to BCCI political policy, which strictly allied the bank with the hard-line Iraqis, but it seems that the policy was erratically policed. In 1984 the Iranian-backed Hezbollah group was found to have an account in BCCI's High Street Kensington branch, where the group was being looked after by an Iranian officer of the bank. The account was closed and the officer was fired. Still, nobody at the bank tried to stop Najmeddin from selling equipment to Iran.

Nonetheless, Qassem thinks that Abu Nidal may have seen to it that Iran didn't always get the arms it thought it was buying. "Sometimes [the terrorists] would sell out-of-date products by changing the expiration date on the boxes," he said. "Sometimes they would pretend to be selling large amounts of equipment and would negotiate for a long time, so that Iran did not receive anything while Iraq did. But sometimes the organization needed money, so they had to sell arms."

It is perfectly possible, however, that Najmeddin was applying the philosophy of the marketplace and not asking any questions. Iran was regarded as a pariah in the West, and it was desperate to find arms for its war with Iraq. BCCI was never one to turn away a profit, whatever the source of funds.

In 1985, Syrian officials approached Najmeddin to purchase a riot-control weapons system. Najmeddin contacted Britain's Royal Ordnance, the sole manufacturer of this item and said he wanted to purchase the weapons system on behalf of the Syrian government. The application was turned down, apparently at a high level of the British government, for political reasons. Undeterred, Najmeddin scoured the embassies of London and within a week, an official at the Sierra Leone embassy had been paid £20,000 to authorize an end-user certificate stating that the weapon system's destination was Sierra Leone rather than Syria. The new documentation was presented to Royal Ordnance, and the sale and shipment were approved. Soon afterwards, Royal Ordnance realized that it had been duped, and called in Scotland Yard to investigate. By this time, however, the shipment already had left the country, bound for Rotterdam and from there to the Middle East.

Najmeddin worked with Qassem for four years, apparently keeping the young bank manager in the dark about his real business the entire time. But in 1985, Najmeddin seemed to have an attack of conscience, according to Qassem. "He tried to hint to me indirectly that he had put me in a wrong position, trying to apologize," Qassem said. "He used to say things to me sometimes, indirect things that made no sense. For example, we used to talk about Palestinians sometimes, while having dinner. He used to quote things and examples just to be heard saying it. . . . He couldn't say anything to me openly because he did not know what the reaction would be, what danger he would put himself into—whether it would cease the operation with the bank."

Najmeddin's cover finally was blown in 1985 by the French magazine L'Express, which quoted information on him from a leaked FBI report and openly accused him of being Abu Nidal's financier. Najmeddin told Qassem that the article was false and went to court to clear his name. Because the magazine could not summon the FBI to substantiate the leaked report, he won.

Still, Najmeddin no longer felt safe dealing through BCCI in London, and in early 1986 he began to withdraw large amounts of money from his BCCI accounts. The smallest of these withdrawals was $5 million, and the money was transferred to banks in Switzerland and Poland. Within two months, Najmeddin had left BCCI completely. He continued to trade from Poland for another two years until the U.S. government pressured the Poles into expelling him. In January 1988, Samir Najmeddin left Poland, and his days as an international arms trader came to an end. Today, he is believed to be living in Libya, along with Abu Nidal. Both men are wanted by Interpol.

BCCI's role in another large smuggling operation was laid out in detail in a trial in Florida and in congressional testimony late in 1991. The bank was alleged to have helped a Jordanian businessman, Munther Ismael Bilbeisi, to smuggle tens of millions of dollars worth of coffee beans into the United States and to provide a wide variety of covert arms sales to governments around the world. BCCI is said to have known of Bilbeisi's activities and to have aided them by supplying letters of credit and other documents that most other banks would not have provided. The bank then looked the other way at what it had to know was illegal activity.

"Without BCCI, Bilbeisi would have had a really difficult time organizing and financing his deals," said James F. Dougherty II, an investigator for Lloyd's of London, which successfully sued Bilbeisi for insurance fraud in connection with some of the transactions. "With BCCI, they were a snap. . . . BCCI prepared documents which were essential to the shipment and then interpreted them loosely so that a false destination would not impede payment." Perhaps not coincidentally, Bilbeisi's cousin reportedly ran the Jordanian branch of BCCI, one of the few branches not affected by the July 1991 shutdown of the bank.

Dougherty's tale, told to a congressional committee, shed new light on the way BCCI did business with one of its many questionable customers. He said his investigation had turned up hints of bribery and kickbacks, allegations of evasion of U.S. laws governing arms sales, an apparently abortive attempt to deal in weapons-grade uranium and a simple but effective coffee-smuggling scam in which tons of coffee beans were shipped from Central America to U.S. ports in room-sized containers that unsuspecting Customs officials believed to be empty. Almost all of this was made possible by financing and other services provided by BCCI, according to Dougherty's testimony and other evidence. An internal report from Lloyd's of London said BCCI provided Bilbeisi a "flexible system of payments to foreign associates in Central America."

BCCI provided financing for Bilbeisi's arms deals through $79 million worth of letters of credit, although he drew on only about $8.5 million of that. According to Dougherty, the transactions financed by BCCI ranged from shipments of small arms to tanks to fighter jets. In one 1987 deal, Bilbeisi bought three civilian Sikorsky S-76 helicopters from Jordan—including King Hussein's personal helicopter—and sold them to Guatemala along with parts needed to turn them into gunships. Such a transaction would be contrary to American law governing arms sales, and as such would be avoided by most honest banks because it took place without documents ensuring that it was legitimate. But Dougherty said BCCI provided a $5.2 million letter of credit for the transaction, and he alleged that documents show that some of the proceeds were used to provide kickbacks to Guatemalan government officials and even to BCCI's Miami branch, which allegedly received $400,000 for helping out on the deal. "BCCI was the conduit through which the funds to finance the arms deal were funnelled," according to Richard Alan Lehrman, an associate of Dougherty.

BCCI also backed several other illegal arms sales by Bilbeisi during the 1980s, according to Dougherty. Documents obtained from Bilbeisi under discovery in the Lloyd's lawsuit included an offer by South Africa to sell enriched uranium through Bilbeisi to an unnamed Middle Eastern nation, believed by Dougherty to be either Iraq or Iran. The sale never took place.

Bilbeisi's main business was somewhat more mundane, but allegedly no less illegal—and certainly lucrative. His firm, Coffee Inc., would ship bargain-basement coffee from Central America to Miami, Tampa and New Orleans in huge containers listed in shipping documents as being empty or partly filled. BCCI financed the shipments with $100 million worth of letters of credit. Customs agents never checked the containers, Dougherty said. If they had, and discovered them full of coffee beans, Bilbeisi's employees—backed up by falsified documents—were prepared to tell Customs that a mistake had been made. The smuggled beans were relabeled as higher-priced coffee, worth twice as much or more than the original purchase price, and sold to processors, Dougherty said. By doing so, Bilbeisi allegedly sold $34 million worth of coffee for more than $100 million—and that counts just the deals Dougherty was able to uncover. Many others were hidden by the destruction of documents, he claims.

In a story that echoes other early attempts to raise alarms about BCCI's activities, Dougherty said he reported the alleged coffee-smuggling scam and arms deals to Customs Service and Justice Department officials repeatedly beginning in late 1989, but received no response. He said there are indications that the Customs Service knew about Bilbeisi's alleged coffee smuggling activities in 1983, but did not act. Finally, in the summer of 1991, days before the last of the statutes of limitations on Bilbeisi's alleged wrongdoing were to expire, the Justice Department brought tax-evasion charges against the alleged smuggler. Lloyd's of London later won its lawsuit against Bilbeisi, in which it sought to void— on the basis of fraud—an insurance policy it had issued Coffee, Inc. to cover some of the coffee shipments. The judgment in the case was entered as a default against Bilbeisi, who declined to return to the U.S. from Jordan to answer the charges. Lloyd's still has a claim outstanding against BCCI for its role in the alleged scheme.

BCCI's list of shady customers wasn't limited to those on the wrong side of the law. For example, it assisted the CIA in the financing of arms sold to Iran and transferred the proceeds to Nicaraguan contra rebels, greasing the wheels of the affair that rocked the Reagan administration. Adnan Khashoggi, the Saudi arms dealer, indicated in testimony before the congressional panel investigating the Iran-contra affair that $17 million worth of financing for the scheme passed through accounts that he kept in BCCI's Monte Carlo branch, and that some of the profit was kicked back to the bank itself. As part of the same arrangement, Lt. Col. Oliver North opened three accounts at BCCI's Paris branch in 1984 in the name of a Panamanian-registered shell company, Devon Island. The accounts were allegedly used to handle the $10 million sale of American TOW anti-tank missiles, and the profit from the deal was then transferred to a Saudi Arabian branch of BCCI and paid to Adolfo Calero, the head of the contras.

BCCI's willingness to turn a blind eye in order to make a profit perfectly complemented the operations of intelligence agencies that would break the law to further what they saw as the national interest. The CIA, for instance, transferred funds to Mujaheddin rebels in Afghanistan during the Soviet occupation, using BCCI's branch in Pakistan. As it turned out, the money was embezzled at every stage of its passage and used by some of the rebels to finance their own drug-smuggling operations—the profits being laundered back through BCCI, naturally.

The CIA also used BCCI for routine business: Through its Cromwell Road and Edgware Road branches in London, it reportedly paid 500 British CIA contacts, including senior figures in politics, industry, academia, banking and the media. These contacts, or "monitors," provided the agency with information—for instance, details of British arms sales and overseas contracts, sometimes even before the deals were made. The CIA is believed to have run many other covert accounts out of BCCI. More innocently, the CIA used BCCI's Washington bank, First American, for payroll and operational accounts at its suburban Virginia headquarters.

The CIA's use of BCCI is not in and of itself suspicious—it had to bank somewhere, and BCCI and First American may merely have been the most convenient outlets. But it appears that the CIA knew who it was dealing with. During the 1980s, it circulated intelligence reports to other federal agencies concerning BCCI's arms dealing and money-laundering activities, as well as about the bank's alleged illegal ownership of First American. And in the mid-1980s, Robert Gates, then deputy director of the CIA and later its director, described BCCI in a report as "the Bank of Crooks and Criminals International"—an apt description that was to stick many years later.

Nevertheless, there are indications that the CIA did not try very hard to expose BCCI, especially in the United States. Although it says it circulated "hundreds" of intelligence reports about the bank to other agencies in the latter half of the 1980s, some of these reports were misdirected—the Federal Reserve, for instance, doesn't seem to have been told what the CIA knew about BCCI's alleged ownership of First American Bank. CIA officials later conceded that they made an "honest mistake" in not trying harder to blow the whistle on BCCI, especially to the Federal Reserve. Some investigators suggest that the CIA had decided that BCCI was worth much more to it alive than dead, although CIA officials have denied that they were so reliant upon BCCI.

In 1988, U.S. Customs Commissioner William von Raab sought information on the bank from Gates. Von Raab claims that he was given no access to the earlier CIA memos, particularly a detailed September 1986 report on the BCCI-First American connection, and received little more than what he calls "well-written pablum"—information that was already widely available. Several weeks later, von Raab found out from Customs agents in Britain about the CIA's use of BCCI, and he has since accused Gates of being "less than candid" about the affair. He complained that Federal Reserve and Customs investigations into BCCI were consistently stonewalled by other U.S. government agencies. He accused the U.S. Treasury—then headed by George Bush's pal James Baker III—of being "lackadaisical and worked over" by "some of Washington's most blue-chip influence peddlers" and he said that the Department of Justice had been "pounded" by lobbyists for BCCI.

Von Raab's complaints, made to a congressional committee shortly after BCCI was shut down in the summer of 1991, received wide attention and seemed to add more evidence of BCCI's ability to influence those in power to its own ends. But many investigators have discredited his griping by pointing out that there was evidence that the Customs Service under von Raab had fumbled its own BCCI investigation, the 1988 Tampa money-laundering case against the bank, also possibly for political reasons. Besides, it was noted, von Raab had a different reason to carry a grudge: His wife had lost her job at First American Bank.

Other governments also had close links with BCCI, but none was more intimate than Pakistan. In the 1970s, BCCI was heavily involved in the financing of Pakistan's attempts to build its own nuclear arsenal. This came about through Abedi's close ties with Gen. Zia al-Haq, then president of Pakistan. Over the next 15 years, a series of attempts was made to obtain nuclear components for Pakistan, with varying degrees of success. BCCI transferred cash and gold in order to finance the operation and arranged air freight, shipping and insurance.

In 1983, the head of Pakistan's nuclear program, Dr. Abdul Qadir Khan, was arrested in Holland on charges of trying to steal blueprints for a uranium enrichment factory. BCCI provided his defense, paying all the expenses of his legal counsel.

BCCI also is thought to have underwritten the illegal export of nearly $1 million worth of computer equipment for Pakistan's nuclear program in 1982 and 1983. Moreover, in 1987, a Pakistani-born Canadian was indicted in the United States for conspiring to export specialty metals to Pakistan for use in a nuclear bomb, and documents found in his house showed that the deal involved the use of London and Toronto branches of BCCI.

Although the rumors of the existence of BCCI's own internal intelligence and espionage service, the notorious "black network," have generally been discounted, BCCI seems to have been no stranger to the techniques of espionage and surveillance. For example, BCCI's protocol officers were responsible for making sure that whatever the bank wanted, it got—sometimes by means of either bribes or terror. BCCI also appears to have been willing to terrorize its own managers if they showed disloyalty. Former BCCI officials have said they were threatened with financial ruin, injury or death if they testified against the bank. Often, they have taken that risk.

Since the bank's closing, two free-lance journalists investigating BCCI have died under mysterious circumstances. Joseph Daniel Casolaro was researching aspects of the "October Surprise" and theories of a grand conspiracy involving BCCI and several other scandals when he was found dead in a hotel room in West Virginia, an apparent suicide—although his family and some friends believe he was murdered. Another reporter, Anson Ng, was found dead while working to uncover BCCI's activities in Guatemala. There has been no solid proof of any connection between BCCI and the deaths. But conspiracy theorists believe that these journalists may have discovered that BCCI's tentacles stretch farther and are far more dangerous than anyone had imagined.

Chapter 10

===

Drug Money

The wedding of Robert Musella and Kathleen Erickson was scheduled for 10 a.m. on Sunday, October 9, 1988 at the Innisbrook Golf Club and Hotel in Tarpon Springs, Fla.; naturally, there was a bachelor stag party the night before. Ten limousines delivered the party guests to the NCNB Bank building in the center of Tampa that Saturday night—an appropriate site, given that the guest list included a large number of bankers and their well-to-do clients.

The party was to be held in a private club on the bank building's top floor, but the elevator didn't go that far. It stopped at a lower floor, where the guests were met by federal agents—and arrested on money-laundering charges. They then were driven in the same limousines to the county prison. Supposedly, one of the guests turned to the agent arresting him and said, "Boy, this is really some kinky bachelor's party."

BCCI finally was being brought to justice.

Among those arrested that night were several senior BCCI executives, including Amjad Awan, one of BCCI's top U.S. officials and the personal banker of Panamanian strongman Gen. Manuel Noriega. Indictments unsealed over the next few days named more than 80 BCCI employees and customers, including members of the Medellin drug cartel.

The arrests were the culmination of Operation C-Chase, a two-year undercover Customs Service investigation led by

Musella—actually Customs agent Robert Mazur. His supposed fiancee also was an undercover agent. Their ruse had been so complete that the BCCI men had even become social friends of the man they believed to be a big-time money-launderer, comfortable enough to attend his "wedding"— which Customs agents had arranged to gather the BCCI suspects in one place and keep them from fleeing.

The Tampa case, which led to a record $14.8 million fine against the bank and the conviction of several of its executives, was a landmark in the history of BCCI. For the first time, the bank's criminal wrongdoing was publicly and dramatically exposed. The case spurred BCCI to a last-ditch attempt at influence-buying on a grander scale than ever before, with a $21 million legal effort, organized by Abedi's friends Clark Clifford and Robert Altman, that brought some of America's best legal minds to bear in drawing up the bank's defense. The Tampa bust also triggered investigations elsewhere into the bank's activities, and the reverberations from the arrests and the bank's exposure hastened Agha Hasan Abedi's departure from the top of the bank he had founded.

The Tampa arrests also sent shudders through those who knew about the relationship between BCCI and First American Bank. Concerned that the Tampa case might lead to discovery of the secret ownership of First American, BCCI officials worked frantically to put some distance between the two institutions, according to former BCCI executive Abdur Sakhia, who oversaw the bank's U.S. operation at the time of the Tampa arrests. Among the "damage control" done in the months after the arrests, Sakhia said, was an attempt to build a "fire wall" between BCCI and First American by cutting off communications between the two and reducing First American's business ties with BCCI.

In retrospect, BCCI's involvement in money-laundering and drug dealing is hardly surprising. Its relationships with arms traffickers and other smugglers put it only a short, logical step away from the drug trade, and its desperation for new deposits made drug money particularly attractive.

BCCI operated branches throughout Central America to handle the drug kingpins' business, and went so far as to purchase a bank in the Medellin cartel's backyard in Colombia. The handling of billions of dollars in drug money gilded BCCI's books for nearly a decade, and the bank turned money-laundering into a high banking art.

Drugs are a cash business, and that's a problem for those who produce and sell them. The sale of large quantities of drugs produces large quantities of cash, and regulators in the United States and several other nations have attempted to squelch the drug trade by putting tight restrictions on the amount of cash that banks can accept from any one customer at one time—$10,000 per transaction, under U.S. law. Anything more has to be reported in detail. As a result, drug traffickers need to find a way to "launder" their money—to move it into the legitimate financial system undetected or to convert it into another form of negotiable asset. Customs agent Mazur later told Congress:

> Literally every conceivable method had been discovered as being used, from the simplest forms of depositing currency in banks, which either occurred in large sums due to relationships with individuals in the banks, or . . . [in smaller amounts] by what is commonly termed in the law enforcement community as "smurfs"—dozens of people who would be given several hundred thousand dollars a day to go around to banks and deposit amounts under $10,000 so that funds could get into the banking system; also, the use of private aircraft, where tens of millions of dollars would be flown out of the country on one occasion to haven countries, where the deposits could be hidden due to bank secrecy laws; and even the concealment of currency in commercial goods, such as cutting out the insides of air-conditioning units and filling them with cash and shipping them to different areas of the world.

The key to such schemes, often, is the participation of a bank willing to handle large amounts of cash without asking any questions, preferably in a nation that doesn't regulate such transactions very closely. BCCI, eager to get deposits anywhere it could to prop up its financially ailing operations, was happy to oblige.

BCCI's money-laundering business apparently had its origins in Panama, where Noriega allegedly held forth over the drug business. The bank opened up in Panama in April 1980 with royal fanfare at the Hilton in Panama City. The country's then-president, Aristides Royo Sanchez, was on hand to hear a paean of praise for Panama personally delivered by Abedi. Panama was well-positioned for the rogue bank. It was a short aircraft ride from Miami and the U.S. mainland, and an even shorter flight over the Caribbean to BCCI's financial center on Grand Cayman Island. Panama also adjoins Colombia, one of the world's largest cultivators of cocaine.

Panama gained notoriety when Noriega came to power in 1981. Noriega is believed to have been recruited by the Central Intelligence Agency as early as 1966, when he was a corporal in the Panamanian army. It appears that U.S. officials permitted Noriega's wilder excesses in the belief that he supported U.S.-backed contras against Sandinista guerrillas in nearby Nicaragua and that he helped the U.S. cause by backing Oliver North's arms dealing in the Iran-contra affair. He became a regular player in the worldwide market for illegitimate arms. But drug-money-laundering allegedly became Noriega's favorite business. At least a half-billion dollars in drug money passed through the Panamanian banking system every year, out of which Noriega allegedly demanded a substantial cut.

Among BCCI's early customers in Panama was Noriega's secretary, Marcela Tason, who opened several accounts at the bank's new branch in Panama City. Noriega quickly exerted his influence by having the branch manager removed because he was not sufficiently compliant. That made way for the man who would come to be known as Noriega's banker, Amjad Awan—whose father reportedly had been head of the Pakistani secret police. As soon as Awan arrived, he made it clear to his deputy, Daniel Gonzalez, that they should go for deposits from the Colombian drug barons, and he said Noriega would help with some introductions. Awan had no scruples about the origins of the funds. He told Gonzalez that BCCI would accept any amounts of cash or checks without asking, and that to get the business rolling, the bank would not charge fees on the transactions.

The approach worked. Drug money poured in and a branch of BCCI was quickly opened in Colon, Panama. Many others followed. Noriega clearly developed a close relationship with Awan—so close, in fact, that when Awan was transferred to the United States in 1984, Noriega personally protested the move to Abedi, in vain. But Awan continued to serve Noriega from Miami and then Washington, providing BCCI funds to pay for the dictator's regular visits to the United States, where he was entertained on a lavish scale on the BCCI tab.

Vital to the success of BCCI's Panamanian operation was Noriega's total grip on authority and power in Panama, which included the issuing of passports and visas, the running of the Panama Canal and the government and, most importantly, the oversight of the National Bank of Panama. His progress from lowly National Guard non-com in May 1962 to chief of the notorious G-2 intelligence branch and ultimately commander-in-chief of the Panamanian Defense Force was accomplished ruthlessly and efficiently—opponents, it is alleged, simply disappeared. In this atmosphere, BCCI's business was able to flourish without interruption.

Among the early clients who took advantage of BCCI's new money-laundering facilities were two Americans, Steven Kalish and Bruce Ritch, who had $12 million to be laundered. They were introduced to the bank by three close associates of Noriega, who claimed that for a 12 percent cut, they could collect money from Florida, transport it to Panama and make deposits in the bank. Kalish and Ritch accepted the deal, and they were taken to see Awan with their cash following behind them in an armored van. They opened three accounts in the name of Frank Brown, a pseudonym for Kalish. "Brown" had a passport, driver's license and credit cards to verify his new identity.

That night, Noriega entertained his American guests at his mansion in Altos del Golf, and Kalish made him a present of a case containing $300,000 in cash. The following morning, this money was deposited in BCCI in an account for Noriega under the colorful name "Zorro." Kalish continued to ingratiate himself with Noriega; he allegedly helped the Panamanian leader buy a Boeing 727 for his armed forces and a helicopter for smuggling out drugs.

The Panamanian operation flourished for three years. In the course of one month, drug launderers brought $300 million into Panama. Much of this went into local banks, but BCCI took $50 million. BCCI's commission on the deal was $1 million. Noriega's cut allegedly was $15 million.

A particular star of the Panamanian operation was the Colon branch of BCCI, whose manager, Wilfredo Glasse, reported receiving $30 million in a single week from a group of drug-money-launderers. Five days later, another $9 million came in—but the bank was so busy counting the $30 million worth of notes that it had to stick the new money in the vault.

Financially, the bank did very well on the Panamanian operation. BCCI allowed these customers to borrow only up to 80 percent against the money they deposited, enabling the bank to profit from the interest on the rest. The bankers themselves also did well on personal commissions from their associations with the drug kingpins. Awan, for example, was able to buy a $700,000 house even though he officially earned only around $60,000 a year.

BCCI strengthened its Central American presence in 1983, when it bought Banco Mercantil, a Colombian bank with branches in Medellin and Cali, centers of the cocaine trade. At the time, the Colombian press praised BCCI for bailing out the struggling bank, which was renamed Banco de

Credito y Comercio de Colombia and staffed with aggressive BCCI managers. But BCCI wanted the bank for its customer base, which included drug smuggler and launderer Pablo Escobar, who claimed to have been introduced to Noriega by Cuba's Fidel Castro and U.S. fugitive Robert Vesco. Escobar was one of the leading players in the Medellin cartel, the largest gang of Colombian drug growers and dealers, which takes its infamous name from the industrial city in Colombia's Andes.

Colombia was a canny expansion move for BCCI. Its trade in drugs is vast, involving billions of dollars a year in revenue. Together with a smaller cartel in Cali, Medellin is reputed to account for the production and shipment of some 60 to 70 percent of Colombia's cocaine. This provided still more money-laundering opportunities for BCCI.

By 1985, however, the noose was tightening around Noriega's lawless operation in Panama. Noriega sought to appease American officials by raiding the main Panamanian banks in an operation run by American agents and dubbed Operation Pisces. Although this netted some $350 million, the money is thought to have gone straight into Noriega's coffers. The time was now ripe for the U.S. to mount its own direct assault on the drug-money-launderers: Operation C-Chase.

C-Chase was Mazur's idea. The veteran federal agent, who had worked for the Internal Revenue Service before joining Customs in 1983, had specialized in money-laundering cases for most of his career. Like others in law enforcement, he knew that the Central American drug cartels were using money-laundering services on an unprecedented scale, and he proposed a major attempt to infiltrate these operations over a long period of time. Discussions of the plan had begun as early as 1984, and by 1986, Operation C-Chase—named after a Tampa apartment complex called Caliber Chase, in which the Customs agents kept an undercover outpost—was underway. C-Chase was the largest operation ever undertaken by the Customs Service, and its every move was carefully documented on tape and film for later use in court.

BCCI was by no means an initial target of the C-Chase probe. The operation was aimed more at individuals who facilitated money-laundering by offering investment scams and other "front" businesses through which the dirty money could be passed. Such businesses dealt with banks as a matter of course, but there was no reason to believe, at the outset at least, that BCCI was operating illegally.

Mazur and the handful of other federal agents involved in the case set up a series of fake investment services, hotels, restaurants and other front companies to establish themselves as potential handlers of large amounts of cash. Using the name Robert Musella, Mazur went undercover as a businessman who ran a string of investment and mortgage companies that could be used to launder drug proceeds. Like the "Miami Vice" television series come to life, Mazur and the other agents fostered the illusion that they were wealthy, if shady, individuals by tooling around South Florida in luxury cars and even a Cessna Citation II jet—all seized from criminals in other operations. Several legitimate businesses also contributed services and facilities to add verisimilitude to the investigation.

The Operation C-Chase team made contact with the Medellin cartel via Tampa exporter Gonzalo Mora Jr. in December 1986. Mora, a one-time Colombian prosecutor, told the agents that he had been importing drug money into the United States for a long time under the guise of lentil shipments, but he said the group with which he worked was running short of places to put the cash. Mazur replied that he could oblige, because he was supported by a large organization with offices around the United States. To prove the point he took Mora to New York and introduced him to other purported members of the organization—actually more undercover Customs agents. Mora, suitably impressed, gave Mazur the business at a seven percent commission.

A short time later, Mora led Mazur to an even larger player in the drug trade. Roberto Baez Alcaino owned a jewelry shop in Los Angeles and was a major dealer in Colombian cocaine. Mazur met him in style, flying into Panama's international airport accompanied by his "fiancee," Kathleen Erickson, played by another undercover agent. The next day, Mora took Mazur and Erickson to a BCCI branch in Panama. He explained: "It is easy to work with them; they have branches all over the world and have no objection to receiving large amounts of cash."

Back in Tampa, Mazur visited BCCI's office to open an account. He told officials at the bank that he was a businessman with a large number of Colombian clients for whom he transferred funds. To anyone with any sophistication, that was a thinly disguised description of a drug-money-launderer, but the BCCI account officer didn't bat an eye. "At that very first meeting in February 1987, I was the recipient of what appeared to me to be a rather well-polished pitch by the officer that he could assist and the bank could assist in the secret transfers of funds," Mazur testified to a Senate subcommittee in late 1991, his identity hidden by a screen and his voice electronically altered to protect him in future undercover work.

The bank helped Mazur open an account in Panama without ever leaving Tampa. The agent said he found this unusual, but it was being made clear that BCCI was glad to have the kind of business he was offering and happy to help him conduct it smoothly:

> I was very surprised at the intense interest that BCCI had in demonstrating to me what the unique—what they felt unique—characteristics of their banking were and how it was that they could assist in the laundering of drug money. . . . I found it rather peculiar that the bank had such a polished marketing approach. . . . Everything fit with an institution that might have an ulterior motive for its [branch] locations.

Indeed, Mazur said, the BCCI officials suggested several different ways that money could be laundered through the bank and its branches abroad.

As in other instances, BCCI seemed to be doing little to maintain a law-abiding facade—when Mazur told Akbar Bilgrami, BCCI's manager for Panama, point-blank that his clients' funds came from cocaine sales, "Bilgrami told [Mazur] that he and the bank did not care where [Mazur's] money came from," according to an affidavit in the Tampa case. Mazur later said: "The fact that the monies were derived from the sales of drugs in the United States on behalf of very powerful drug loads in Colombia was something that ultimately became rather commonly discussed amongst the officers with whom I had contact in BCCI."

If it wasn't a target at the beginning of Operation C-Chase, BCCI was moving quickly into the Customs agents' crosshairs. The undercover operation expanded dramatically, collecting suitcases full of cash from Mora's operatives in cities around the U.S., then depositing it in American banks and finally sending it by cable to the account with BCCI in Panama. Mazur sent signed, blank checks to Mora in Medellin to allow the drug dealers to withdraw the money that had been deposited in the account. It was then further laundered through a friendly foreign exchange house—altogether, a typical money-laundering scheme. Because the checks were signed and blank, they could be passed through several hands, as if they were currency, before the name of the ultimate beneficiary was filled in. By then, they were virtually untraceable—and BCCI was happily making it all possible. Mazur testified that BCCI made about $250,000 in fees on the $14 million that the undercover Customs operation passed through the bank. More importantly to the bank, Mazur said, the money deposited on behalf of the drug dealers helped swell BCCI's coffers at a time when the bank desperately needed deposits—indeed, he said, BCCI used to urge him and other customers to substantially increase their deposits every six months, even for as little as 24 hours, when the auditors were looking more closely at BCCI's financial condition.

Not everything in Operation C-Chase went flawlessly. In one memorable incident, one of Mazur's Customs partners asked him to help run the recording equipment at a meeting with some subjects of the investigation. Mazur stationed himself in the closet of a small apartment near the Miami airport with the equipment, taped the meeting, let the agent and suspects leave, and then waited for the agent to return to pick up the tapes. But the agent returned with one of the suspects, who insisted on spending the night in the apartment—stranding Mazur in the closet. Mazur had to wait for the suspect to fall asleep before he could sneak out of the closet, across the apartment and through a window to escape.

To penetrate deeper into the Medellin organization, Mazur told Mora in November 1987 that he wanted to expand the scale of his money-laundering efforts for the cartel. Mora could not make the decision himself, but said he would contact his two immediate masters, Gerardo "Don Chepe" Moncada, one of the leaders of the Medellin cartel, and Rudolph Armbrecht, who ran Pablo Escobar's finances. Bigger deals meant more sophisticated laundering, and Mazur set up a meeting with Amjad Awan, BCCI's laundering expert. The two men met at the Carlos on the Grove Restaurant in Miami, and Mazur explained to Awan that these new clients would be "as important to Awan's bank as Lee Iacocca was to Chrysler, the only difference being that Iacocca sold cars and [these] clients sold cocaine."

Awan swallowed the bait, but said the laundering technique used by the Medellin barons was too risky. The bank officer told Mazur that he could offer a safer alternative. Cash would be collected and deposited in the U.S. and transferred electronically to France or London, where it would be used to buy certificates of deposit. These certificates would then be used as collateral to obtain loans, which would be wire-transferred to Panama to be credited to Mazur's account. Thus laundered, the money would be free for Mazur or his Medellin clients to tap.

In March 1988, Mazur and another undercover agent met with representatives of the Medellin cartel at the Hotel Cariari at San Jose in Costa Rica. The cartel's top man, Escobar, was absent, but his representative, Javier Ospina, attended along with Mora. The money-launderers occupied four suites at the hotel, one of San Jose's largest. When they met by the pool at six in the evening, Mazur explained the laundering arrangements to the druglords and the part BCCI would play. "BCCI is a very powerful bank," Mazur told them. "Our contact there [Awan] has great experience in dealing with VIPs, and he has also had many years as General Noriega's personal banker." That was enough to convince Ospina, who said the organizations he worked for had between $12 million and $20 million to launder.

Ospina and Mora were told that Armbrecht and Moncada or their representatives would need to go to London and Paris to open accounts at BCCI. In May 1988, the cartel godfathers had a final meeting at the bank's offices in South Florida to check the details of the laundering operation and to receive letters of introduction.

The Colombian party that eventually made it to Paris on May 22, 1988, included Mora and his wife; Armbrecht; and Ospina, representing Moncada and Escobar. The group was met at BCCI Paris by Nazir Chinoy, the manager of the Paris branch, accompanied by two colleagues: Ian Howard, who despite his name is a Pakistani, and Sibte Hassan. Chinoy explained to the men from the cartel how the system worked: Couriers carrying suitcases of dirty money would go to BCCI offices around America at a prearranged time and swap them with identical but empty suitcases carried by bank officials. The money would then be transferred by wire to BCCI in London with instructions to credit the Paris branch. They in turn would issue fixed-term certificates of deposit in the name of Armbrecht, who had opened three accounts at the branch. BCCI branches in the Cayman Islands and Nassau would create a loan guaranteed by these certificates of deposit, and the loan would then be transferred by cable to Panama and credited to Moncada and Mazur's company. Mazur would then send signed blank checks drawn on these funds to Mora.

The cartel's appreciation of Mazur's skills and laundering system increased, but the political situation in Panama was worsening as the United States cracked down on Noriega. Mazur suggested changing the system to cut out Panama, and Mora shifted his business, making Tampa and Europe the two focuses of the laundering system.

A complex new money loop was devised to beat regulators—who probably could not possibly check so many transactions in any event. All funds collected in the United States would be sent to Tampa by cable. They would then be wired to BCCI Luxembourg, through a New York bank. From Luxembourg the funds would go to London, where fixed-term certificates of deposit would be issued. The CDs would be used to guarantee loans made to different companies that the cartels controlled. The cartels would then move the borrowed money to accounts in Tampa, from which it would be sent to BCCI Uruguay. At this point the druglords could get their hands on the money either by going directly to the bank or by writing a check, which they could negotiate on the Colombian black market through foreign exchange dealers.

Central to the laundering system in London was Capcom Financial Services, the trading company that was run by the bank's former treasury manager, Syed Ziauddin Ali Akbar. Capcom was a handy vehicle for money-laundering, because its constant trading in commodities made it difficult to trace the many transactions into which tainted money could disappear. Much of the money laundered by BCCI apparently went through Capcom at one stage or another. Mazur shifted some of his business to Capcom in mid-1988 because he was told by Awan and Bilgrami that they planned to leave BCCI, taking some high-powered clients—including Mazur—with them to form a private bank in Miami under Capcom's auspices.

By summer 1988, however, Mazur's drug-dealing customers were getting nervous. The exposure of other federal money-laundering "stings" had made the drug dealers nervous about the legitimacy of Mazur's operation, and Sen. John Kerry (D-Mass.) had begun an investigation into money-laundering that was to include the issuance of a subpoena to

BCCI's Awan. What's more, the ever-suspicious Colombian cartel had assigned its own agents to conduct surveillance of the people laundering its money, and it was beginning to suspect that Mazur's operatives actually were law enforcement agents. Mazur was threatened with death, but he was able to convince the druglords that his operation was genuine.

Even BCCI was nervous about the large volume of drug money passing through its coffers. One overzealous bank clerk is reported to have told a bank executive, Bashir Shaikh, that some of the Mazur accounts were drug-related and should be closed. But Shaikh's response betrayed the bank's desperate greed for the drug money—to do so, he said, BCCI might as well shut down its entire Panama branch. Even Naqvi had been involved in discussions in Bogota about the legality of BCCI's money-laundering activities as early as 1984—but he had no intention of closing down such a lucrative source of business.

One hint that the federal agents were getting close was the September 1988 arrest of Alcaino, the Los Angeles jeweler and cocaine importer. Alcaino had become one of Mazur's best customers. A few months before, Alcaino told Mazur, who was visiting the Alcaino family's Pasadena mansion, that he wanted him to launder $500,000 so that he could build a covered tennis court and an underground garage for his two Rolls Royces and two Mercedes Benzes. To do so, Mazur created a number of companies through BCCI, which made "home improvement loans" to Alcaino.

In a further demonstration of the creative ways in which money could be laundered, Alcaino used Mazur's services to handle $50,000 in drug profits used to finance a super flyweight world title fight between Gilberto Roman and Sugar Baby Rojas in Miami in April 1988. Hundreds of screaming, flag-waving Colombians attended the bloody fight, which ended in a 12-round decision for Rojas over Roman, the champion. Behind the scenes, Mazur had accepted and deposited the drug money and then used it to make laundered loans to finance the fight.

But Alcaino was arrested five months later, following the seizure in Philadelphia of 2,400 pounds of cocaine packed into anchovy tins imported by his family's sardine company. The arrest ruffled some feathers among the cocaine cartel chiefs, who again had to be reassured that their dealings with Mazur were not threatened.

The Customs agents were, indeed, ready to pounce. Although Mazur wanted the investigation left open a little longer in an effort to catch more high-level BCCI executives, Customs officials made the decision to wrap it up in October 1988—both because two years is a long time to keep an undercover investigation a secret and, some critics have suggested, to provide a high-profile drug-money arrest to help George Bush on the eve of the 1988 presidential election. There also were indications that the druglords, suspecting that something was afoot, were starting to withdraw their money from Mazur's operation. BCCI, indeed, had warned its customers to lay low after the bank and Awan received subpoenas from Kerry's subcommittee in late summer.

The bachelor-party bust nabbed a handful of BCCI's officials and customers, and in the days after the sting, federal agents arrested others involved in the scheme. Indictments announced in the days following the arrests named BCCI itself, nine bank officers, including Awan, Bilgrami, Chinoy, Hassan and Howard, plus dozens of others not employed by the bank but allegedly involved in the laundering operation, including Capcom. They were charged with conspiracy to launder more than $32 million of the Medellin cartel's drug money through BCCI. The feds might have netted an even bigger fish, but Naqvi had warned a BCCI general manager not to attend the wedding or bachelor party because he didn't want such a high-ranking officer to be seen associating with people involved with illegal accounts.

Abedi and Naqvi turned immediately to BCCI's American lawyers, Clark Clifford and Robert Altman, for help with the case. They in turn assembled a veritable all-star team of legal help for the BCCI defendants, all paid for by the bank—at a final price of a whopping $21 million, including support services such as accountants and the copying of 100,000 documents involved in the case. On the face of it, the bank doesn't seem to have gotten much for its money; while there was initial talk of attempting an entrapment defense, in the end the bank itself decided to settle the charges with a guilty plea and a $14.8 million fine. The bank officials went to trial, were found guilty and were sentenced to up to 12 years and seven months in jail. Awan, for instance, got 12 years and was fined $100,000; Armbrecht got 12 years, seven months and a $200,000 fine.

But some cynical observers suggest that the millions in legal fees were well spent. Almost from the moment the plea bargain was announced, there was debate over whether the bank had been treated too leniently, even though the fine was a record. Justice Department officials defended the agreement by arguing that there were indications that the judge in the case would severely reduce any fine, but some critics suggested that Clifford and Altman and the high-powered legal team had again worked their magic. "There wasn't a single influence peddler who wasn't being used to work this case," former Customs commissioner William von Raab later complained. "The result is that senior U.S. policy-level officials were constantly under the impression that BCCI was probably not that bad because all these good guys that they play golf with all the time were representing" the bank.

In one apparent effort to derail the investigation even before the indictments, Altman advised Awan to leave the U.S. for Paris after the bank executive was subpoenaed by Sen. Kerry's subcommittee. Altman said he advised Awan to leave the United States because of death threats from Noriega and drug dealers who feared Awan's testimony. Mazur, however, later said that he was unaware of any threats and that Awan had told him he had been asked to leave the country specifically to avoid the subpoena. Any other suggestion, he pointedly told Kerry's subcommittee in 1991, "appears to be a recent invention." Altman denied that there had been any impropriety in his advice to Awan.

In retrospect, there is little doubt that the federal prosecutors were overmatched and outgunned by the gargantuan defense effort; in one meeting, a government lawyer found himself outnumbered 23-to-1 by attorneys for the defense. Preparing for trial and keeping up with the waves of pre-trial motions filed by the defense before the BCCI guilty plea in early 1990 so distracted the feds that almost no effort was made to digest and follow up on the mountain of leads into other potential cases that C-Chase had produced—among them more information on alleged wrongdoing by BCCI and Capcom. During this "time out," as Mazur later described it, tens of thousands of documents went unread by investigators and hundreds of tapes of wiretaps and witness interviews went untranscribed as the short-staffed federal agents and prosecutors worked on trial preparation.

Among other things, little effort was made to follow up on a piece of information that Mazur had gleaned from Awan during the C-Chase investigation: that BCCI owned First American Bank in Washington. A grand jury was briefly convened in 1989 to investigate this allegation, but the probe was dropped because investigative resources were needed to prepare for the money-laundering trial.

"I felt as though we were somewhat of a reconnaissance squad that had been out in the middle of the desert and counted the enemy, sent word back to the fort that we needed some help, and waited and waited and fought and fought, but no help came," Mazur said later. He became so frustrated by the failure to follow up on the many leads that he finally quit the Customs Service and went to work as an undercover agent for the Drug Enforcement Agency, leaving behind a strongly worded letter of protest to his former bosses at Customs. "The outcome of the [C-Chase] case, while notable, was considerably less than what it could have been," Mazur wrote:

> The indictment of additional defendants and the seizure of substantially more drug proceeds was lost, directly as a result of the application of inade-

quate resources. . . . If the followup investigation is well-organized, supported and coordinated, it should produce the most significant money-laundering prosecution ever achieved in the world community.

Instead, it was nearly three years after the C-Chase arrests in October 1988 before the federal government brought additional charges in the case.

Chapter 11

Noriega

Among the loose ends left by the termination of Operation C-Chase was the probe into the bank's relationship with Noriega. In spite of Altman's suggestion, Amjad Awan did not go to Paris after receiving his Senate subpoena in the summer of 1988. He actually appeared before Sen. John Kerry's subcommittee in a closed hearing just a week before the Tampa arrests, where he testified frankly about his role as Noriega's personal banker at BCCI. "I made an effort to cultivate him," he told the committee. "When he came to the United States, I used to take care of his expenses here." Together with the Tampa indictments, Awan's testimony demonstrated Noriega's strong links to BCCI, a relationship that investigators were to piece together more completely later.

Documents recovered in 1991 from BCCI's defunct Washington office revealed that the bank treated Noriega like a most valued customer. Whenever Noriega traveled to the United States, for instance, he received the red-carpet treatment, with BCCI paying his hotel and limousine bills with tens of thousands of dollars of checks drawn on the Washington office's account at First American.

As befitting a head of state, Noriega went first-class: He stayed at New York's luxurious Helmsley Palace Hotel and was transported by limousine, all paid for by BCCI, which also provided him with thousands of dollars in spending money out of the Washington account. "Cash: For Mr. Noriega" was a common entry in the Washington office's checkbook ledger during 1986 and 1987. It is not clear whether Noriega reimbursed BCCI for these expenditures.

Payments also were made out of the Washington account into Noriega's accounts at BCCI's London branches, and money also apparently was transferred to BCCI's Panama, New York and Los Angeles offices for Noriega's use, according to information found by investigators. It is not known what these payments—as much as $60,000 at one time—were for. BCCI, through Awan, also appears to have been deeply involved in handling Noriega's personal finances—apparently using Panamanian government money to do so. Awan would fly to Panama monthly to review Noriega's account, once bringing back with him a cash deposit of several hundred thousand dollars from the strongman. For the record, it is thought that Noriega's annual salary never exceeded $50,000 during his 28 years with the National Guard and the Panamanian Defense Force, yet it is alleged that he managed to amass a net worth in excess of $300 million.

With help from the bank, Noriega apparently systematically plundered his country's treasury. On January 19, 1982, it is alleged, Awan accepted instructions opening an account in Noriega's name but using more than $1.3 million of Panamanian National Guard funds. The instructions specified that the details of the account—No. 03002781—should be kept secret at all times, and Awan later described it as a "secret account, a secret service account." Only Noriega was authorized to give instructions about the handling of the money. Most of the deposits to the account were made by Noriega in cash, and Awan said the account balance later grew to as much as $25 million.

Where was the money coming from? Allegedly, some came from the Panamanian treasury. Much of the rest, apparently, were the proceeds of payments made to Noriega for services he rendered to various shady friends and business associates. No opportunity, it seems, went begging when Noriega wanted to make an extra few million dollars.

On one occasion he allegedly instructed the former chief of the Panamanian Air Force to sell eight military aircraft for $7 million and pass the money on to Noriega. On another occasion, the man who had pledged himself to "honestly" exercise his power as leader of Panama ordered that $800,000 be diverted from a government fund set up to help struggling Panamanian farmers. It is alleged that Noriega then instructed the general manager of the Banco de Desarrollo Agropecuario to endorse the checks and bring him the cash. This bank proved to be an exceptionally rich source of cash for Noriega, who is said to have removed more than $1 million from its vaults in this way.

BCCI's willingness to accept customers and money without asking questions had made it the natural bank for Noriega, and it handled the delivery and movement of so much hard currency in as cavalier a way as it conducted all its business, according to a report by Jack Blum, a former investigator for Sen. Kerry. "BCCI stayed out of the cash-handling business because it was too expensive," Blum wrote. "The bank did not use armored cars to handle the transfer of excess cash." Instead, Blum wrote, a BCCI employee "carried the cash [from Noriega] himself in the trunk of his car and did not worry about being robbed. He said that Panama at the time was quite safe."

Once the money was in his personal account, Noriega had it laundered. Between 1982 and 1986, money was regularly transferred to BCCI's Cromwell Road branch in London (account No. 03016120), until February 1986, when $3.3 million was moved to another BCCI branch, Edgware Road, at which account No. 03001734 had been opened for the dictator.

Another Edgware Road account (No. 01010571)—ostensibly belonging to the Panamanian Defense Forces—was used for personal expenses such as the payment of Noriega's own Visa cards, as well as those of his wife, Felicidad, and daughters Thays, Sandra and Lorena, who were regular visitors to the United States. Between February 1986 and January 1988 the family managed to run up credit card bills of $223,281.73 in such American stores as Toys R Us, Saks Fifth Avenue and Jordan Marsh—not the sort of shopping the Panamanian Defense Forces would reasonably have been expected to undertake.

According to court documents, the shopping sprees took the family from Panama to Las Vegas, Tokyo, Hawaii and Venezuela during the summer of 1987. Sandra Noriega managed to charge $24,946.43 on her gold card in November 1987 alone, including $5,000 at Christian Dior in Paris. The case against BCCI is that the bank was well aware of the personal nature of these expenditures. Shopping wasn't all of it: some of the money in this account allegedly was used by Noriega to fund payoffs to Panamanian politicians.

Noriega's money was moved regularly around BCCI's branch network and occasionally into other banks, apparently to avoid suspicion about the accounts and to provide still more laundering. Both Edgware Road accounts were moved to Luxembourg, first into one account and then into another (No. 01164492); the balance in February 1988 was $14.9 million. But the funds scarcely had a chance to earn more than a few thousand dollars' interest there before they were on the move again, this time to the Union Bank of Switzerland in Zurich and the Deutsche Sudamerikanische Bank in Hamburg, Germany.

Just in case anyone at the Panamanian National Guard dared to check on the state of the funds, the National Bank of Panama opened an account for Noriega under an assumed corporate name, reportedly Finley International, and allegedly showed a false deposit of $23 million to cover the actual whereabouts of the money. The BCCI-Capcom connection also is said to have come into play in laundering Noriega's money, allegedly with the personal knowledge of top BCCI executives Swaleh Naqvi and Dildar Rizvi. Noriega was given an account at Capcom, under the Finley International name, and the money allegedly was laundered through Capcom commodity accounts in its journey around the BCCI system.

In September 1988, the money was again traveling the world: From Germany, the balance of more than $12 million moved to an account at the Middle East Bank in London under the Finley cover name, to be joined by a little over $11 million from the Swiss bank. The money spent the next six months oscillating between London and New York, although most of it went through Capcom rather than through BCCI itself. All the time, BCCI was making funds available to the Noriega family. It is claimed that other funds were channeled through BCCI accounts in the name of Noriega's wife and daughters in the bank's Sloane Street and Hyde Park Corner branches in London and at BCCI's Leadenhall Street headquarters.

While Noriega's money was on the move, the strongman himself was on the run from the law. In February 1988, Noriega was indicted in Miami for drug and money-laundering offenses, including an alleged conspiracy to import more than 1 million tons of marijuana into the United States. The chief witness in the case said he had paid Noriega almost $1 million in bribes between 1983 and 1984 in return for a diplomatic passport, a multimillion-dollar letter of credit and safe passage for large quantities of hashish. Noriega also was charged with accepting $4.6 million to allow Colombian ships containing over 4,000 pounds of cocaine to pass through Panama to the United States. It also was alleged that he permitted the Colombians to establish a cocaine processing plant in Panama.

The U.S. government caught up with Noriega in 1989, mounting an unprecedented military invasion of Panama to overthrow his government and return him the United States for trial. For good measure, Noriega, who has languished ever since in the Municipal Correctional Center in Miami, also faces a catalog of murder, theft and corruption chrages. In the legal jargon of one of the indictments, Noriega and others conspired "unlawfully to convert and cause to be converted to his or their own use money, funds, property and other valuable assets belonging to the plaintiff [Panama]." In 1991, the U.S. expanded its original indictment of BCCI in Tampa to bring racketeering charges against Naqvi, former BCCI treasury and Capcom chief Syed Ziauddin Ali Akbar and other top BCCI executives for their part in allegedly supporting Noriega's money-laundering activities at the bank. The indictment issued the same week that Noriega went on trial in Miami on charges of taking bribes from the Medellin cartel to facilitate the trafficking of drugs charged that:

> The BCCI enterprise was a group of banking and financial institutions whose relevant policies . . . involved the knowing quest for, and acceptance of, narcotics proceeds and the laundering of these proceeds, as well as the acceptance and laundering of the criminally derived property of Manuel Antonio Noriega, including narcotics proceeds.

Panama also has brought charges against Noriega and BCCI, whose disregard for the law when conducting business is succinctly summarized in one of the indictments:

> The operations of the BCCI Group in its dealings with Manuel Noriega constitute a racketeering operation of unparalleled scope, international in its reach and totally ruthless in its evasion of banking, fraud, disclosure and common and code laws of numerous nations, including the United States.

Panama charges that BCCI maintained its branch office in Miami "for the purpose of expediting these and other transfers of funds" and that Awan's position as regional manager and as Noriega's personal banker were "essential to these transfers."

Chapter 12

Bailing Out the Bank

The money-laundering accusations, while dramatic, barely scratched the surface of BCCI's wrongdoing. Regulators and law enforcers were beginning to catch on to the magnitude of what the bank had been up to all these years. But inside the bank, at its top levels at least, there was knowledge of an even greater problem than anyone on the outside might have imagined: by the time of the Tampa indictments, in late 1988, BCCI was on the verge of financial collapse.

The bank's problems were not wholly a secret. Bank of America, an early investor, had pulled out of BCCI in the late 1970s because of its executives' private misgivings about BCCI's loan practices and other operations, although they scarcely knew the half of it. BCCI also was considered something of a pariah in the world financial community, in spite of its many efforts to win acceptance. In part, this may have been the result of a sort of xenophobia—the conservative world of banking did not take kindly to the Third World upstart in its midst, and thus did not take BCCI very seriously even though it had grown to be one of the world's largest banks. At the same time, there were whispers that BCCI was not being run by the same standards as other banks, and as a result most international banks tried to minimize their dealings with the bank—although Bank of America continued to trade with BCCI on a large scale right up until it was shut down.

Some of these misgivings spilled over to regulators, although there is little evidence that much action was taken as a result. Still, hints were being dropped around the financial world that all was not right with BCCI. By 1984 Bank of England officials were quietly putting out the word that BCCI was best avoided. On one occasion, the chairman of a bank with links to the Middle East was given a confidential piece of advice by a senior Bank of England supervisor to steer clear of BCCI.

There were plenty of other signs that all might not be well with BCCI's operations. For example, police officers in Britain investigating a mid-1980s bank failure had found that a number of their suspects had accounts at BCCI, which stonewalled investigators when they asked questions about the funds. There was little or no followup about BCCI's involvement in the bank failure, although one source suggested that in the course of the investigation, arrests of senior BCCI officials had been considered.

A scandal in India in 1986 provided some more early smoke, although quick action by BCCI succeeded in stifling the fire. It may have been an anomaly that BCCI was able to do business in India, given its Pakistani roots, Abedi's closeness to Pakistan's leading politicians and the historic political hostility between India and Pakistan. But Abedi had ingratiated himself with Indian Prime Minister Indira Gandhi, using his family connections with the rajah of Mahmudabad and possibly even bribes. The bank was allowed to set up a branch in Bombay in 1985, shortly after Gandhi's assassination. But, within a year, BCCI ran afoul of Indian authorities. The allegations had a familiar ring—money-laundering and links with espionage.

According to the former director-general of India's Revenue Intelligence, B. V. Kumar, BCCI tried to get around the country's foreign exchange regulations, which prohibited anyone from sending foreign currency out of India without prior permission of the Reserve Bank of India. Kumar said BCCI staff members were engaged in "some underhand dealings" and that the bank had violated India's foreign exchange and smuggling laws by selling unsigned and unrecorded travelers checks to people leaving the country to enable them to dodge foreign exchange controls. Revenue Intelligence officers raided the BCCI branch in Bombay, and its general manager and three members of his staff were arrested and put in jail. BCCI in London reacted with urgency, even panic, and sent over Nadir Rahim, the executive who oversaw the bank's Indian operations. He hired Bombay's top lawyer, who had the BCCI men quickly released and the charges dropped.

Rahim told the Indian authorities that the alleged violations were a misunderstanding, and further, that BCCI had been entrapped by law enforcement officials. The bank had been supplying travelers checks to travel agents for pilgrims going to Mecca, and Rahim claimed that the Revenue Intelligence agents had unfairly moved in on the busy operation before the checks could be properly signed and recorded in the travelers' passports. The bank would later be accused of improperly exporting travelers checks from Brazil to Paraguay. Those charges also were dropped.

Indian Customs subsequently investigated charges that the bank had assisted in other breaches of Indian foreign exchange controls. Indians were obliged to return unused foreign currency to the Bank of India when they returned to the country, but it appeared that BCCI was buying back the surplus at a hefty premium.

BCCI also got involved in the underground network run largely by expatriate Indians living in Hong Kong who used the bank to slide illegally obtained money past the exchange controls by buying and selling Indian companies. "We had the corporate raider, non-resident Indians who were trying to take over big corporations in India," according to Kumar. "They had their deposits in Hong Kong, and against that deposit the advances were being given in India. So actually it was their own money that they were borrowing and the bank had no risk at all. In other words, tainted money deposited in Hong Kong was used through Bombay."

Naturally suspicious of BCCI's pro-Pakistani political leanings, Indian officials also claimed that the bank was operating an undercover espionage network for the Pakistani government, according to Kumar. He said members of BCCI's staff were put under surveillance "to establish what their real business was about, and the Indian government was informed. It was only a watch-and-learn operation by the authorities. We alerted and cautioned the government agencies. Once you know that a person is doing this kind of work, you caution others and say beware of this kind of bank. The alert was given. These people were helping to spy on India."

Kumar said he was in touch at this time with other international intelligence and security services, which may have included the CIA, and Kumar confirms that he met with U.S. Customs Commissioner William von Raab, who shared with him his deep suspicions about the bank.

Authorities in Luxembourg, where BCCI's holding company was officially incorporated, also had doubts about the bank in the mid-1980s. In 1985, the Luxembourg Monetary Institute decided to commission BCCI auditor Price Waterhouse to carry out a detailed investigation of the bank's operations. BCCI hid most of its malfeasance from the auditors, but Price Waterhouse still found significant losses that had gone unrecorded. Most of these, however, were attributed to incompetence by BCCI's managers. Although they did not have a reputation as the world's most stringent bank regulators, the Luxembourg authorities were generally suspicious about the speed of BCCI's growth and were convinced that the bank did not have the management to control it. BCCI's assets had increased almost eight-fold in seven years, from $2.2 billion in 1977 to $16 billion in 1984, and even the best-run organization experiencing that sort of growth would creak at the seams.

In reality, BCCI was bursting at the seams. Only brilliantly deviant management had kept BCCI's house of cards from collapsing already. The huge losses from the bank's treasury operation had badly eroded its financial foundation in 1985, and the mounting collection of bad loans to customers like the Gokal brothers' Gulf Group were further draining BCCI's coffers. Only the constant search for new deposits—including those from drug dealers and the illegal acquisitions of the U.S. banks—and creative manipulation of accounts were keeping BCCI afloat.

The losses from the treasury operation were serious enough to have attracted the attention of Luxembourg authorities by 1986, and Abedi was told to clean up the bank's act. As a stopgap, he raided the BCCI pension fund in the Cayman Islands for $150 million, and the bank's nefarious practice of account manipulation was ratcheted up another couple of notches. But Abedi needed to look elsewhere for a more lasting fix.

Abedi turned for help to Saudi financier Khalid bin Salim bin-Mahfouz, who controlled the National Commercial Bank of Saudi Arabia and had many other investments in that nation. The bin-Mahfouz family agreed to help bail the bank out, but at great cost. Abedi had made a strategic blunder that left him little negotiating room with his new benefactors: He already had assured Luxembourg officials that he could obtain the new financing and that they should not worry any further about BCCI's solvency. When that information slipped out—perhaps through Abedi's own bragging—the bin-Mahfouz representatives had BCCI in the palm of their hands. Said a close associate of Abedi:

> I differed with him over the need to find new funds, since we could have stopped expanding and begun consolidating. But he had made the promise [to the Luxembourg officials]. We were negotiating with Mahfouz's lawyers when the capital terms were being discussed. Because Abedi had committed himself, they knew the commitments, so they dictated the terms.

After a hard fight, Abedi gave the bin-Mahfouz family an indemnity against loss—if the family decided to sell its shares in the bank, BCCI would agree to buy them back at the original price or more. Thus warrantied, the family began buying BCCI stock in 1986. Part of the deal, apparently, included a sham transaction involving shares in First American Bank's parent company, CCAH. In late July 1986— a couple of days after Clifford and Altman had bought their shares in CCAH—the bin-Mahfouz family purchased more than 22,000 shares from Mashriq Holding Co., one of the alleged BCCI fronts that held stock in CCAH. Since those shares actually belonged to BCCI, investigators said, that provided BCCI with a badly needed $135 million cash injection.

At first, the bin-Mahfouz family purchased 10 percent of BCCI's stock, providing the bank with a new round of capital, but then it increased its holding to 20 percent, and Abedi started to worry that the rescue would turn into a predatory raid. It is now believed that the family wanted at least 30 percent of the shares, which might have given the bin-Mahfouz clan control of BCCI. Abedi's guarantee that the bank would buy back the bin-Mahfouz shares at any time was coming back to haunt him, since the guarantee was underwritten by ICIC, the BCCI affiliate that served as "the bank within the bank." ICIC did not have enough resources to buy back the bin-Mahfouz shares, putting the family in the driver's seat. "It was too big a commitment for ICIC," an Abedi associate later said. "Abedi's commitment laid the bank wide open. . . . It was a very rash promise."

The bin-Mahfouz family stopped at 20 percent, but the deal sealed the future of the bank as an independent entity, since from the moment the family took over, it sought to oust Abedi. The family members had him over a barrel, because they knew that even if he didn't like them, he would have to make sure they did not lose money on their investment. Abedi was in desperate straits. His dream for the bank depended on his keeping control, but the money was draining away and he could see the bin-Mahfouz plan to gain creeping control over BCCI. "At one stage, Mahfouz wanted to buy the whole thing," Abedi's associate said."That scared Abedi, who didn't want to part with BCCI."

At the same time, Abedi's health began to falter, probably not coincidentally. Fighting off the powerful and predatory Saudi family had taken its toll. His bank was failing financially, and many other pressures, accumulated over the years, also were besieging BCCI. Ernst & Whinney, one of BCCI's two auditing firms, resigned in early 1987, apparently in protest over the bank's shoddy internal accounting practices. That left BCCI's other auditor, Price Waterhouse, to solely oversee the bank's books.

A few months later, regulators had begun to mobilize, at long last. In December 1987, an international "college" of regulators was formed to look into BCCI, comprising officials from Britain, Luxembourg, the Cayman Islands, Hong Kong, France, the Netherlands and the United Arab Emirates. By banding together, the regulators hoped, they could have more clout over BCCI than any one nation acting alone.

Agha Hasan Abedi suffered his first heart attack in February 1988. As usual, his workload had been heavy, but he insisted on flying to New York for a staff meeting. Nadir Rahim, the bank's head of human resources, tried to intervene. "When he was leaving the office, I was aware that he wasn't well and I got up from my desk and I said, 'You are not looking well. Why don't you cancel your visit to New York?' " But Abedi brushed him aside, saying people were expecting him and there was no question of cancellation. He flew to New York in the BCCI corporate jet and returned overnight to put in a full day's work in the office working on decisions about staff postings.

At five o'clock that evening, looking close to exhaustion, Abedi prepared to fly to Lahore, where he had arranged a dinner with President Zia in honor of their old friend, Abu Dhabi's Sheik Zayed. Abedi always insisted on personally meeting his most important customer when he arrived in Pakistan. But his eyes were bloodshot, he was running a fever and everyone in the office seemed to be aware of the risks. Again Rahim, feeling responsible for his president's health, spoke up:

> I felt he was taking chances with his health, and I wasn't wrong. He again said, "Mr. Rahim, you know that there is no way I cannot go. It is the president of Pakistan, it's a command performance. I can't not be there."

Abedi arrived in Lahore, and as he was dressing for dinner he collapsed with a heart attack. President Zia and Sheik Zayed rushed to his hospital bedside, and they were aghast at the machines being used to keep their banker alive. For the sheik, it must have been an even greater shock as he looked down on the man who had guided him through the financial jungles of the world and advised him on his investments. Theirs was no ordinary banker-customer relationship.

The sheik ordered that his own plane, equipped with the latest life-support technology, should remain in Lahore. It was a life-saving decision. Abedi's personal physician, in consultation with a heart-transplant expert sent to Pakistan by former President Carter, decided that Abedi would be dead within hours unless he was moved directly to London. He was carried there aboard the sheik's jet with the BCCI corporate 727 flying close behind. They arrived in the middle of the night and Abedi underwent immediate surgery.

Another heart attack, a stroke and other operations over the next few months—including a heart transplant, an operation to repair a detached retina and surgery to improve breathing difficulties—all left Abedi an enfeebled man. On top of everything, his vocal chords had been damaged and his speech seriously impaired. The inspiration and driving force behind BCCI was now confined to a wheelchair, scarcely able to communicate and thus shielded from the storms of controversy that were about to break around him.

Chapter 13

Going Down in Flames

If anybody from outside the bank should have known the depth of BCCI's problems, it was Price Waterhouse. As one of the bank's auditors from the beginning—and the sole auditor since 1987—Price Waterhouse should have had access to enough detail about BCCI's books and the bank's worsening financial condition to raise red flags to management and regulators on many different occasions over the years.

But for one reason or another—in the wake of the scandal, theories included incompetence, deliberately turning a blind eye and lack of accurate information from management—Price Waterhouse had missed the bulk of the bank's problems. Sure, it had raised questions about the treasury trading activities and the loan exposure to the Gokal family—billion-dollar problems far too large for anyone to cover up, no matter how artfully the books were juggled. But by and large, Price Waterhouse continued to give BCCI a mostly clean bill of health even as the bank was virtually insolvent.

A November 1989 audit report by Price Waterhouse is illustrative. While it gently chided the bank's management for not sufficiently increasing provisions for loan losses, Price Waterhouse also wrote:

> Overall the bank has performed reasonably over the past year, considering the significant repercussions

that could have resulted from the U.S. [money-laundering] indictment.

The bottom line, according to the auditors: a $9 million profit over the nine months ended Sept. 30, 1989, an improvement over the $49 million loss the year before. It was a report that might have belonged to any big-name international bank.

As usual, the situation behind the scenes was much different. Two days after the end of the period covered by the report, the bin-Mahfouz family, apparently working off of better data than the auditors, walked away from its attempt to bail out the bank. The family exercised its guaranteed option to sell its 20 percent stake back to the bank, and BCCI's management, deftly sidestepping what could have been a fatal buyback requirement, convinced Abedi's old friends in Abu Dhabi to purchase the bin-Mahfouz shares.

Various members of the Abu Dhabi royal family and government paid a total of $596 million for the bin-Mahfouz family's 20 percent stake, raising the percentage of BCCI stock held by various Abu Dhabi entities—but ultimately controlled by Sheik Zayed—to more than 55 percent. Over the next few months, Abedi arranged the sale of other bank stock to Abu Dhabi—often in exchange for fresh capital infusions—so that, combined with earlier stakes, Abu Dhabi owned more than 77 percent of BCCI by April 1990. By selling to Abu Dhabi many of the shares he had controlled secretly, Abedi was giving up his precious hold on BCCI's ownership in an effort to salvage his crippled creation.

Sheik Zayed himself played only a small part in the purchases. His son Khalifa bought most of the shares, some 35 percent of BCCI's equity, and the Abu Dhabi government's finance department took 29 percent. The Abu Dhabi Investment Authority chipped in for 9 percent. The sheik himself had 3.5 percent, but it is generally believed he formally or informally exercised control over most of the rest held in Abu Dhabi's name. Among other remaining shareholders, BCCI's own ICIC Foundation held 7 per cent of the bank that was technically its parent.

Abedi, his health poor, was a virtual recluse, and his involvement in the bank's management was limited. Swaleh Naqvi, his deputy, took over most of the bank's operations. But Naqvi, it appeared, did not have the same absolute command over BCCI's affairs as Abedi. Cracks were beginning to show in BCCI's healthy facade, and Price Waterhouse, at long last, was beginning to see them.

It's not clear what finally tipped Price Waterhouse off, but one factor may have been what happened when it asked BCCI's largest customers to confirm the amounts they had in the bank or on loan as of the end of 1989—a routine step in the annual audit. In the past, Price Waterhouse had asked bank officials to obtain these confirmations, which had always come back favorably—perhaps not surprisingly. This time, however, Price Waterhouse sent confirmation requests to the customers itself—with surprising results.

The rulers of two small Arab nations, Fujairah and Ajman, who were listed on the BCCI books as having borrowed a total of $270 million to buy stock in CCAH, First American Bank's parent company, told Price Waterhouse they were unaware of the loans. Other customers also questioned the information the auditors had gleaned from BCCI's books. On February 14, 1990, Price Waterhouse official wrote a concerned letter to Naqvi asking for an explanation of these and other irregularities it had come across:

> We place heavy reliance upon confirmation procedures, and where disagreements do arise, we need to investigate the reasons why these occur and the implications. . . . I am concerned about the number of outstanding issues on major accounts and the time that it may take to resolve them satisfactorily.

The auditors also took their concerns to BCCI's chief financial officer, Masihur Rahman, who received a call at home one weekend from a top official at Price Waterhouse, urgently asking for an appointment to talk about the 1989 audit. "I went to their offices," Rahman later recalled:

> and they produced for me a whole list of what they thought were irregularities, illegalities, misuse of funds. . . . They presented this list of huge problems whose potential loss could be a billion-plus, so I said, "I will not receive a casual presentation like this from the [Price Waterhouse] partners. You make the same presentation to the chief executive and to the board." So this was arranged.

In the wake of the scandal, many observers were skeptical that Rahman, as chief financial officer, should have been so surprised by what the auditors had found about the bank's financial shenanigans; he, in turn, claims that he relied on Price Waterhouse to keep watch on the bank's finances and blames the accountants for belatedly discovering the problems. Whatever the reason, the BCCI board apparently was as shocked by the revelations as Rahman and appointed him to head a task force of senior executives to look more closely at BCCI's financial condition in tandem with Price Waterhouse.

The results were astounding. The bank that the auditors had been giving good grades for years suddenly took on a much different appearance. On March 14, 1990, Price Waterhouse gave the task force and BCCI's directors a first glimpse at its findings. Virtually all of the news was bad— very bad. The auditors wrote that nothing at the bank was what it seemed. Loans that had been on BCCI's books for years as assets had never existed or now were being denied by the alleged borrowers.

The rulers of the Arab states of Ajman and Fujairah, for example, rejected out of hand responsibility for $270 million worth of loans that were listed in BCCI's files under their names. The bank also seemed to have come into possession of more than 100,000 shares of First American Bank's parent company, CCAH, which had previously been listed as collateral on loans to various customers but now appeared to be an illegal ownership stake—the loans, it appeared, were bogus. Large customers who were supposed to confirm their loan exposures each year had not been heard from in years, it turned out. Account confirmations that previously had been provided to the auditors by BCCI executives apparently were false.

Time after time, the auditors found loans for which there seemed to be no documentation. "The files maintained by the bank are sparse and do not in our view support the level of lending," Price Waterhouse wrote:

> There is a general lack of third-party evidence or customer acknowledgement. . . . Loan agreements have not been drawn up or signed for many of the loans.

Frighteningly, some of the worst situations involved people who were major customers or shareholders of BCCI. "There are no loan agreements with the customer or formalized repayment terms," Price Waterhouse said of BCCI's transactions with Kamal Adham, the former head of Saudi intelligence who was a major customer and shareholder in CCAH.

At least BCCI knew how to get in touch with Adham. It had somehow lost track of another big customer, Saudi businessman Abdul Raouf Khalil, who was listed as owing BCCI $150 million. "Since the cessation of A.R. Khalil's treasury trading relationship with BCCI in 1985, there has been little, or no, direct contact with this borrower," Price Waterhouse reported. Attempts by the bank to reach Khalil had been to no avail, even though Khalil was a prominent business executive in the Middle East and by no means inaccessible. Still, there were indications that bank officials had continued to manipulate his accounts for their own ends. According to the Federal Reserve Board, most of the loans to Khalil were sham transactions through which BCCI secretly owned First American stock in Khalil's name. The frustrated auditors wrote:

> There are no signed loan agreements with the customer. There is no correspondence with the customer. There are no net worth statements or cash flow information. There is no documentation.

The books on loans to such key customers as the bin-Mahfouz family and the Gokals also were a disaster. The bin-Mahfouzes may have generously helped bail out the bank, but that didn't stop BCCI from playing games with their accounts behind their backs. The bank apparently had created $146 million for itself by putting it on the books as loans to the bin-Mahfouzes, than shifting the money elsewhere in BCCI. "The drawdowns of $146 million have not been supported by requests from the customer, nor were payment instructions received from the customer," Price Waterhouse reported. "The purposes of the lending is not known. There are no loan agreements, promissory notes or security documentation for the advance."

Things were even messier when it came to the Gokals. The auditors found dozens of companies, apparently spinoffs of the Gulf Group, that had borrowed money from the bank, but on which there was little or no documentation. At least two of these accounts had been misidentified on BCCI's books as belonging to other companies that had no ties to the Gokals or the bank. The multiple accounts indicated that BCCI—apparently under Naqvi's direction, it would later be learned—had lent increasing amounts to the Gokals, contrary to good banking practice, by funneling the money through Gokal subsidiaries to hide the concentration of loans. The result was an extremely confusing and dangerous web of deceptive loan practices that left the auditors scratching their heads. "We cannot be sure of the extent of the Gulf Group lending," Price Waterhouse wrote, but it appeared to be at least $700 million, with sketchy collateral and long-overdue interest payments. Examining one corner of the

Gokal empire, the auditors' report took on a tone of exasperation: "What is the business of these companies? What is the relationship between these companies? Who controls these companies?"

Good questions all. As the spring of 1990 wore on, there were to be even more. Price Waterhouse had finally cracked the secrets of BCCI, and, perhaps motivated by embarrassment at being made to look so foolish for so long, the auditors pulled no punches.

Reports from Price Waterhouse cascaded into the bank during April 1990, each one worse than the one before. The modest profit seen after the first nine months of 1989 was an illusion; instead, Price Waterhouse reported, the bank had lost a massive $498 million in 1989. The bank's total assets had risen to $23.5 billion from $20.6 billion, but loan-loss provisions had jumped to $600 million from $145 million— and probably still were way too low. What's more, Price Waterhouse said that it was so unsure of the actual state of the bank's financial condition that it was refusing to sign off on BCCI's annual report for 1989—perhaps the ultimate expression of pique by auditors, and one that was bound to attract the attention of regulators and the public. BCCI could only forestall the auditors' actions by convincing them that the bank was on the road to recovery.

The accountants had finally awoken to the huge exposure to the Gokal brothers' Gulf Group, the string of disputed loans worth $870 million to CCAH and the equally doubtful loans worth $477 million to other BCCI shareholders. The Gokal problem was at the heart of the affair. For years, BCCI's accountants had gone along with Naqvi's ingenious ways of papering over the problems at the Gulf Group, but now they wanted some explanations out of Naqvi. Board meetings turned acrimonious as the directors grasped the size of the loans that were causing problems. Even more terrifying, there wasn't much they could do about it. If they called in the Gokal loans, they would have forced the collapse of the Gokal empire and with it the failure of BCCI.

The directors were "fooled by Naqvi ,who time and again came to the meetings with some new proposal to give the Gokals more credit," said one insider. These proposals purported to show that the family's main debt was being reduced, but "all the proposals were phony." This inside source said Price Waterhouse went along with Naqvi's evasiveness and "never adequately investigated what was really being suggested." Price Waterhouse also is said to have failed to check that credit lines were cleared and vital documents signed. "Price Waterhouse often told the directors that the loan was a big one, but never that it was a bad one," the insider said. The same applied to countless other loans that went unchecked but, because they were all kept just below $10 million, were not considered important enough to be discussed at the board level.

It was clear that the Gokals were spending BCCI money like water, failing to account for it and losing all management grip on their network of companies. What had been a drive for profitable growth in the early days had turned into a push for business at any price. Gulf Group head Abbas Gokal had also lost touch with his staff, either through delusions of grandeur or because he could no longer cope. It was now rare for managers who formerly had been treated as equals by Abbas to get to speak to him at all.

One manager who had a conversation with Gokal at this time mentioned that senior Gulf Group executives, including members of Gokal's own family, were "stealing blind." Gokal is reported to have said, cryptically:

> I don't mind people stealing from me, because if they are holding down a position which enables them to steal for themselves, then they're going to try very hard to hold that position. I will only allow them to stay in that position if they're making money for me. Therefore, by stealing for themselves, they're also stealing for me.

This paradoxical position made sense only if Gokal could control everything that was being stolen, and it quickly became obvious that he could not.

As far back as 1983, Gulf Group managers had discovered that when the company went to BCCI to increase its loan, it received only some 90 percent of the money. It was assumed that the missing part went to the bank's branch managers and to people working for Gokal as kickbacks and payoffs. Former BCCI bank officers on the Gokal payroll are thought to have engineered the loans and then taken their cut. In 1984, there was a rumor that the Gokals paid BCCI $25 million in return for a bank loan of $200 million. No matter how you looked at it, Gulf Group was a financial can of worms, and BCCI had its hands in deep.

Facing up to its problems for the first time as a result of the Price Waterhouse findings, the bank attempted internal damage control. The task force led by Rahman reported back to BCCI's directors that it concurred with Price Waterhouse's disastrous findings. "The Task Force simultaneously expresses considerable surprise and disappointment at such obvious flaws in basic banking procedures and documentation," it reported. The bank had no current personal net worth statement on Kamal Adham, for instance, even though he had been allowed to borrow more than $300 million from BCCI through more than 40 thinly documented accounts. Abedi's old friends in the Saigol family were found to have borrowed more than $40 million, with little indication that the money could be paid back. "Task Force is of the opinion that in the past [the] Saigols have not honored their commitments," the report said:

> Due to unsatisfactory conduct of the accounts . . . [the] existing situation cannot be allowed to continue.

And about the Gulf Group, the task force lamented that it had been "surprised and dismayed at the very poor quality of supporting documents."

The case of the elusive A.R. Khalil, the task force reported, "makes really sorry reading." And even when BCCI was in touch with a customer, there was no guarantee that his account would be up to date. Faisal Saud al-Fulaij, a Kuwaiti businessman and investor in First American, held $147.9 million in BCCI loans by 1990, according to Price Water-house, with "very little performance on any of these ac-counts" and "generally no loan agreements, customer instructions or promissory notes supporting this lending." In other words, the bank apparently was giving him millions of dollars in loans without asking for the kinds of applications and financial records that the average customer would need to borrow money to buy a car. Again, in al-Fulaij's case, many of the loans were to buy First American stock, supporting later allegations that BCCI had used sham loan deals to secretly acquire First American shares through al-Fulaij, Khalil and other front men.

Indeed, the task force report laid out the first real details of BCCI's odd practice of secretly buying interests in banks through front men, or nominees. Not only had it purchased control of First American and other U.S. banks in this way, but it also had purchased stock in itself, through convoluted arrangements involving nominee shareholder arrangements and its Cayman Islands operations. At one point, inves-tigators said, BCCI subsidiaries may have owned more than half of the parent company itself. According to the task force

> there is little doubt from the sparse records available and inadequate explanations given by the accounts executives/officers that there must be some "inter-locking" arrangements between the shareholders of both BCCI Holdings . . . and CCAH, whereby in several cases the 'nominee' route may have been taken to front each others' investment in these two banking groups.

* * *

The Task Force . . . recommends that in [the] future there should be no interlocking or nominee relationships for shareholders of BCCI and CCAH, if such exists at the moment.

Questions were raised by the task force about what else was going on in the Cayman Islands, where BCCI apparently had shifted many shady loans and accounts to avoid scrutiny from regulators and auditors. Some of them had been moved to the mysterious ICIC affiliate, "the bank within the bank." Nobody, it seemed—except perhaps Abedi, Naqvi and a few others—could figure out where BCCI ended and ICIC began, but it was clear that the situation in the Caymans was a mess. In a briefing paper prepared for BCCI's directors during the task force investigation, Price Waterhouse commented:

Our enquiries . . . have indicated that certain accounting transactions principally booked in Cayman and other offshore centers have been either false or deceitful. Whilst we and the task force have sought to identify all problem transactions, it is impossible, without an exhaustive inquiry, to know whether this has been achieved.

Looking for a scapegoat, the task force report pointed the finger at Price Waterhouse. Much as Rahman would later charge in his Senate testimony, the task force contended that the auditors had been asleep on the job. "The task force feels that the regular annual audit . . . should have easily detected and corrected such haphazard transactions several years ago," it griped. "Any reasonable audit process should have tracked down, identified and stopped [the problems] forthwith."

The task force concluded by urging that action be taken quickly to recapitalize the bank and tighten its operating procedures to prevent further damage. "It is in the interest of all concerned who are involved in safeguarding the existence of BCC Group—the shareholders, the directors, the management, the auditors and finally the regulators to 'close' this matter urgently," the task force wrote in its report:

> Without this there is now a grave and real danger of a serious "run" on the bank worldwide, resulting in an uncontrolled situation which would even close the entire Group, with serious consequences to the 1.3 million customers, the $17 billion-plus deposits . . . as well as the future of over 14,000 employees, all of which will be in serious jeopardy.

Abu Dhabi, it seemed, had bought into a major financial disaster. It still is not clear whether Abu Dhabi fully appreciated the scope of BCCI's problems when it agreed to purchase the bin-Mahfouz stake in October 1989 and then broaden its holding. Some cynics suggest that Abu Dhabi, as a shareholder from the start—and with Sheik Zayed's close relationship to Abedi—hardly could not have known that BCCI wasn't operating ethically. Regardless, Abu Dhabi was finding out just how bad an investment it had made. Price Waterhouse, reporting to the people who paid the bills, wrote a letter to the chairman of the Abu Dhabi finance department on April 25, 1990, to summarize the findings of its close examination of the bank's books. Price Waterhouse wrote:

> We advised the directors that there remain uncertainties over the recoverability of a number of major loans, in particular Gulf Group, CCAH and shareholder loans, and that further significant provisions in excess of the amount of $500 million already provided in 1989 were required in absence of a commitment from the government of Abu Dhabi that any losses arising from realization of these loans would not impair the [BCCI] group's capital base.

But Abu Dhabi, it seems, was prepared to do what it could to improve the situation. "Your representative . . . has confirmed to us that you are fully aware of the nature and magnitude of the uncertainties," Price Waterhouse wrote Abu Dhabi, "and are prepared to provide the necessary financial support in the event that losses arise from realization of these loans."

BCCI needed hundreds of millions of dollars of fresh capital, and Abu Dhabi, the new owner, seemed the most logical source. Price Waterhouse held the ultimate accounting sword over the bank: The threat that the auditors would not sign off on the bank's 1989 annual report.

Price Waterhouse also had flagged BCCI's problems to regulators in London and Luxembourg—although there is no indication that the auditors shared with U.S. regulators their findings about the bank's ownership of First American. The revelations concerned the British and Luxembourg regulators, but they still didn't grasp the magnitude of the problems. "Our view was that even if these transactions added up to individual acts of fraud, it did not add up to systematic fraud," Robin Leigh-Pemberton, the governor of the Bank of England, later told an investigative committee in the House of Commons. "If we closed down a bank every time we had a fraud, we would have rather fewer banks than we have."

Somehow, nobody was seeing the big picture. The Tampa drug-money-laundering bust was hardly a secret; ditto the persistent reports about BCCI's cozy relationship with Manuel Noriega. It is known that information about BCCI's terrorist ties and money-laundering activities had been passed to the Bank of England in 1989 by intelligence officials, who had based their Operation Q investigation on the information. The CIA, the British intelligence service MI5 and other intelligence agencies around the world had been collecting string on BCCI for several years. But due to a lack of communication or perhaps a deliberate desire to keep the bank alive for political or intelligence reasons, government officials still were making no efforts to take harsh action against the bank.

The Bank of England, along with the Luxembourg authorities, Price Waterhouse and BCCI itself, continued to regard the bank as salvageable. The BCCI management task force, despite its harsh words of criticism about the bank's practices, recommended only the stiffening of loan-loss reserves and a relatively small injection of new capital.

Naqvi went hat in hand to the new majority shareholders in Abu Dhabi in spring 1990 in an effort to raise money, but Sheik Zayed refused to see him—he wanted to see his friend Abedi. So Naqvi turned around the BCCI corporate jet and flew to Karachi to collect the wheelchair-bound and barely coherent Abedi to put the arm on the sheik. Abedi was so ill that he had to be coached to mouth the right words before he went in to see Sheik Zayed, but when he did, it was a request his old friend could not refuse. Abu Dhabi agreed to recapitalize the bank.

Price Waterhouse wanted assurances that there was money to underwrite the bad Gokal loans and the treasury losses of the mid-1980s before it would finally complete and sign off on the 1989 audit. The auditors got such a pledge from the sheik's chief financial adviser, Ghanim al-Mazrui, himself an investor in BCCI. That was enough for the accountants, and they approved the 1989 annual report in early May 1990. As far as the outside world of depositors and investors was concerned, all was well again with BCCI.

Except that there was some fine print involved. Price Waterhouse added to the report what amounted to an escape clause:

> They [the Government of Abu Dhabi] have advised the directors of their intention to maintain the group's capital base whilst the reorganization and restructuring necessary for its continuing development is undertaken.

Later, that was to be the accountants' excuse when accused of missing the gigantic holes elsewhere in the bank's books—whatever happened, the auditors were saying, Abu Dhabi would cover it. This form of "weasel words," whose meaning is far from clear, did not provide the outside world a clear warning of the precarious state of the company. Price Waterhouse later said that if it had done that, it would have started a run on the bank.

BCCI was continuing to hemorrhage capital. Abu Dhabi put $400 million into the bank in an attempt to stabilize its position in late spring 1990 and stepped in to take more operational control of BCCI. Abu Dhabi wanted to get the regulatory position sorted out once and for all. Its idea was to set up a London holding company answerable to British regulators, a second company, based in Hong Kong, to handle BCCI's Asian business, and a third in Abu Dhabi to handle the rest of the world, including the Cayman Islands operation. Each would deal with the others at arm's length, and the bank's main center of operations would be shifted from London to Abu Dhabi.

The sheik summoned the bank's top executives from London in late spring to tell them of his plans. Naqvi, in a last-ditch attempt to hang onto power, loaded several key managers into a chartered jet and set off to talk Sheik Zayed out of the reorganization scheme. It was a gloomy trip. One of the passengers recalls how Naqvi gave the executives a pep talk, suggesting that they apologize to the sheik and attempt to convince him that nothing like this would ever happen again. If they failed, he warned them gravely, they could be "dropped down a well."

But Naqvi's efforts were to no avail. The sheik was angry, and he appointed a committee in Abu Dhabi to take control of the bank, all but bypassing Naqvi and the by now incapacitated Abedi. The new management began to arrange for customers to alter their accounts to fit in with the new tripartite structure, and there were indications that BCCI was finally coming under professional management—quite contrary to the bank's history of phony paternalism.

The move to Abu Dhabi started a massive shake-up at BCCI that included significant layoffs at the bank as the new leadership attempted to pay for the bad loans by slashing operating costs. In the early summer of 1990, as the head-quarters operation was shifted to Abu Dhabi, BCCI laid off 4,000 of its 18,000 workers, including 800 of its 1,460 British staffers. Those who remained in Britain were told that the British business would remain a vital part of the BCCI structure, and "it can be made more profitable through a slimming down."

That wasn't enough explanation or solace for some BCCI employees, and one bank official sat down and wrote an angry letter that would not have significant reverberations until a year later. Vivian Ambrose, a member of BCCI's British regional inspection department, wrote to Member of Parliament Tony Benn on June 19, 1990, with the bitterness of someone whose dreams had been dashed. "The apparent incompetence of the bank's executives and higher management is surpassed only by the widespread corruption and nepotism within the organization," Ambrose wrote. The letter was a fairly scathing indictment of BCCI, but it promptly got lost in the maw of the British government bureaucracy. Benn passed it onto the British Treasury, on the grounds that it was about banking, but it went from there to the Department of Employment, on the theory that the letter had more to do with employment conditions at the bank than with finance. Once there, it got lost in the shuffle. When the fate of the letter came out in the House of Commons in the summer of 1991, after the scandal had broken, it was evident that government officials had passed the buck on BCCI.

Sheik Zayed continued to throw good money after bad. The sheik put another $600 million into BCCI to cover bad debts during the summer, and that was followed in October 1990 by a whopping $1.5 billion cash infusion. BCCI had become a black hole. The Gokal brothers—customers of the bank from the start—were now, towards the end, being identified as the bank's principal bad debtors. Price Waterhouse eventually estimated that the Gulf Group had defaulted on $1.2 billion worth of loans from BCCI.

The decline of BCCI was watched with growing anxiety by the Gokal brothers from their base in Geneva. They became particularly concerned when Sheik Zayed came firmly into control of the bank. There had been bad blood for years between the Gokals and the sheik. No one knew exactly why, but there was a suspicion that Abedi had told the sheik about the bribery a decade before that had led BCCI to dramatically increase its lending to the Gulf Group. Now the sheik was in charge. "You could feel the fear go through the company. It was a tangible thing," one Gulf Group employee said.

Fear turned to irrationality in the Gulf Shipping boardroom, and Gulf staff members sought an Islamic solution to their financial problems. "As things got worse, going to the mosque got more and more important," observed one manager. "I used to say, 'What's going to happen here?' and they would say, 'If God is good, such and such will happen.'"

The religious enthusiasm also infected the Gokals' business, and some managers prayed before they did a deal. This practice, called kaddesh, involved the manager opening the Koran at random three times, with the passages that turned up determining whether and how the deal would be done. On one occasion the company actually paid more than was necessary to charter a ship because the reading of the Koran dictated it. Senior executives were unperturbed by the excess cost and in fact promoted the manager for his wisdom.

The problems of the Gokals in particular and the shipping business in general in the late 1980s added to the panic. No longer could the company attempt to cover its indebtedness by churning out new shipping contracts. As it became harder for Gulf Group to find people who would do business with it, the firm cut its prices to a point where the deals were no longer profitable. The widespread view at Gulf was that BCCI's new Abu Dhabi leadership would call for repayment of the company's huge loans. Gulf Group officials desperately went to BCCI to attempt to remortgage everything they could lay their hands on, and they madly sold assets to raise cash. But it wasn't enough.

For at least 10 years, Naqvi had played the game of hide-the-Gokal-loan with remarkable success. No one knew better how to use corporate structures, paper companies, legal niceties and the like to slip bad business through the cracks. He did it with nothing more than a sharpened pencil and voluminous paper files.

On July 28, 1990, Naqvi packed the whole collection of files into a few suitcases and took them to BCCI's new head-quarters in Abu Dhabi. When Price Waterhouse prepared its next report—on Oct. 3, 1990—the accountants had gotten hold of Naqvi and his files. Now they could outline fully 30 pages of "inappropriate transactions" by senior officials of BCCI.

The Price Waterhouse report gave Sheik Zayed a picture of the antics that had gone on at his bank, and the day after it was produced, he decided to act. On Oct. 4, Abedi and Naqvi were forced to resign and the sheik launched his own inquiry into the bank's affairs under the auspices of account-ants Ernst & Young—who as Ernst & Whinney had quit as BCCI's auditors in disgust just three years earlier. Regulators in Britain and Luxembourg also were becoming more aware of the scope of BCCI's problems, courtesy of the increasingly ominous Price Waterhouse reports, which were being for-warded to the regulators. Still, banking officials around the world were apparently reluctant to move too quickly on BCCI as 1990 drew to a close: With Iraqi leader Saddam Hussein playing a game of chicken with Allied forces over Iraq's occupation of Kuwait, no one in the West wanted to risk a political misstep over BCCI that might anger Abu Dhabi or other critical Arab members of the anti-Saddam coalition. So thoughts of action against the bank were put on hold.

But Sheik Zayed was clearly angry. On Christmas Eve 1990, he warned darkly that his government would ter-minate any agreements to save the bank "if any criminal or illegal activity was involved."

There didn't seem much question that BCCI would meet that qualification. It already had settled the Florida money-laundering case, paying the $14.8 million fine and agreeing to five years of probation. But there were other legal problems around the world, and they seemed to steamroll over the first few months of 1991. In Argentina, the central bank already had ordered BCCI to start winding up its activities. BCCI found itself linked to Italy's Banca Nationale de Lavoro, whose Atlanta office was implicated in providing fraudulent loans to Iraq. And in the United States, the Federal Reserve Board finally had figured out the links to First American.

The Fed had been poking around First American for more than a year. It had written to Altman in late 1989, asking about rumors that BCCI had made large loans to some of the shareholders in CCAH and reports that BCCI, as a consequence, had an ownership position in First American. Altman had turned this inquiry away, saying that there were no loans and thus no relationship. In May 1990, however, *Regardies*, a Washington business magazine, published a long story noting the many coincidences between the shareholders of BCCI and First American and saying this raised questions about the actual ownership of the bank. The *Wall Street Journal* followed with a similar story, and then, in February 1991, *Washington Post* investigative reporter Jim McGee broke a detailed 6,000-word story that probed even deeper into the relationship. McGee's story reported Awan's statement to Customs investigator Robert Mazur boasting that BCCI owned First American, and it disclosed that BCCI and First American had "had an extensive, long-term relationship that appears contrary to what regulators say they understood it would," including BCCI's involvement in laying strategy for First American and in hiring executives for the bank.

The Federal Reserve, *The Post* reported a few days later, had begun an investigation into the BCCI-First American relationship. Acting on a tip from New York District Attorney Robert Morgenthau, who was already deeply involved in his own BCCI investigation, the Fed in late 1990 had gotten a look at some of the Price Waterhouse audits that confirmed the BCCI "loans" to the First American investors, despite Altman's denials.

McGee's story was a virtual blueprint for the action taken by the Fed a month later, in early March, when it ordered BCCI to sell its secret stake in First American. The Fed was to bring more serious charges against BCCI and its alleged nominee shareholders five months later, but in the meantime it ordered BCCI to close its offices around the United States. First American and its leaders, Clifford and Altman, professed shock about the revelations of secret ownership. The Washington bank issued a statement saying, "If the Federal Reserve has been misled or misinformed in any respect regarding the stock ownership of First American . . . First American has been equally misled."

Things were starting now to move very fast. The same day that the Federal Reserve took action on First American, the Bank of England commissioned a detailed report on BCCI's affairs, tipped off by a peek at the internal audits that showed the bank to be in such disarray. "It appears to the Bank [of England] that significant accounting transactions undertaken by the company, or other companies within the same group, may have been either false or deceitful, or that their underlying purpose may have been disguised or otherwise misstated," R.A. Barnes, head of the British central bank's banking supervision division, wrote to the newly hired auditors.

The Bank of England's choice of examiners seems strange, to say the least: none other than Price Waterhouse, already facing its share of blame for missing the scandal for years. But then, who else knew as much about BCCI as Price Waterhouse? A new group of auditors from the firm descended upon BCCI to check the work of their colleagues.

While the auditors and regulators were building their case, Sheik Zayed was pumping money into the bank. In May, the Abu Dhabi government agreed to hand over promissory notes worth more than $3 billion to cover problem loans at

BCCI. The sheik also found himself propping up something he didn't even know he owned: First American Bank. Beset by years of mediocre management exacerbated by the problem real estate loans that were plaguing most Washington-area banks, First American needed a handout, and the sheik contributed $200 million to this cause in 1991.

On June 28, the Price Waterhouse report commissioned by the Bank of England landed on the desk of Robin Leigh-Pemberton, the governor of the British central bank. This report, perhaps not surprisingly, was the worst yet. It told of unimaginable frauds in every section of the bank, ranging from treasury trading to Islamic banking, and found billions of dollars in unaccounted-for loans. It revealed $600 million in deposits not properly recorded on BCCI's books, but instead diverted elsewhere. It described the fakery perpetrated by the secretive "special duties" department. It exposed the existence of "the bank within the bank" at ICIC in the Cayman Islands. And it spelled out in the most detail yet the mechanism of the secret ownership of First American and other U.S. banks. There was particular criticism of senior management, especially Abedi, who it was said had commanded "blind loyalty" from subordinates who then corrupted the bank. Members of BCCI's board of directors, as well, "appear to have been taken in by, and trusted, dominant, deceitful management, in the form of Abedi and Naqvi," the report said.

Sheepishly, Price Waterhouse had to admit, many of these revelations were "based on records which have previously been concealed from us, as auditors, and only came to light as a result of our insistence on the files of Mr. Naqvi being [made available], such records having been in his personal possession."

The 45-page Price Waterhouse report to the Bank of England is a fascinating document, revealing the inner workings of a major international bank in ways never previously seen, in some cases with detailed customer-by-customer breakdowns. It is replete with rich irony: In the interests of security, several key entities were given code names by Price

Waterhouse in the draft of the report, most notably BCCI itself, which went under the quite appropriate moniker "Sandstorm." But there was nothing funny about the information contained in the report: Taken as a whole, it was a portrait of a major financial debacle.

"From the investigation work it is apparent that the senior management of Sandstorm have abused their responsibilities to depositors, shareholders, investors, regulators and to the bank itself," Price Waterhouse wrote:

> The accounting records and financial position of the Group have been falsified in relation to the above transactions for a substantial number of years. In fact, these transactions represent only a part of the wholesale deception to misrepresent and falsify the financial position of Sandstorm over the last decade through a series of complicated manipulations. These include the use of a related bank (Fork Overseas [a codename for ICIC]), which now appears to have been controlled by Sandstorm management; nominee and hold-harmless arrangements with a substantial number of prominent Middle Eastern individuals; the fraudulent use of funds placed under management . . . ; the formation of a significant number of companies and operation of bank accounts outside the Sandstorm Group used to disguise the nature of transactions and route funds . . . and a significant falsification of accounting records (involving false loans, transactions and confirmations) on such a scale that the true financial history of "Sandstorm" is unlikely to be able to be recreated.

"In recent years, these activities have continued on a significant scale in an attempt to conceal total losses of several billions of dollars," Price Waterhouse reported. "The total amount cannot be established both because of the problems of untangling the complex web of deception and because we have had no access to the losses of funds under management within [ICIC]." Nevertheless, the report said, "On the basis of the losses which have been concealed, it would appear that the bank has generated significant losses over the last decade and may never have been profitable in its entire history."

It was clear that strong action finally had to be taken against BCCI. After receiving the report, Leigh-Pemberton met with the chancellor of the exchequer, Norman Lamont, and the prime minister, John Major—who had been chancellor of the exchequer during some of BCCI's worst wrongdoing—and told them of his decision to shut down the bank. The British officials consulted with their American counterparts at the Federal Reserve, who were preparing their own case against the bank in connection with the First American takeover, and Fed officials traveled to Britain to coordinate the two efforts.

Supervisors at the Bank of England worked around the clock to iron out the logistics of shutting down and seizing BCCI on a coordinated basis around the world. Across the Atlantic, the Federal Reserve Bank was likewise getting ready. On July 3, BCCI's biggest debt burden hit the rocks, as the Gokal family's Gulf International Holdings was taken over by Luxembourg authorities under bankruptcy law.

At BCCI's old headquarters at 101 Leadenhall Street, a five-minute walk away from the scene of some of the top-level discussions among regulators, Leonard Kingshott, former chief executive of Lloyds Bank International, had been preparing for the greatest challenge of his banking career. On July 1, he had gone to work for BCCI to shake up and reorganize the bank on a salary of more than $250,000 a year. Four days later, officials in Britain and elsewhere moved in and seized the bank, and he was left without a job.

And what of the man whose genius had created BCCI? On July 15, 10 days after the shutdown raid, Agha Hasan Abedi broke his silence in Karachi. In his 70th year, his health broken, his dreams crumbled around him, he summoned up the composure that colleagues had come to know and worship and said, "I don't hold myself responsible, because I have not had anything to do with the affairs of BCCI for the past three years." Unfortunately, that still left the previous 16 years unaccounted for.

Chapter 14

Victims and Villains

In January 1991, Naresh Chada's small computer export company, based in the British town of Wokingham, cut a deal to buy computer equipment from a supplier in Germany and resell it in the Middle East. Payment for the sale came in German deutsch marks, and Chada decided to leave the money—about $110,000 worth of marks—sitting in his company's bank account in BCCI until foreign exchange rates improved.

As the early months of 1991 passed, Chada was aware of the increasing turmoil at BCCI, but he received assurances from the bank that his money was safe. "The irony is that in March one of their people came to see me," Chada remembered later. "I took him out to lunch and talked about the problems and he said, 'Everything had been sorted out; you don't have to worry. The sheik has taken personal control and is trying to put the house in order.' So that gave me a little reassurance to continue."

That decision cost him most of his money. When BCCI was shut down in July 1991, Chada and thousands of other innocent depositors in the bank saw their holdings all but wiped out overnight. British banking insurance covered the deposits only up to £15,000, about $25,000. The rest was gone. Chada doubted he'd be able to recover any of his deutschemark deposits.

The shutdown of BCCI took Chada and BCCI's 1.25 million other customers around the world almost completely by surprise, and the action set off a global firestorm of outrage that virtually matched the controversy over the bank's operations. After fumbling their oversight for years, it was charged, regulators had bungled their most important action against the bank. Thousands of businesses like Chada's were virtually wiped out; thousands of individual depositors saw their life savings go up in smoke.

BCCI employees got a double whammy, losing both paychecks and the deposits that many of them loyally had kept in the bank. Many of the employees and customers, like Chada, were natives of Third World nations who had been attracted to BCCI by its close ties to their home regions. BCCI staff members spoke many languages, understood small businesses' need for quick decisions and made modest customers feel cared for and affluent. When the bank was closed, these customers received a slap in the face. Many lost a substantial part of their savings and liquid assets, while politicians and the authorities appeared to do all they could to bury the problem, along with these victims' right to a hearing and fair compensation.

For his part, Chada had to lay off three of his company's four employees and accept that it might be months or years before he saw any of his money—if he saw it at all. The business that he started with his own savings was stopped in its tracks. "Now I don't have anything to put up front. My customers in the Middle East want the products. They won't wait," Chada said in late 1991. "It won't take long before the business closes. We are talking weeks.".

The timing of the shutdown of BCCI took almost everybody—even some of the regulators—unawares. Most people assumed that another infusion of cash from the sheik of Abu Dhabi and at least one more accountants' report would keep the BCCI hulk afloat for a while. In the rush to the courts, even the Bank of England's law firm, Freshfields, was caught off guard. Freshfields' reputation for immaculate presentation was marred by the crossings-out and handwritten passages on the documents requesting the closing of the bank July 5, and some of its affidavits had yet to be sworn. For an institution with a reputation for stateliness rather than speed, this precipitate action indicated that something was afoot.

So it was. It is generally believed that the Bank of England feared being upstaged by American authorities, particularly New York District Attorney Robert Morgenthau, who had a grand jury moving quickly toward an indictment of BCCI. The American officials also were competing among themselves. Morgenthau was generally believed to have taken the lead on the BCCI prosecution, much to the embarrassment of the Justice Department, which had been very slow to move on the case.

Morgenthau's people had been pestering the Bank of England for information for months, and in the process had obtained copies of the damaging Price Waterhouse audits from April 1990, which offered Morgenthau a considerable roadmap in making his case. Also pending in the United States was an action by the Federal Reserve, which had seen some of the audits and had moved in March to shut down BCCI's U.S. operations and to separate the bank from First American Bankshares. The Fed now was on the verge of bringing charges against BCCI, its executives and associates for the First American takeover.

The thought of being beaten by the American prosecutors apparently spurred the British authorities to move more quickly—in part because they feared that a criminal indictment in the U.S. might spark an uncontrollable run on the already jittery bank. "What appeared to galvanize the Bank of England into action was the acute embarrassment it would have felt if the New York District Attorney had acted first against BCCI," the *Banker*, a British magazine, wrote in September 1991. "Morgenthau had his evidence and was determined to use it. But if the indictments he brought against BCCI on 29 July had been made before the Bank of England had moved, there would have been a run on BCCI and U.K.

regulators as chief supervisors would have looked incompetent. Timing was critical."

Robin Leigh-Pemberton, the governor of the Bank of England, later said that he had decided to move against the bank mostly because of the contents of the June 28 Price Waterhouse report. "The culture of the bank was criminal," he declared in a famous statement that wound up angering BCCI's new owners in Abu Dhabi, as well as thousands of quite innocent bank employees around the world. But he seems to have been pretty close to the mark, as Morgenthau and the Fed demonstrated on July 29.

In the end, the two actions were taken virtually simultaneously. That morning in New York, Morgenthau unsealed an indictment naming the bank, Abedi and Naqvi and charging them with fraud, money-laundering grand larceny and falsifying documents. They also were charged with paying $3 million to two top officers of the Peruvian Central Reserve Bank in exchange for deposits and with snookering American Express Bank Ltd., an offshoot of the travelers-check and credit card giant, out of $20 million by leading American Express to believe that BCCI was a reputable bank in which to deposit its funds.

"The essence of the scheme was to convince depositors and other banking and financial institutions, by means of false pretenses, representations and promises, that the BCCI group was a safe financial repository and institution for funds," Morgenthau said in a strongly worded statement:

> The corporate structure of BCCI was set up to evade international and national banking laws so that its corrupt practices would be unsupervised and remain undiscovered. The defendants systematically falsified the capital structure of BCCI to make it appear as though it was a solvent, profitable bank secured by the backing of wealthy businessmen from the Middle East. In fact, much of the bank's capitalization and assets were fictitious and its backing illusory.

The pricetag on the swindle? "The best estimates indicate at this time that upwards of $5 billion has been lost through this fraud," Morgenthau said. That estimate was later to double, then triple, and even quadruple. Morgenthau said he wanted Abedi and Naqvi extradited from Pakistan and Abu Dhabi, respectively, to face the charges, which could mean prison terms of up to 25 years.

Some critics wondered what a local district attorney was doing prosecuting an international bank and its foreign managers, but Morgenthau responded that New York's position as the center of the world financial trade gave him unusually wide scope. Besides, BCCI had had an office in Manhattan, and First American Bank had branches throughout New York. "The simple truth is that the wire transfer and the bank book are as much the tools of the drug trade as the scale and the gun," Morgenthau later explained. "The nexus between drugs and money means that if we are to succeed in the war on drugs, we must be as vigorous in our prosecution of rogue bankers as we are of street dealers. That is one reason that our office has pursued BCCI so relentlessly."

There was no questioning the jurisdiction of the Federal Reserve, whose duties include regulating the U.S. banking system. Its thick July 29 complaint detailed how BCCI allegedly had used Kamal Adham and others as front men, or nominees, to illegally purchase stock in First American on behalf of the bank, and how they had received millions of dollars in payments for their services. Similar schemes were used in Ghaith Pharaon's takeovers of National Bank of Georgia, Independence Bank and CenTrust Savings on BCCI's behalf. BCCI, Abedi and Naqvi were named in the Fed's complaint, along with the alleged nominees. The proposed penalty: a $200 million fine and lifetime ban of all the defendants from the U.S. banking business. The fine was later dropped in exchange for BCCI's forfeiture of its $550 million in U.S. assets in a plea bargain in which the bank also pleaded guilty to Morgenthau's most serious charges and a sweeping federal racketeering charge.

"This is a case of systematic and deliberate criminal fraud," Virgil Mattingly Jr., general counsel to the Fed's board of governors and the head of the Fed's BCCI-First American investigation, told a congressional hearing a few weeks after the Fed brought its charges. "BCCI took maximum advantage of an unsupervised corporate structure to conceal and warehouse, in bank secrecy jurisdictions overseas, hundreds of millions of dollars in fraudulent transactions."

The Fed was angry—according to its charges, it had been grossly lied to when it approved the takeover of First American in 1982. Clark Clifford and Robert Altman, who had represented BCCI and First American, were not named as defendants by the Fed, and they were hardly mentioned in the complaint's detailed narrative of the alleged crimes. But there had been more about them in an earlier draft of the complaint, and sources said their role had been minimized in the final version only to save ammunition for potential later actions against them by the Fed. Like Morgenthau, the Fed said its investigation of the BCCI affair was continuing, and it did, mostly in secret.

As often happens in official Washington, the actions against BCCI set off a wave of congressional hearings. At least four separate committees set out to investigate what had happened, each with sweeping powers to obtain documents and to summon and question witnesses. Some of these were little more than publicity stunts to make congressmen appear to their constituents to be on top of the high-profile scandal, but others represented a real desire to uncover the truth about the bank, particularly the long string of hearings held over the next few months by Sen. John Kerry (D-Mass.) and his subcommittee on terrorism, narcotics and international operations.

Kerry, though a former prosecutor, had had a reputation on Capitol Hill as something of a lightweight, but he and his subcommittee had been doing serious and impressive work on BCCI since 1988 as part of an ongoing investigation of money-laundering. Kerry's former chief investigator, Jack Blum, had developed numerous leads on the bank. Blum, in fact, had triggered Morgenthau's investigation by visiting Morgenthau and his staff in New York in 1989 to complain that the Justice Department and Customs Service were not doing enough to chase BCCI. Blum said later that he had

> concluded that they [the Department of Justice] weren't interested in or didn't have the capacity to go after these issues of capitalization, or other illegal activities regarding the control of First American by BCCI. . . . I took the matter to Morgenthau in New York and told them I wanted an investigation into the capitalization of BCCI and First American.

Morgenthau complied.

During the summer of 1991, Kerry and others on Capitol Hill began subpoenaing the many documents already obtained by the Federal Reserve and other investigators. Early on, this caused a diplomatic flap when congressional investigators obtained, and released to the press, Price Waterhouse audits and other sensitive BCCI documents that the Bank of England had given to the Fed in confidence. Newspaper reports on those documents added further fuel to the developing scandal by providing even more detailed illustration of BCCI's alleged wrongdoing. A series of congressional hearings beginning in August also brought new attention to the scandal and produced new evidence of its breadth and depth.

Following the indictments, and the blistering press assault on BCCI and all associated with it, the spotlight was turned on a number of public figures in the United States. Jimmy Carter, Andrew Young and the U.N.'s Javier Perez de Cuellar found themselves scrambling to explain their close relationships with BCCI, which now looked extremely embarrassing at best. All denied that they had known of the bank's malfeasance. Rumors swirled, some fed by irresponsible press reports, of bribery of other public officials by BCCI on a massive scale; to date, there is no solid proof of that.

Clark Clifford and Robert Altman, BCCI's lawyers and the head of First American, also were under intense heat in the wake of the scandal. They continued to argue that they had known nothing about BCCI's alleged ownership of First American, even though the evidence now tumbling out of BCCI's files seemed to cast more and more doubt on their story, especially given their close ties to BCCI. In spite of all the negative publicity, Clifford and Altman continued to cling to their positions at the top of First American in the weeks immediately after the eruption of the scandal, arguing that they saw no reason to step down if they were innocent men.

In the two weeks following the July 29 charges, however, the Federal Reserve put increasing pressure on the two to leave their posts at the bank, or for First American's board to oust them—although it was not clear that the board actually had the power to do that, given the bank's convoluted corporate structure. During marathon meetings in the First American boardroom in Washington—a room dominated by a large portrait of the distinguished-looking Clifford—regulators and bankers negotiated the futures of Clifford and Altman until finally, on Aug. 13, the two men agreed to resign as chairman and president, respectively, of the bank. Former Attorney General Nicholas deB. Katzenbach, himself a longtime fixture as a Washington insider almost on the scale of Clifford, was named as First American's caretaker chairman.

Congressional hearings into the BCCI affair in the late summer and fall of 1991 heard testimony from bank executives, investigators and officials of the CIA and the Justice Department. Some of the most stunning revelations came from Abdur Sakhia, the former head of BCCI's American operations, who testified that BCCI had always treated First American and the other U.S. banks as full-fledged subsidiaries, regardless of the representations to the Fed. At one point, Sakhia revealed in a startling piece of testimony, he had been in a meeting with Clifford and a newly promoted BCCI executive when Clifford jokingly told the executive, who was overseeing BCCI's U.S. operations from London, "Welcome aboard. We will tell more lies now." Clifford adamantly denied that the conversation took place.

Another key witness was Masihur Rahman, BCCI's former chief financial officer, who had resigned from the bank a year earlier. He said he had been forced to hide in London after death threats to himself and his family. BCCI officials and the liquidators appointed by a British court to oversee the affairs of the bank managed to stop him from testifying to British authorities on the grounds that he would damage the attempts to salvage the bank, but eventually he and his family came to the United States, where he appeared before the Kerry subcommittee in August 1991 as the first inside witness to testify publicly about BCCI. He seemed a desperate figure, looking older than his 57 years, with only his well-cut suit suggesting better times.

Rahman testified that Abedi and Naqvi and other executives had overseen the looting of $2.5 billion from BCCI's coffers through theft, bad investments and insider loans. Pointing his accusing finger far and wide, he criticized the Bank of England, calling it "grossly negligent," argued that the bank's internal management controls had been lax and ineffective and charged that Price Waterhouse had been incompetent in overseeing the company's books.

The motives behind Rahman's accusations were open to question—after all, as chief financial officer he could be blamed both for the sloppy management and for not seeing that Price Waterhouse got better data to audit. Ghassan Qassem, the former bank executive who had been a key source of British Intelligence's investigation of the bank was among those criticizing Rahman's testimony. "That man was deeply involved in the restructuring of the balance sheet, the fiddling and the cover-up," Qassem said. "And suddenly he goes out in the open and says, 'I did this and that.'" Rahman's real motive for talking, Qassem believes, was pique over not receiving enough severance from the bank to buy his silence.

"He was with the bank 17 years," Qassem said. "He was with Naqvi, with Saleem Sidiqi [in charge of internal audits], the top policy-makers for 17 years, and you tell me that that man was so stupid he didn't know what was going on?"

By far the most eagerly expected congressional hearing was Clifford's and Altman's voluntary appearance before the House Banking Committee on September 11, 1991—the first chance the two men had been given to respond publicly and first-hand to the increasing amount of innuendo against them for their role in the BCCI-First American scandal. The elder statesman and his young protege testified for several hours in a packed hearing room, their wives sitting dutifully behind them along with a battery of expensive lawyers. Their testimony—as well as a later session they had with Kerry's subcommittee—ultimately was inconclusive. But it was great Washington political theater.

Clifford led off with a long, rambling history of his life, dropping names of presidents and celebrated friends left and right, a tour de force performance for a man 84 years old. When the questioning finally began, after Clifford's noon-time nap, the two men, not surprisingly, stuck to their story: Despite their longtime dual role as BCCI's lawyers and First American's top executives, they said they were not aware of any connections between the two outside of BCCI's role as investment adviser to some of First American's Middle Eastern shareholders. They said they found out about BCCI's malfeasance at the same time as almost everyone else, when the bank was named in the Tampa money-laundering indictment in 1988—a case for which they organized the defense on BCCI's behalf. And while they conceded that they regularly met with BCCI officials, often traveling to London to do so, they insisted that they did so only under the impression that they were dealing with Abedi, Naqvi and others as legal clients or as the representatives of the Middle Eastern shareholders—even though the shareholders, who were successful businessmen and government officials, were easily reachable directly by phone or telex.

Clifford and Altman said they never suspected a thing about the bank until stories questioning the BCCI-First American relationship began appearing in the press—and even then, they said, they received assurances from BCCI that the stories were in error. Clifford even said he was "mystified" as to why BCCI would secretly purchase stock in First American.

"The reports we get are very disturbing. They are embarrassing. They are even shocking," Altman testified. "We've dealt with people in good faith for more than a decade, and it's hard to square our dealings with them. They always seemed completely honest and straightforward. There was never anything slippery about it."

"Our consciences are clear," Clifford intoned. What's more, the two men testified, proof of their innocence could be found in the fact that little or no BCCI-style wrongdoing had been found at First American—an argument investigators said was erroneous, citing evidence of money-laundering and other sins. Besides, the pair noted, the bank, under their management, had more than quadrupled in size to $11 billion in assets, making First American the Washington area's largest bank holding company. That could not have happened, they argued, had BCCI been pulling the strings behind the scenes.

Their testimony did not convince many members of the committee, and Clifford and Altman faced some sharp criticism during the hearing. Like many other observers, some of the congressmen felt that the two men's credibility had been badly damaged by their $9.8 million in profit on BCCI-financed trading in First American stock.

"Mr. Clifford and Mr. Altman, I've looked at the facts presented to this committee and studied your statements," Rep. Toby Roth (R-Wis.) told the two men. "It pains me to say this, [and] others may believe your story, but I must say I don't believe a word of it. I've looked at this case and my conclusion is that you knew and that you made millions."

Clifford, the man who had been laying his previously sterling reputation on the line for clients for years, conceded to the committee that maybe he had allowed his reputation to be used one time too many. Clifford said:

> One of the reasons I believe that these people came to us originally was because they felt that our standing and our reputation would be an asset to them. So that the fact is when someone says to me, "I really think you should have known," the true fact is I believe we would have been the last people to know. ... So it has been a deeply regrettable experience. But ... looking back on it, with all of the experience I have had, I did not detect any element in it that would have warned me that we were being deceived.

The upheaval and negative publicity surrounding First American was hardly reassuring to its depositors in the Washington area, many of whom had seen other local banks fail in recent months as the shock waves from the region's real estate slump rocked the banking industry. During the third quarter of 1991, when headlines about BCCI and First American were appearing almost daily, depositors withdrew more than $1 billion from First American, further weakening its already tenuous financial position. There also was a run on First American of Georgia, the former National Bank of Georgia, which lost significant deposits because of the scandal.

Regular customers weren't the only ones making sure their deposits at First American were safe. On the same day that Clifford and Altman resigned from the bank, Altman's wife, actress Lynda Carter, appeared at a First American branch and rearranged $500,000 held in an account under the name of her movie company, Altman Productions, *The Washington Post's* Sharon Walsh reported. Carter split the Altman Productions money into several smaller accounts, according to bank employees—each containing less than $100,000. That way, if the bank failed, her money would be insured by the federal government, which covers amounts up to $100,000 per account. Better to be safe than sorry, no doubt.

In Britain, the closing of BCCI set off a political storm. The Bank of England thought it had been rather brave to close down the bank, and it now apparently hoped that BCCI would go away. BCCI was not the first instance of fraud the Bank of England had encountered and, according to Governor Robin Leigh-Pemberton, "Our experience in the past is on the whole that we have been able to correct that sort of thing by the dismissal of management and closer supervision."

But new management and closer supervision weren't going to be nearly enough in BCCI's case. Depositors were livid and former employees distraught. British government officials were feeling the heat from politicians such as Keith Vaz, an Asian member of parliament who had become the depositors' friend—sort of the British equivalent of Sen. Kerry, as far as ferreting out BCCI's wrongdoing was concerned. Vaz was well-suited to the legal fray; he had studied law at Cambridge University and he long had battled for the Muslim cause. He had, for example, supported calls for the withdrawal of Salman Rushdie's controversial novel, "The Satanic Verses," while others said that smacked of censorship.

The chancellor of the exchequer at last acceded to Vaz's demand for an inquiry into the supervision of BCCI. Shortly after, it was announced that Lord Justice Thomas Bingham would hear evidence on the case in private. Depositors wanted something stronger, but Prime Minister John Major reassured them that the inquiry would be very thorough and that even he would not be allowed to escape questions about his role.

The government's approach found few supporters. Major seemed to miss the point that most people who had real evidence about the fraud would be unlikely to attend the Bingham hearings voluntarily. Nonetheless, advertisements were placed in British newspapers appealing for witnesses to the crime. The ads read:

"The Inquiry's terms of reference are: To inquire into the supervision of BCCI under the Banking Acts; to consider whether the action taken by all the UK authorities was appropriate and timely; and to make recommendations."

That approach clearly wasn't sufficient, and Prime Minister Major's opposition in the Labour Party had a field day, pointedly contrasting the public posture of the U.S. congressional inquiry with the private nature of the British investigation. One Labour MP, Roy Hattersley, complained that BCCI's British customers would learn more by watching the congressional hearings on television than they would from the Bingham inquiry.

In one particularly heated exchange in the House of Commons, opposition leader Neil Kinnock accused the prime minister of being "utterly negligent" in his handling of the affair and said Major had known of "grave irregularities" at BCCI as early as 1990. Major, nearly speechless with rage at the accusation, stared straight at Kinnock and broke with Commons etiquette by not addressing his comments through the Speaker of the House when he replied, "If you are saying I am a liar, you had better say so bluntly." However, there has not yet been concrete evidence that Major, even as chancellor of the exchequer, had significant early knowledge of BCCI's wrongdoing.

BCCI depositors were unhappy about the seeming lack of aggressiveness of the Bingham inquiry and the degree of understanding of their case at the political level—an attitude that perhaps reflected the British establishment's dim view of the minorities that dominated BCCI's lists of depositors and employees. "There is a large area of government which says it's a fringe bank, it's mainly for ethnic minorities," one critic said. "It's not a fringe bank. At the time of closure it was not a fringe bank. The Bank of England had prime responsibility as regulator. The informal inquiry was the least they could get away with."

British officials also were much slower than their American counterparts in prosecuting the perpetrators of the alleged crimes at BCCI. The Serious Fraud Office (SFO) was said to have put 22 investigators into the probe, but there was a widespread view that the British would at best be bit players in the inquiry. There was a brief flurry of activity when the SFO raided the London offices of Capcom Financial Services in August. Shortly after, Syed Ziauddin Ali Akbar, the founder of Capcom, was arrested in Calais, France, but that was a joint operation with the French and outside British jurisdiction.

The immediate effect of the closing of the bank around the world in the days and weeks following the action can best be described as confused. In the Seychelles, the bank was allowed to stay open just long enough to allow depositors to withdraw all their money. Then it was closed, three days after most of the rest of the world. In Sri Lanka, officials decided to reopen the bank under the management of one of the country's own banks. In Jordan, Brazil and a handful of other nations, the bank was allowed to keep operating, although authorities in some of these finally acted against them a few months later.

In Canada, Michael Mackenzie, superintendent of financial institutions, told a parliamentary committee in Ottawa that both he and the police authorities had closely monitored BCCI's operations for years and had found nothing untoward. He said he wished he had been kept better informed: "We asked repeatedly—the police, the English, the Americans, the whole damn world—and nobody told us anything," Mackenzie said. In Abu Dhabi, meanwhile, an attempt was made to get around some of BCCI's problems by changing the name of the bank from BCC Emirates to the Union National Bank.

There also were important diplomatic and political ramifications of the Bank of England's handling of the shutdown. At first, the government of Abu Dhabi was so incensed by the abrupt shutdown in Britain that Sheik Zayed let it be known that he had no intention of bailing out the bank's customers outside the Persian Gulf region. Private depositors and businesses in the United Arab Emirates with an estimated $1 billion on deposit would receive refunds; everyone else would be left out in the cold.

On behalf of the majority shareholders in Abu Dhabi, the sheik took out full-page newspaper advertisements outlining his displeasure with the British authorities. It is very unusual for any government to communicate with another in this highly public way, but for the secretive and retiring sheik, it was quite extraordinary.

"The majority shareholders of the BCCI Group were shocked by the abrupt action taken by the Bank of England, the Luxembourg Monetary Institute and other regulators on Friday, 5 July 1991, to freeze the assets of the BCCI Group and close its operating branches," the advertisements read. "This action was taken without any consultation whatsoever with the shareholders of the Central Bank of the United Arab Emirates, a member of the College of Regulators. Since April 1990, the government of Abu Dhabi and related institutions have held a majority shareholding in the BCCI Group."

The notice continued:

> The majority shareholders feel that they cannot absolve Price Waterhouse from all responsibility since they have been auditors of a major subsidiary [BCCI Overseas] for 15 years and auditors of the whole group since 1987. . . . The action taken on 5 July has resulted in severe problems (involving financial hardship in many cases) for more than 1.25 million depositors of the Group worldwide, and some 12,000 staff are likely to lose their jobs. It has resulted in the destruction, at a stroke, of what the majority shareholders believe was a well-structured and viable future plan. If the restructuring plan had been allowed to proceed, the majority shareholders have no doubt that no depositors' money would have been lost. In view of all the above, the majority shareholders deplore what they consider to be the unjustified action taken by the Bank of England, the

Luxembourg Monetary Institute and other regulators.

Robin Leigh-Pemberton did not need the advertisement to know the extent of the sheik's displeasure. He responded with courtesy, and traveled to Abu Dhabi to meet with the sheik. Leigh-Pemberton did more than merely build bridges; he also asked the sheik for yet more funds to help fund the liquidation of the bank, which was being overseen by a team of experts from Touche Ross & Co. He personally delivered the damning June 28 Price Waterhouse report, which until then the sheik and his advisers had not been allowed to see, since it had been commissioned by the regulators rather than the bank.

The Abu Dhabi government felt it had been tricked into supporting BCCI, that it should have been informed and warned off. After all, the sheik was pumping hundreds of millions of dollars into something that everyone else apparently knew would eventually have to be shut down. Abu Dhabi's final contribution had come just days before the July 5 action.

Keith Vaz, the member of parliament who was championing depositors' rights, also visited Abu Dhabi after the shutdown. "We met a couple of members of the royal family and the senior officials. Their prime hate target was the Bank of England," he said:

"We felt there was a tremendous sense of betrayal. They had trusted the Bank of England. They had traded with the British for years and years. If the Bank of England had said jump, they'd have jumped. If the Bank of England had said sack this person, they would have sacked him. They wouldn't argue with the Bank of England. They had put an awful lot of money in BCCI and then to be cheated in this rather incredible way they found impossible to believe." Vaz returned with a promise of $5 billion from Sheik Zayed, sufficient to avoid immediate liquidation. But as 1991 wore on, the sheik's financial commitment seemed to diminish, and in October Zayed gave up his attempts to salvage the bank.

Still, the sheik seemed willing to contribute something to the bailout of the BCCI depositors and other creditors, if only out of pride and diplomacy. By the end of 1991, it appeared that the sheik would agree to a plan to contribute $2 billion and assume around $3 billion in BCCI liabilities to make good a Touche Ross-organized liquidation plan under which BCCI's creditors would receive 30 or 40 cents on the dollar. Without the sheik's participation in such a plan, the liquidators from Touche Ross warned, the creditors might receive only about a dime on the dollar after many years of litigation.

For many BCCI depositors and employees, the sheik's money may be small consolation for lost savings and ruined businesses. Most of BCCI's 40,000 British depositors, for instance, were a mixture of large and small businessmen from the Third World who were doubtless tempted by the bank's heritage and its higher-than-average interest rates and took them at face value. There is a large number of naive and certainly unlucky investors who thought any British bank was a safe place to park their funds—only to find out the hard way that the British statutory guarantee of £15,000 worth of deposits didn't go very far. Many of the depositors had hoped that Abu Dhabi would make good on all their losses.

Chan Chowdry, a North London businessman who had seen close friends lose "literally thousands" in the BCCI failure, spoke for many depositors when he said: "People had hoped to get something out of it and now the reality has proved to be the worst of all. Everything is lost. They are sure the Bank of England didn't make an attempt to help. They made no effort at all." According to Chowdry, many customers had felt certain that a bailout package would be worked out once Sheik Zayed had intervened and the BCCI ringleaders were rounded up. "They feel they have been led up the garden path," he said.

Mohammed Anwar, who ran an international shipping agency and electrical products outlet in Manchester, said he could not quite believe what had happened. "I'm totally shattered; we were hoping Abu Dhabi would help us out," he said. "Sixteen years of hard work has just gone down the drain."

Third World customers weren't the only ones burned by BCCI. As it turned out, the bank also had drawn many other unwary British depositors, including many of Britain's local council governments. The councils had been attracted to the bank by its high interest rates and reassured by its appearance on a list of banks put out by the British government as approved to hold municipal funds. (In fact, the list included at least two banks that actually were under bankruptcy protection.)

One local council, the tiny Western Isles community in the remote Outer Hebrides off the Scottish Coast, had £23 million—$40 million—in BCCI, mostly borrowed from institutions paying lower rates. Ironically, the last £1.3 million apparently had been deposited just minutes before the Bank of England shut down the bank. "It's easy to say with hindsight we were wrong to put all our eggs in one basket," said Donald Macleod, the head of the council's finance department.

Perhaps the saddest victims of BCCI's failure were the bank's loyal, law-abiding employees who lost both their jobs and their savings when the bank was shut down. They found themselves in the same boat as other depositors, hoping that Sheik Zayed would make good on at least some of the bank's debts, but their employment prospects were not good, not with time spent at BCCI on their resumes. It was guilt by association. "A reference from BCCI is almost worthless," said Richard Lynch of the British Banking, Insurance and Finance Union. "Some workers may become almost unemployable in banking."

Chapter 15

<hr>

While The Regulators Slept

Sen. Hank Brown was exasperated. For hours, he and Sen. John Kerry had been grilling officials of the Central Intelligence Agency about the way they had handled information they received during the 1980s on wrongdoing at BCCI, in particular evidence that the bank illegally owned Washington's First American Bank. The CIA officials had explained to the senators that they forwarded the information to various agencies in the federal government, but conceded that somehow they had failed to pass the information about First American onto the Federal Reserve—which oversees bank ownership. To Brown, that was a significant error. "If you know there's a fire, you don't call the city manager's office, you call the fire department," the Colorado Republican complained. "They called the city manager's office."

The BCCI saga is rife with examples of similar errors on the part of authorities who might have derailed the scandal in its early stages. Time and time again, regulators, auditors, intelligence agencies and law enforcement officials missed chances to uncover the bank's pattern of illegality. More aggressive sharing of leads by the CIA might have broken the bank scandal open in the mid-1980s. More skeptical questioning by the Federal Reserve might have prevented the secret takeover of First American. More detailed examination of BCCI's books by Price Waterhouse might have revealed the bank's financial house of cards at any time during the 1980s. Tougher regulation by officials in Britain and Luxembourg might have exposed the bank's gigantic losses from treasury trading and bad loans. Better followup on evidence obtained in the Tampa money-laundering case by officials at the Customs Service and Justice Department might have uncovered the scandal a year or two earlier. And so on.

"It wasn't just that BCCI was rumored to be bad," said Rep. Charles E. Schumer (D-N.Y.), whose House Judiciary subcommittee studied the handling of BCCI by U.S. law enforcement agencies. "It was that professional investigators in the agencies had hard evidence that they were bad, and bad in a big way, and nobody did anything about it."

The kindest explanation for such omissions is neglect, caused by a lack of resources or misunderstanding of the wrongdoing involved. More serious are charges of incompetence or, worst of all, deliberate decisions to look the other way, perhaps in exchange for money or other favors. No doubt, BCCI's habit of ingratiating itself with the rich and powerful served it well over the years—how could a bank with such famous and powerful friends be so corrupt? It was not an illogical assumption to believe that smart people like Clark Clifford and Jimmy Carter would not associate themselves with an institution that could so seriously damage their reputations. Such favorable associations doubtless helped deflect suspicion from the bank in many subtle ways.

For whatever reasons, the overseers blew it. Part of the problem lay in BCCI's very unusual corporate structure. Brilliantly set up to straddle many different jurisdictions, the bank took advantage of the parochial regulatory set-up that governs international financial institutions, with each nation looking at only the part of the bank that it could see and no one stepping back to look at the whole picture—something like the old story about the five blind men feeling different parts of an elephant and coming up with wildly different assessments of the beast.

BCCI was, in effect, a stateless bank, with no main regulator. Its headquarters were in Luxembourg, where bank regulation is lax; it had a major bank in Grand Cayman Island, where bank secrecy laws rule; its center of operations was in London, where regulators have a reputation for sloth; and its main shareholders were in Abu Dhabi—where the owners and the regulators were basically the same people. Such an arrangement is hardly made for close scrutiny of a rogue bank with farflung operations.

And yet, there had been questions around the world about BCCI for years. It was run by people who weren't part of the usual old-boy banking network, operated in nations populated by shady characters and had grown at unprecedented speed—all of which made it an easy object of suspicion. It had been whispered in financial circles for many years that BCCI was at the very least an unsound base for deposits.

By the end, virtually no major international banks were doing enough joint business with BCCI to have a lot of money sitting on the bank's books when the shutdown came—an unusual state of affairs, given that major international banks cooperate on business all the time and routinely keep money on deposit with each other. Bank of America had known enough to sell its ownership position in BCCI in 1980, although it maintained business ties over the years. Unique among big banks, BCCI also did not have a lender of last resort, a home-country central bank that could back up its operations. And more publicly, the money-laundering case in Tampa was a sure sign that something was wrong at the bank.

For all that, regulators still seem to have missed the boat. Rumors were one thing, they said after the scandal hit, but they never really had enough hard information to move against the bank until the Price Waterhouse report in June 1991. "There was a lot of talk about this bank and it was rumor and it was suspicion, maybe, but certainly not information on which the Bank of England could necessarily act,"

Bank of England Governor Robin Leigh-Pemberton told the House of Commons.

Like Sen. Brown and Sen. Kerry, many on Capitol Hill found fault with the handling of BCCI by regulators and law enforcers in the wake of the scandal. The House Judiciary subcommittee, in a report in September 1991, said that its investigation of the actions of the Internal Revenue Service, the Customs Service, the Drug Enforcement Administration and the Justice Department had found that as early as 1983 incidents had come to light in which criminals were using BCCI "as a conduit," or in which the bank itself was an "active participant in possibly criminal activity." The report went on: "The government simply overlooked the repeated run-ins that it had with BCCI, its officials, customers and accounts. Any reasonable review of those historic files would have led a knowledgeable investigator to BCCI far earlier. Perhaps it would have uncovered sooner the staggering international proportions of BCCI's illicit business, and put it out of business."

There were many instances in which investigations involving BCCI had gone no further than the case at hand, even though they raised important questions about the bank's operations. In 1985, a federal investigation of money-laundering in Chicago turned up an employee at the BCCI office there who offered to launder money and hosted meetings on the scheme in a BCCI conference room. The case was ultimately dropped. In another instance, an agent of the Drug Enforcement Agency was taken to BCCI's Los Angeles office by an alleged drug dealer during undercover negotiations for a big heroin sale in 1985 and was told by a BCCI officer that he could "conceal and launder accounts at a foreign bank," according to an affidavit in the case. The DEA turned the reference over to the IRS, but there apparently was no followup. In all, the Judiciary subcommittee found 15 BCCI-related cases in the IRS files, but incredibly, "no one at the agency appeared to have noticed the pattern," according to the congressional report.

The CIA also had found repeated evidence of wrongdoing at BCCI, and officials there said they sent "several hundred" intelligence reports on the bank to other federal agencies during the 1980s. Some were little more than newspaper clippings, but at least one, in mid-1986, was a fairly extensive report on the bank's activities. In that document, the CIA said:

> In late 1981, BCCI made an unsuccessful attempt to acquire or gain control of Financial General Bankshares, a Washington, D.C.-based multi-state bank holding company; BCCI achieved its goal half a year later, although the exact nature of its control is not clear.

But the CIA, apparently not understanding the Fed's role in bank regulation, failed to forward the report to that agency; others who got the reports, apparently, failed to see the breadth of BCCI's activities.

One person in government who apparently did understand what was going on at BCCI was Robert Mazur, the Customs agent who created and directed the Operation C-Chase probe that produced the Tampa money-laundering indictments. In the course of the investigation, Mazur came across not only the money-laundering case but also a boast from BCCI's Amjad Awan that the bank illicitly owned First American Bank. Mazur also believed that BCCI's money-laundering operations were not a local phenomenon—he attempted to pursue a theory that top executives of the bank were aware of, and encouraged, the bank's money-laundering activities.

Mazur was talking with his BCCI contacts about a trip to London to discuss money-laundering with higher-level BCCI executives when the two-year undercover investigation was "taken down," or ended, with the October 1988 arrests. The timing of the termination of the investigation has been the subject of some dispute. Customs officials insist that they had been considering ending the case in October for several months, and internal Customs documents confirm this. But the documents also show that Mazur lobbied hard to postpone the ending of the case, arguing that he believed he had an opportunity to implicate higher executives at BCCI. There has been speculation that he was overruled so that the Reagan administration's Justice Department could bring a high-profile drug-money case shortly before the 1988 presidential election to aid the candidacy of Vice President George Bush.

There is no hard evidence to support that contention. But the ending of Operation C-Chase seemed to leave many loose ends. Busy assembling the case for trial against BCCI's expensive phalanx of lawyers, Mazur and the other Customs agents, as well as Justice Department officials in Tampa, were unable to sift through the huge amount of evidence gathered during the investigation. Mazur, Sen. Kerry and others have complained that this evidence—some of which apparently still has not been evaluated—might have greatly expanded the case against BCCI long before the revelations of 1991. One key piece of evidence: Mazur's secretly taped conversation with Awan at the Grand Bay Hotel in Miami, made in September 1988, in which Awan said:

> I have [a] totally different, uh, uh, assessment of the situation. And it might be farfetched, it might sound stupid, but my assessment is that we own a bank in Washington. I may have mentioned it to you before.

Awan went on to describe how BCCI had purchased the bank through front men: "BCCI was acting as adviser to [the shareholders], but the truth of the matter is that the bank belongs to BCCI. Those guys are just nominee shareholders."

Awan told Mazur during their conversation that he was concerned about the subpoena from Kerry's subcommittee requiring him to testify, which had arrived a few days before. "I don't think the bank can stand up to any sort of publicity," Awan said. "It's gonna hit them bad." When Mazur suggested that BCCI had powerful friends in Washington, Awan responded, "Well, our attorneys are, are, they're heavyweights. I mean, Clark Clifford is, is sort of the god-father of the Democratic party." Clifford has since said that Awan was only speculating about BCCI's ownership of First American during the conversation with Mazur.

Despite such tantalizing bits of evidence, the Justice Department officials apparently were intent on making a money-laundering case, and nothing more, out of the Operation C-Chase investigation, at least for the short term. They later said they hoped eventually to use information gathered in that case, and testimony from those convicted, to expand the scope of the inquiry. Using a colorful analogy, Mark V. Jackowski, the assistant U.S. attorney in Tampa who prosecuted the case, told Kerry's subcommittee:

> We were at dinner, and the first course was to eat the money-laundering plate. . . . That was what was on our plate. We ate that meal. We didn't ignore the dessert, which was First American Bank. We simply put it aside.

To Kerry, however, the prosecutors had missed the main course. The illegal ownership of one of the nation's 50 largest banks, he argued, was of at least equal importance to the money-laundering case. "That's the problem," Kerry said in sharply rebuking Jackowski during the subcommittee hearing. "It wasn't a money-laundering case. It was a case that was much bigger than that."

Kerry himself attempted to push the Justice Department to expand the scope of the case in early 1989, sending his then-chief investigator, Jack Blum, to Tampa to try to persuade prosecutors that there was more than just money-laundering at stake. Blum was a burly lawyer known around Washington for his penchant for conspiracy theories, but this time he was onto the real thing. Blum, who had joined Kerry to investigate drug dealing and money-laundering activity, had been sniffing around BCCI for a couple of years, curious because he kept running across the bank's name in strange and at times criminal contexts. At a 1988 subcommittee hearing, for instance, a witness had displayed a chart labeled "Noriega's Criminal Empire." At the center of the chart was the name BCCI. "Suddenly, the information I had parked in the back of my head years before became relevant," Blum later said. "I began to seek out more information about BCCI."

Blum came across a former BCCI official who had stories to tell of illegal activities at the bank and, at Kerry's behest, he urged the Tampa prosecutors to interview him. But the prosecutors, after two days of questioning, concluded that Blum's witness did not have first-hand information and therefore was of little value. Frustrated, Blum then took his information to Robert Morgenthau, the New York district attorney.

Morgenthau had a more open mind. Over his long career, he had earned a reputation as a tough, maverick prosecutor with a particular appetite for cases involving white-collar crime, money-laundering and drug-dealing. The BCCI affair was right up Morgenthau's alley, and he put some of his top investigators on the case. They ran smack into the Justice Department, which did not seem at all interested in cooperating. Morgenthau's men found that documents and witnesses routinely were withheld by their federal counterparts, in a fashion that seemed to be beyond the bounds of normal turf wars among prosecutors. For one reason or another, Justice seemed to be deliberately hampering Morgenthau's probe. Some have seen sinister political motives in this, but others believe that the feds knew they had mishandled the case in Tampa and didn't want to be embarrassed by Morgenthau's investigation.

Morgenthau's office took the clear lead in the investigation, and its indictments of the bank in July 1991 completely upstaged the Justice Department. Federal officials maintained that they were working hard on the case, and promised indictments to prove it, but the handful of cases they brought in 1991—including an expansion of the original Tampa charges to include Abedi, Naqvi and other top BCCI executives—were relatively minor. In some cases, key witnesses said they had not even been contacted by federal investigators. Still, Robert S. Mueller III, the assistant attorney general overseeing the Justice Department's BCCI probe, argued that his office would not succumb to pressure and bring half-baked cases against the bank, a gentle jibe, perhaps, at Morgenthau's indictment of the bank. By the end of 1991, however, the ice between the feds and Morgenthau's office finally had thawed, and the two were said to be working hand-in-hand on the BCCI investigation.

By slipping between the crevices of international regulation BCCI has been a debacle for the world's leading banking supervisors. Belatedly they are learning some of the lessons.

In Luxembourg, for example, banking authorities do not scrutinize bank holding companies like BCCI because they are not formally considered to be banks. The Grand Duchy now wants to plug that gap. Pierre Jaans, head of the Luxembourg Monetary Institute, has called for the law to be changed so that any banking group would be barred from establishing its headquarters in Luxembourg through a holding company if its main operations were in other nations. BCCI was something of a unique case in Luxembourg, where none of the other 180 banks, with total assets of $350 billion, had a similar structure. That's one reason many regulators around the world believe—and pray—that BCCI was a one-of-a-kind scandal. But that has not stopped the banking fraternity from opposing tougher regulation because of the possible threat to their prized banking secrecy laws.

In the United States, there has been a call for a more unified approach toward regulating banks operating across national boundaries. With commendable prescience, the Group of Thirty, a Washington-based think tank, wrote just before the BCCI closing of the difficulties of supervising banks that have branches in many countries. It recommended that foreign operations either should be regulated as extensions of their domestic business in which they would be subject to home country control, or they should be treated as local banks and subject to the host country's regulations.

The moment BCCI was closed, legislators began pushing a Foreign Banking Supervision Enhancement Act through Congress, taking advantage of coincidental legislative work on a major banking bill. The final bill, approved in late 1991, included several new regulations designed to help prevent a scandal like BCCI from happening again, including greatly enhancing the Federal Reserve's authority over foreign banks doing business in the United States.

Things moved at a more leisurely pace in the United Kingdom. John Maples, the economic secretary to the Treasury, told Parliament that the government had ruled out any immediate increase in the Bank of England's regulatory powers, but he observed that the central bank would be reflecting on any lessons that the BCCI case held for future regulation.

The creation of Europe's single market in 1992 might actually make matters worse for banking supervision. Under the EC's second banking directive, which is due to take effect on Jan. 1, 1993, each European nation will have to assume greater responsibility for assuring the safety of its own banks. Only a gentlemen's agreement exists among the European Community to cover the joint sharing of information and coordination of banking regulation. That may have to be formalized in the wake of the BCCI affair.

Like the scandal that rocked the savings and loan industry and the failures of many of the leveraged buyouts of the 1980s, the BCCI scandal raised serious questions about the roles of independent auditors in checking corporate books. Price Waterhouse has been singled out for criticism for not blowing the whistle sooner on BCCI. The accounting firm's defense is two-fold: First, it argues, Price Waterhouse shared the auditing responsibilities with Ernst & Whinney and assumed total control only toward the end of 1987, and second, the firm says, auditors are not there to investigate.

The first line of defense, that there were two auditors, sounds a little hollow, since Price Waterhouse had prime responsibility for the Cayman Islands operation, where ICIC—the powerful "bank within the bank" was housed and where much of BCCI's funny business took place. Price Waterhouse probably should have noticed something amiss over the years.

The second point increasingly is becoming a vital management issue. The big auditing companies generally are held accountable only to management, and serve at management's pleasure. There's no incentive, then, to look any more closely at the books than is needed to file a favorable, or at least neutral, report. A negative, or "qualified," rating from the auditors could cost an accounting firm millions of dollars in business. So a go-along, get-along philosophy often prevails.

British auditors are required to form an opinion as to whether a set of accounts is true and fair, and even if they stumble across fraud they are not obliged to report it to the regulators, although under the British Banking Act they have a right to do so if they feel so inclined. Above all, auditors in Britain have a duty of confidentiality to their clients, which must be broken only if they uncover treason or terrorist offenses relating to Northern Ireland.

Was there a degree of naivete about the way Price Waterhouse went about the examination of BCCI's books over the years? Perhaps. Reportedly, on one occasion the auditors wanted to look at the books relating to the BCCI affiliate KIFCO (Kuwait International Finance Co.), which was being audited by a local Kuwaiti firm. But they were told by BCCI management that under Kuwaiti law they could not visit Kuwait to examine KIFCO's books themselves. The auditors went along with this until they discovered from Kuwaiti officials that there was no such law.

According to Jahangir Masud, an investment banker who was familiar with BCCI's operations, the internal auditors were "not allowed anywhere near the treasury," which was the source of one of the bank's major losses, or into the department handling loans to insiders or shareholders of BCCI, another black hole. But such unusual exclusion does not seem to have troubled Price Waterhouse.

Masud told a British television interviewer that preparations for Price Waterhouse's arrival at BCCI every year were quite intense. "Mr. Naqvi headed a committee of senior executives that would decide what to tell Price Waterhouse, what not to say to them, what management analyses to present and what files were to be presented," he said. Such careful preparation was bound to limit what Price Waterhouse would see.

Indeed, there is a third defense for Price Waterhouse: that the firm's auditors consistently were given false information by bank executives, so that there was no way to do an accurate audit. The discovery of Naqvi's personal set of records in July 1990—in effect, a second set of corporate books—revealed details of BCCI's operations that Price Waterhouse hardly could have imagined, finally making it possible for the auditors to raise serious warnings about the bank's financial situation and operational practices. On the other hand, some sources suggest, the Naqvi files might have been available to the auditors much earlier if they had been more aggressive in asking for information from the bank.

For Ian Brindle, who became senior partner at Price Waterhouse five days before the scandal broke, BCCI was something of a baptism by fire. Brindle hammered home the difficulties his firm faced when it came to signing off on the accounts in 1987, 1988 and 1989. There could be no half-measures, he said. "You simply can't go around qualifying the accounts of a bank without creating all sorts of problems, without the whole thing collapsing," he said. The result was annual negotiations with BCCI management that led each year to another financial band-aid on the bank's growing problems—enough to get the audit reports safely out the door.

There has been frustration in the Price Waterhouse camp that the firm's pledge of confidentiality to the Bank of England has prevented it from fully answering some of the criticisms of its work. Unofficially, Price Waterhouse staffers say there was a sense of accomplishment that once they took full charge of BCCI's books, they were able to get to the bottom of things so quickly.

Nevertheless, as revelation after revelation spilled out of BCCI's files in the latter half of 1991, one was particularly embarrassing to Price Waterhouse: the disclosure that an arm of the accounting firm also had been a customer of BCCI, an apparent conflict of interest. Documents showed that Price Waterhouse's Barbados branch borrowed several hundred thousand dollars from the bank in the mid-1980s to pay for the refurbishing of its offices and some general operating expenses.

The transaction may have been innocent enough—Price Waterhouse, like most accounting firms, is actually a confederation of independent firms around the world, and the Barbados unit had nothing to do with the auditing of BCCI. But it helped fuel speculation that the real story behind BCCI was even worse than what was already known—a tale of bribes, payments and influence peddling that deliberately delayed prosecution of the bank and kept it operating for years after it should have been shut.

Like all good conspiracy theories, it is possible to make the facts of the BCCI case fit this fantastic scenario. BCCI certainly had friends in high places—Jimmy Carter, Javier Perez de Cuellar, Andrew Young, Clark Clifford. It didn't hesitate to cultivate people who might have helped it in times of trouble, such as Bert Lance, Ed Rogers and Sen. Orrin Hatch (R-Utah), who issued a ringing defense on the floor of the Senate of BCCI's handling of the money-laundering case after a meeting with Robert Altman and other lawyers for the bank in early 1990—at the same time he was sitting on the Senate Judiciary committee, which oversaw the Justice Department and its investigation.

There is no evidence that any of these American officials received payoffs from the bank, but certainly, BCCI has shown its ability to spend money to make things go its way, as in the expensive lobbying of the Georgia legislature and the alleged bribes paid to officials of foreign central banks in exchange for their business.

Together with the seeming ineptness of the investigation of BCCI, particularly by the Justice Department and other U.S. government agencies, it is not hard to posit that somehow, somewhere, powerful influence was being brought to bear to turn attention away from BCCI. Taking the theory a step further, there have been suggestions that the CIA and other intelligence agencies used BCCI to their own ends, and interceded to keep the bank open whenever regulators drew too close, in order to take advantage of its Third World contacts and the window it provided into terrorist and drug-dealing operations.

None of these theories is outlandish, but so far they remain largely speculative, dependent on circumstantial evidence that frankly contradicts other information—such as the CIA's repeated warnings to other government agencies about the bank's activities during the 1980s. Investigators have searched far and wide for proof of widescale, systematic bribery and political corruption by BCCI, but so far have found little evidence to support the conjecture.

That doesn't mean it isn't there, however, and some key investigators were left wondering at the end of 1991 whether what was known so far about BCCI was only the beginning of a much larger scandal. Perhaps, they said privately, the BCCI scandal was much, much more than a banking fraud. Perhaps it reached into the highest levels of political power around the world in ways that would dwarf even the wildest conspiracy theory. For now, one can only imagine. But it seems safe to say that the story of the world's sleaziest bank is not over.

"I may have exaggerated when I said we were at the tip of the iceberg last summer," New York District Attorney Morgenthau said at the end of 1991. "We may not be that far."

Chapter 16

Epilogue

In the waning days of 1991, the accountants handling the dismantling of BCCI finally began to get a handle on the losses at the bank. Touche Ross, BCCI's court-appointed liquidators, reported in early December that it had been able to find less than $1.2 billion in assets, while the bank had liabilities of more than $10.6 billion—leaving a total shortfall of more than $9.4 billion. Even that estimate was considered conservative, and the actual amounts of losses at the bank—by some reckonings as much as $20 billion—may never be known.

Abu Dhabi and regulators around the world have moved to make some sense out of the BCCI mess, if only to provide a stable platform for the next round of litigation and investigation. At the end of 1991, Abu Dhabi's on-again, off-again commitment to bailing out what was left of BCCI appeared to be on again, with Sheik Zayed tentatively pledging to contribute at least $2 billion to a Touche Ross-organized liquidation plan under which BCCI's assets would be pooled and depositors paid off at 30 or 40 cents on the dollar. Lawyers involved in the negotiations expected that deal to be completed by January 1992.

For many of BCCI's depositors, the deal was small solace, but it was better than what they might have gotten otherwise—as little as 10 cents on the dollar without Abu Dhabi's help, according to Touche Ross. Brian Smouha, the Touche

Ross partner overseeing the liquidation effort, spent most of the latter half of 1991 shuttling by jet between London, the Cayman Islands, Pakistan and the Middle East in an effort to tie up some of BCCI's loose ends.

A major step in the proposed agreement to liquidate BCCI and distribute its assets came on December 19, 1991, when marathon negotiations among lawyers for the British liquidators and the many U.S. law enforcement agencies involved in the case produced a comprehensive agreement to handle BCCI's U.S. assets. Under the deal, BCCI pleaded guilty to a wide-ranging federal racketeering charge and many of the charges brought against it by New York officials, in the process conceding its involvement in drug-money-laundering and admitting that it had illegally taken control of First American Bank, Independence Bank, National Bank of Georgia and CenTrust. The bank also forfeited all $550 million of its U.S. assets—almost half its known worldwide assets—to U.S. authorities. The money will be split into two funds, one for use in the U.S. and the other going to victims overseas.

Out of the U.S. fund, $100 million was set aside to provide financial support for First American and Independence, saving federal authorities the potential political embarrassment of using taxpayer money to bail out the two scandal-tinged banks. Independence, in fact, was in such dire straits that $5 million was pumped into it within hours of the signing of the plea bargain agreement, and Abu Dhabi already had pumped $200 million into First American during 1991 to keep it propped up.

Other U.S. victims—mostly unwitting depositors in BCCI's American offices, which technically weren't allowed to take deposits—will be able to make claims out of the U.S. fund; law enforcers also will be able to tap it for $10 million in fines owed New York state, for an undetermined amount owed the federal government and for the costs of the investigations. Overseas, the $275 million is expected to be used to supplement the money recovered from elsewhere in BCCI and the contributions from Abu Dhabi in improving the lot of the bank's depositors and other creditors.

Unlike most of the rest of BCCI's affiliates, the illegally owned U.S banks, First American and Independence, were allowed to keep operating in the wake of the shutdown, in part because there was little indication of BCCI-style corruption in their operation, and in part because they represented some of BCCI's best assets and thus were more valuable in the long run as ongoing entities. Ultimately, First American and Independence will probably be sold, as was ordered by the Federal Reserve.

It is expected that First American, the more attractive of the two, will be placed in a trust until a new owner can be found. One potential sticking point: who would indemnify any potential buyer from legal actions that might linger against the bank after the sale. Separately, First American's management announced that it was seeking a buyer for the Georgia subsidiary, the former National Bank of Georgia, because of deposit losses it suffered as a result of the scandal. In January 1992 First American reached preliminary agreement with SouthTrust Corp. of Birmingham, Alabama, that could lead to sale of the Georgia bank to SouthTrust for an undisclosed amount. The problems of the banking industry around Washington, D.C., posed a similar obstacle to the sale of First American of Washington, but many experts said the bank's size might make it a good catch for a large bank seeking a significant foothold in the Washington market.

The salvage operation continues elsewhere around the world, with various jurisdictions handling the closing out of BCCI's affairs in different ways. Some have attempted to pay off depositors, others have waited for the division of the bank's overall assets. In Canada, for instance, authorities ordered BCCI Canada liquidated late in 1991 after an attorney for the Abu Dhabi government said his client was no longer prepared to offer a separate settlement for BCCI Canada. It was to be the first liquidation of the bank.

In some nations, BCCI even continued to operate, under the watchful eye of government regulators. Brazil, however, finally moved to shut down its BCCI affiliate in late 1991 after the publication of articles questioning the role of former ambassador Sergio Correa da Costa in setting up the bank's Brazilian operation. Meanwhile, in the Cayman Islands, officials moved to liquidate all of BCCI's operations, including ICIC—"the bank within the bank."

While regulators tried to wrap up BCCI's financial affairs, law enforcement officials continued to poke away at the many allegations of illegality surrounding the bank. With a newfound spirit of cooperation, investigators in Robert Morgenthau's office in New York and at the Justice Department forged ahead with their probe of the bank's affairs in late 1991.

Grand juries in New York, Washington, Atlanta, Tampa and Miami were hearing evidence about BCCI—another was about to be empaneled in Los Angeles—and U.S. attorneys' offices from New York to Florida to California were working full-speed on the investigation. In a possible hint about the Justice Department's priorities, officials formed an investigative task force in Washington to focus on BCCI's alleged ownership of U.S. banks. One key part of the December 1991 plea bargain deal was an agreement that BCCI's legal keepers, the liquidators, would turn over additional documents and other information to prosecutors, waive attorney-client privilege and otherwise cooperate with investigators, all promises that were expected to greatly advance the case against the men who had perpetrated the bank's wrongdoing.

Rumors abounded about where the prosecutors might strike next. To many, it was a forgone conclusion that Clark Clifford and Robert Altman would be indicted for their role in BCCI's takeover of First American, but the two men continued to vigorously protest their innocence. Both have appeared repeatedly before grand juries and congressional committees investigating the affair, and have pledged to cooperate with all probes—although they have claimed attorney-client privilege to prevent the release of some documents to investigators. Clifford & Warnke, the two men's Washington law firm, broke up in November 1991, a casualty of the controversy, and Clifford and Altman apparently were spending virtually all their time working on their defense. Their legal bills were said to be in the neighborhood of $1 million a month—and Altman's wife, Lynda Carter, was noticed to have renewed her acting career, perhaps to help pay for the defense.

In September 1991, in testimony before the House Banking Committee, Clifford lamented his involvement in the scandal he claimed he was sucked into so innocently. The elder statesman said:

> I've thought about the whole situation many times, and I've thought about my state of mind when I decided to take on this enterprise. It is entirely possible that my judgment was not all that I might have hoped that it would be, as it has turned out. . . . I enjoyed the challenge of the First American case, I'm gratified that we made the success of the effort that we did, but I've wondered some since whether it might not have been better if I'd just stuck to the law.

At the very least, some in Congress suggested, Clifford and Altman appeared to have some fairly significant conflict of interests in their multifaceted roles as attorneys to two banks, BCCI and First American; representatives of First American's purported owners, the Middle Eastern investors; top executives and board members of First American and the shell companies that owned it; and shareholders of First American's parent company, CCAH. The roles were so intertwined that at one point, investigators discovered to their amusement, Altman, as managing director and corporate secretary of CCAH, sent a letter to himself as a shareholder of the company. As more and more embarrassing and even incriminating documents like this surfaced, Clifford and Altman found it harder and harder to explain their supposed innocence of all that had gone on.

Perhaps not surprisingly, Clifford resorted to citing his mentor, President Harry Truman, in explaining the straits he found himself in as a result of the scandal: "The man with hindsight has 20-20 vision," he quoted Truman as saying. "That applies in this instance." And Altman conceded, "There certainly have been failings here, it is evident from the enormous controversy that has erupted here and the dreadful year that Mr. Clifford and I have spent. But the system did not fail."

The official British investigation continued behind closed doors—albeit with occasional leaks. Lord Justice Bingham made it clear that he was determined to speak to everyone, even if that meant traveling to Abu Dhabi, Hong Kong and Gibraltar. He said he would not be bulldozed by the U.S. judicial process into an early and half-baked conclusion, and he said it was inconceivable that he would be ready to report before the end of 1991 and that it would more likely be spring or summer 1992.

Low-key though it might be, the potential impact of Bingham's inquiry cannot be minimized. The implications of a finding by the judge of poor regulation by the Bank of England could prove disastrous for the bank's governor, Robin Leigh-Pemberton, who resisted the inquiry in the first place. It also could prove disastrous for the British Treasury if Bingham decides the government has a liability to the depositors and employees. The Bank of England faces a possible exposure in Britain alone of $3.25 billion, and there could be further claims in Europe against the Bank of England, since it was BCCI's principal regulator—such as one existed.

In Congress, Sen. John Kerry's subcommittee on terrorism, narcotics and international operations has continued a series of hearings into the BCCI scandal, and investigators for the committee have taken advantage of their subpoena power to add to their thick collection of BCCI-related documents. Other committees also are pressing their probes of BCCI and the way it was handled by the CIA, Justice Department and other agencies.

Several former BCCI executives, notably former chief financial officer Masihur Rahman and former head of American operations Abdur Sakhia, have come forward to testify before Congress and grand juries, apparently no longer quite as fearful about threats from the bank against the lives of themselves and their families. Although the former executives' public testimony has revealed new details about BCCI operations, some observers felt the ex-BCCIers were holding back some of their more lurid tales, perhaps to protect themselves against prosecution until they could cut deals for immunity.

Price Waterhouse has continued to take heat for its role in the scandal and has continued to defend itself, limited in the latter effort by confidentiality agreements. Still, in early September 1991, after Rahman blasted the firm in Senate testimony, the auditors issued a statement saying that the former BCCI executive was "aware of the facts but has misrepresented them." In late 1991, Price Waterhouse's American arm, frustrated at the bad publicity arising from the involvement of its British cousin, hired a high-powered New York public relations firm to attempt to put some distance between the two.

The progress of the global investigations has not stopped efforts by some members of the Gokal family to return to business as usual. It appeared that their Gulf Group, whose billions of dollars of loans were instrumental in bringing down the bank, is being rebuilt by a former employee of the three Gokal brothers, Zeyn Aly Mirza, from a safe haven in Tehran. Mirza, who worked for Euro Gulf, a subsidiary of Gulf Group, was said to be setting up deals with German companies trading steel. Mirza denied that his new company had ties to the Gokals. But he maintains close links with ex-Gulf Group employees. Some members of the Gokal family, however, are not having such an easy time. Mustafa Gokal is reported to be very upset and blaming BCCI for his company's problems, and a member of the family living in Singapore has had to auction his house to cover debts. The company's representative in Egypt had to flee the country by dead of night to escape house arrest.

Manuel Noriega, the Panamanian dictator who banked with BCCI, went on trial in Miami in late 1991. He has threatened to make highly damaging accusations about George Bush's knowledge of Noriega's drug smuggling while Bush was head of the CIA in 1976. One player in Noriega's trial is Amjad Awan, his personal banker at BCCI, who is thought to have bargained for a reduced sentence in return for cooperation with prosecutors as a witness against his old client and friend.

Some key figures in the controversy remained fugitives. Swaleh Naqvi was arrested in Abu Dhabi in September 1991, but has resisted American attempts to extradite him for prosecution. Some investigators speculated, however, that Abu Dhabi might eventually turn the former BCCI president over to Western authorities as an act of good faith as part of the BCCI settlement package. In July, before his arrest, Naqvi gave an enigmatic interview to reporters in which the only figure he would reveal was his age—58.

Also a fugitive was Ghaith Pharaon, the highflying Saudi financier who was alleged to have fronted for BCCI in the purchases of National Bank of Georgia, Independence Bank and CenTrust. His whereabouts were unknown. Indicted by federal authorities on a long list of charges, Pharaon's U.S. holdings were ordered seized, leaving some of his neighbors in Georgia worried that his historic mansion, the former home of Henry Ford, would be sold to land developers and turned into condominiums.

Another key figure, Kamal Adham, the former Saudi intelligence chief who was one of the shareholders in First American, took refuge in Cairo, where he finally agreed to meet with investigators from the Justice Department. He told them that he had not been a front man or nominee for BCCI, that he had purchased the First American stock on his own and without help from the bank—in contradiction to the Fed's charges. More cynical investigators noted that Adham was unable to produce documents to support his contentions, while other documents backed the Fed's version of the story.

Another investor in First American whose testimony might have been valuable has come to a strange end.

Mohammed Hammoud, who had purchased First American stock from Clifford and Altman in 1988, was reported to have died in 1990—setting off a battle between his heirs and BCCI over who actually owned the First American stock, thus suggesting that he, too, was a nominee. But there was a strange twist: the *Wall Street Journal* reported in November 1991 that Hammoud's insurance company had declined to pay off on his life insurance policy because his corpse was four inches shorter than the height recorded in the last physical examination before his death. Privately, some investigators said they didn't believe Hammoud actually was dead. Given his age —he was thought to be in his mid-40s— and his key role in the BCCI saga, particularly as the purchaser of Clifford's and Altman's stock, his purported death was seen by these investigators as being just a little too convenient.

Syed Ziauddin Ali Akbar, the former head of BCCI's disastrous treasury trading operation, served time in Britain for his role in Capcom's involvement in money-laundering. In August 1991, after attempting to flee Britain with a false passport, he was arrested again, in connection with the expanded money-laundering charges in Tampa.

Another former senior executive of the bank, Ashraf Nawabi, who headed up the Dubai operation and was very well-connected with the financially powerful al-Maktoum family, has reverted to the old BCCI stomping ground of Pakistani banking. Nawabi's application to set up a new bank in Pakistan was rejected because of his BCCI connections. But in late 1991, with the help of the al-Maktoums, he was believed to be bidding for 49 percent of Abedi's old United Bank.

And what of Agha Hasan Abedi, whose vision had created the Bank of Credit and Commerce International and who oversaw its rise and fall? He spends his days at his estate outside Karachi, protected from the outside world by his wife, Rabia. He still suffers from the effects of his heart operations, stroke and other ailments and can barely talk. In the few words he has uttered publicly, it has become clear that he is confessing nothing and shedding little light on the inside operations of the bank. "The truth will ultimately prevail," he told the Associated Press in late July 1991. "I have full faith in God. He's always guided me."

Pakistani authorities have said Abedi will not be extradited to the United States to face charges; asked why not, the chief minister of Abedi's home district told reporters that it was because Abedi had given him a monthly stipend of £5,000 when he was forced to live in London as a political exile. Abedi's friends are still protecting him.

In 1991, Pakistani officials received an application for a license to open new bank in that country. Listed among the "sponsoring directors" of the fledgling Progressive Bank, Ltd. was Sani Ahmad, the former head of BCCI's Washington office—and none other than Agha Hasan Abedi. BCCI's founder, it seemed, was at it again.

A

Abedi, Agha Hasan,37, 38, 39, 40, 41, 42, 43, 44, 45, 46, 47, 49, 50, 51, 52, 53, 54, 55, 57, 58, 59, 60, 61, 62, 63, 67, 69, 70, 71, 72, 73, 74, 75, 76, 79, 80, 81, 83, 84, 85, 86, 89, 90, 92, 94, 99, 101, 102, 104, 105, 106, 107, 113-115, 117, 119, 121, 122, 123, 137, 138, 139, 140, 141, 143, 173, 176, 178, 179, 189, 200, 203-206, 208, 209, 215, 217, 218, 220, 221, 223, 224, 227, 229, 234, 235, 239, 240, 258, 273, 274

Abedi, Rabia,273

Abedi, Velayat Hussein, 55, 84, 86, 87

Abu Dhabi,37, 41, 42, 43, 44

Abu Dhabi Investment Authority,208

Adham, Kamal,45, 53, 97, 98, 108, 109, 110, 114, 115, 116, 118, 124, 132, 133, 211, 215, 235, 272

Afridi, Aijaz,138, 139

Ahmad, Sani,125, 274

Ahmed, Akbar,70

Ahmed, Imtiaz,55

Akbar, Syed Ziauddin Ali,94, 95-99, 187, 198, 245, 273

al-Banna, Adnan,161

al-Fulaij, Faisal Saud,108, 110, 115, 118, 119, 141, 216

al-Haq, Gen. Zia,58, 70, 173

al-Khaimah, Ra, 42

al-Maktoum family,273

al-Mazrui, Ghanim,220

al-Nahyan, Sheik Khalifa bin Zayed,50, 208

al-Nahyan, Sheik Zayed bin Sultan,37, 50, 41-46, 53, 70, 71, 85, 86, 108-110, 113, 205, 206, 218, 220-224, 226, 245, 247-249, 265

al-Naomi, Humaid bin Rashid,113

al-Sharqi, Sheik Hamad bin Mohammed,113

Alcaino, Robert Baez,182, 188

Ali, Anwar,44

Alistair Blair,65

Altman Productions,242

Altman, Robert A.,103, 104, 105, 111, 112, 113, 114, 115, 116, 117, 121, 129, 135, 137, 139, 140, 141, 142, 144, 146, 147, 148, 149, 150, 151, 152, 176, 189, 190, 193, 204, 226, 236, 238, 240, 241, 242, 263, 268, 269, 270, 273

Alvand Investment Co.,88

Ambrose, Vivian,222

American Express Bank, Ltd.,234

American Express Co.,45

Americas Coordinating Committee,139

Andrew Young Associates,124

Anwar, Mohammed,248

Armbrecht, Rudolph,185, 186, 190

Arms Export Control Act,164

Asnaaf Bank,84

Associated Press,274

Awan, Amjad,175, 179, 180, 185, 187, 188, 189, 190, 191, 193, 194, 198, 255, 256, 272

Ayub Khan,44

Azmatullah, Mohammed,55

B

Bailey, Sidney,114, 115, 117

Baker, James III,172

Baluchistan,42